The Crowood Press

Reinhold
MESSNER

All 14 Eight-Thousanders

Translated by Audrey Salkeld

*Congratulations
on your grand slam!*

Jerzy Kukuczka

1970/78   Nanga Parbat

1972   Manaslu

1975/84   Hidden Peak

1978/80   Mount Everest

1979   K2

1981   Shisha Pangma

1982   Kangchenjunga

1982/84   Gasherbrum II

1982   Broad Peak

1983   Cho Oyu

1985   Annapurna

1985   Dhau

1986   Makalu

1986   Lhotse

Contents

Warmest congratulations! Delighted you made it. I know just what it means to keep going back to these altitudes. If you've never done it, you have no conception what it's really like to be up there!

Marcus Schmuck

Page 1: Reinhold Messner and Hans Kammerlander on the summit of Cho Oyu (5 May 1983).

Pages 2/3: Looking down from the Northeast Ridge of Kangchenjunga. To the left is the summit of Yalung Kang, one of Kangchenjunga's subsidiary summits. Friedl Mutschlechner (blue suit) follows Sherpa Ang Dorje (red suit), who has attached a prayer flag to his rucksack (6 May 1982).

Pages 4/5: Reinhold Messner photographs himself by remote control on the summit of Nanga Parbat. View towards the southwest with the Mazeno Ridge just right of centre (9 August 1978).

Pages 6/7: Mount Everest from the north during the monsoon (summer 1980).

Lhagyelo –
The Gods have Won *11*

1 Nanga Parbat, 8125m *16*
Nanga Parbat – Heaven, Hell, Himalaya *25*

2 Manaslu, 8163m *32*
Manaslu – Two Failed to Return *41*

3 Gasherbrum I, 8068m *48*
Hidden Peak – An Old Style as a New Idea *57*

4 Mount Everest, 8848m *64*
Chomolungma – The Last Step *73*

5 K2, 8611m *80*
Chogori – Lonely Summit *89*

6 Shisha Pangma, 8046m *96*
Shisha Pangma – Mist Obscures View *105*

7 Kangchenjunga, 8586m *112*
Kangchenjunga – Pinned Down by Storm *121*

8 Gasherbrum II, 8035m *128*
Gasherbrum II – Encounter with Death *137*

9 Broad Peak, 8047m *144*
Falchen Kangri – Only Height is Measurable *153*

10 Cho Oyu, 8201m *160*
Cho Oyu – Astride Two Worlds *169*

11 Annapurna, 8091m *176*
Annapurna – The Biggest Hurdles are in the Mind *185*

12 Dhaulagiri, 8167m *192*
Dhaulagiri – The Records Game *201*

13 Makalu, 8463m *208*
Makalu – Happy Feet *217*

14 Lhotse, 8516m *224*
Lhotse – Climbed to be Free *233*

Appendix *240*
List of all Climbers with four or more Eight-Thousanders *240*

Success, Death and the Eight-Thousanders *242*

Index *246*

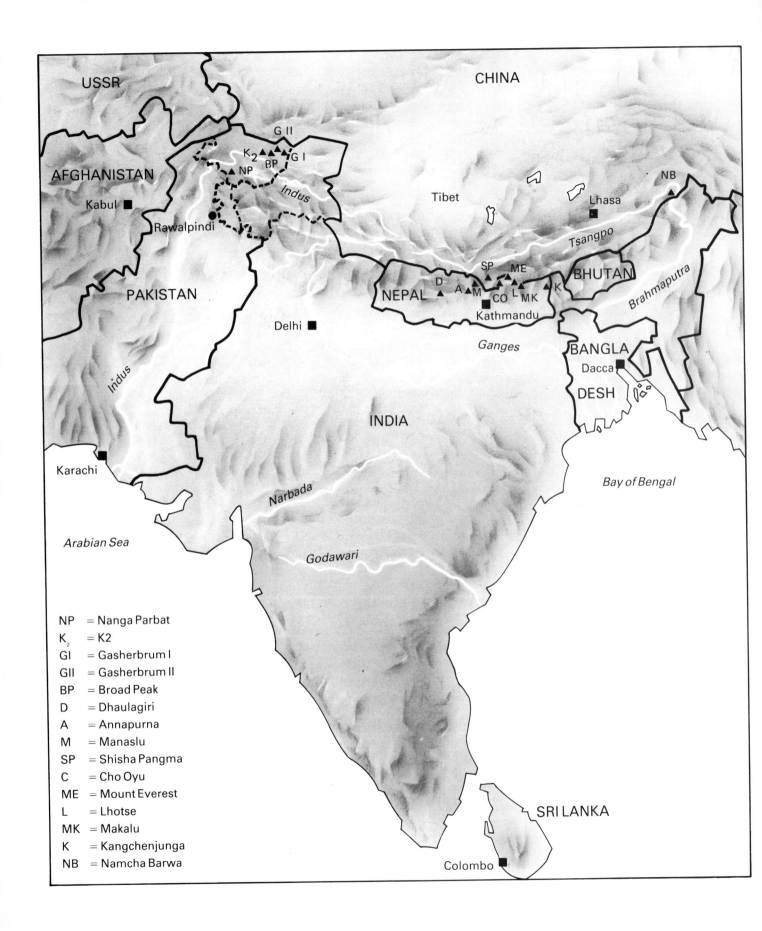

USSR

CHINA

AFGHANISTAN

Kabul ■

Rawalpindi ●

PAKISTAN

Karachi ■

Arabian Sea

K2 ▲   G II
      ▲ ▲ G I
  ▲ NP BP

Indus

Indus

Delhi ■

INDIA

Narbada

Godawari

Tibet

Lhasa ■

Tsangpo

NB ▲

NEPAL

SP ▲ ME
D ▲ ▲ ▲ ▲
   A ▲ M ▲ ▲ ▲ K
      CO L MK

BHUTAN

Brahmaputra

Kathmandu ■

Ganges

BANGLA
DESH

Dacca ■

Bay of Bengal

SRI LANKA

Colombo ■

NP = Nanga Parbat
K₂ = K2
GI = Gasherbrum I
GII = Gasherbrum II
BP = Broad Peak
D   = Dhaulagiri
A   = Annapurna
M   = Manaslu
SP = Shisha Pangma
C   = Cho Oyu
ME = Mount Everest
L   = Lhotse
MK = Makalu
K   = Kangchenjunga
NB = Namcha Barwa

1970–1986

Lhagyelo
The Gods have Won

No one is more irresistible than the dreamer whose dreams have come true.
Tania Blixen

The more we know of something, the smaller appear those obstacles that at first seemed insurmountable. And what is all our wisdom, our wiliness, boldness, our spirit? What else, but what we sense and know?
Max Stirner

Mountain	Country	Height	
		Metres	Feet
Everest	Nepal/Tibet	8848	29028
K2	Pakistan/China	8611	28250
Kangchenjunga	India/Nepal	8586	28169
Lhotse	Nepal/Tibet	8516	27940
Makalu	Nepal/Tibet	8463	27766
Dhaulagiri	Nepal	8167	26795
Manaslu	Nepal	8163	26781
Cho Oyu	Nepal/Tibet	8201	26906
Nanga Parbat	Pakistan	8125	26660
Annapurna	Nepal	8091	26545
Gasherbrum I	Pakistan/China	8068	26470
Broad Peak	Pakistan/China	8047	26400
Shisha Pangma	Tibet	8046	26397
Gasherbrum II	Pakistan/China	8035	26360

The 'eight-thousanders' are an arbitrary accident, determined by the length of a metre. They do not exist in the same way measured in feet. The table includes the most recently accepted Nepalese and Pakistani heights.

On 17 October 1986 Hans Kammerlander and I came down off Lhotse, back towards Base Camp. I felt quietly content, all the emotion of the past days drained away. The others hurried up the icefall to meet us: Friedl Mutschlechner, Renato Moro with his colleagues from *Trekking International*, all our Sherpas and the cooking team. 'Hi, you two! Congratulations!' Mugs of hot tea were thrust into our hands. We received huge hugs from Brigitte and Sabine. Everyone was visibly relieved.

At their pleasure, I too was filled with happiness. But there was no pride. I didn't feel especially heroic to have climbed all fourteen of the eight-thousanders. Not exceptional in any way as a climber. I had seen something through, that was all, a task I had set myself four years before. I was pleased to have done with it. If it meant I had won the 'race', then I was pleased to be done with that, too, and all the people who were making such capital out of it. It was all behind me at last. This was the morning I could start living the rest of my life. I felt light and free. The whole world lay before me.

It had taken me sixteen years to climb all fourteen eight-thousanders. But that hadn't been the object in the beginning, and if it later became an unacknowledged goal, it was only a secondary one. Climbing increasingly harder routes, setting myself new targets, was of far greater importance to me. I have always been on the look-out for new ways to tackle problems, concerned to push the limits of my climbing, and myself, ever further.

The true art of climbing is survival, and the point at which that becomes most difficult is when, having mastered what till then has been considered the epitome of achievement, you try to go one stage further. To venture where no one has been before, and where hardly anyone wants to follow – or even understands what it is you are trying to do. It is there, in that unknown region, where sensations and experiences are found that are of far greater intensity than any from 'well-grazed' lands.

There is now almost 100 years' history of climbing the eight-thousand metre mountains. It was in 1895 that Albert Frederick Mummery made the first attempt on Nanga Parbat; an attempt in a style which would be considered exemplary even today. But Mummery failed to return; somewhere on Nanga Parbat, he vanished. Between 1921 and 1924 British mountaineers made three successive attempts on Everest. They came within close reach of the summit, some even without oxygen masks. There followed unsuccessful attempts on Kangchenjunga, Nanga Parbat and K2. In the 1930s, there were plenty of men with the experience and endurance to climb eight-thousanders, yet at every attempt they failed. The time was not ripe for the highest mountains in the world.

Only after the Second World War, in the period between 1950 and 1964, were the eight-thousanders finally climbed, all fourteen of them. You might even say 'conquered', for in those days it was primarily a matter of planting your flag on the summit and, as first-comer, claiming the right to a small bit of the world's surface, both in a geographic and a sporting sense.

In this phase of conquest interest in the eight-thousanders was intense and nationalistic. Most expeditions were organised by national bodies and financed by governments or local Alpine associations; a country's best climbers were invited to take part, without having to pay much of a contribution themselves into the expedition kitty.

In order to reach the summit practically every conceivable aid was employed. At that time, however, such devices were still modest, some even defective. Eight of the eight-thousanders were first climbed using oxygen apparatus, six without. When people say – as sometimes they do – that I was the first to climb an eight-thousander without using oxygen, it is simply not true. The first-ever ascent of an eight-thousander, Annapurna back in 1950 by the French mountaineers Lachenal and Herzog, was done without supplementary oxygen. And Hermann Buhl, the great solo-climber of Nanga Parbat, also managed without oxygen cylinders. Only on the bigger eight-thousanders did it become normal to employ breathing apparatus, because climbers and doctors still believed it to be physiologically impossible to go above 8,600 metres without extra oxygen.

Once all fourteen eight-thousanders had been climbed, it seemed that interest in the highest mountains might die down. It is true that in 1963 an American expedition under the leadership of Norman Dyhrenfurth traversed

Everest – crossed from the Western Cwm up the unclimbed West Ridge and down the Southeast Ridge (the route taken by Hillary and Tensing on the first ascent in May 1953) – but apart from that, development stood still.

There was one eight-thousander, however, that lost none of its appeal. If anything, it became even more attractive to mountaineers. In 1962 Toni Kinshofer, Anderl Mannhardt and Siegi Löw reached the summit of Nanga Parbat, having followed a new and direct route from the Diamir Valley on the mountain's west side. This, too, was a pioneer event when you consider that it was still not usual for two routes to be opened up on any of the great mountains. The general public, however, remained scarcely aware of these new lines on Nanga Parbat or Everest.

The essential phase of second-routes really began in 1970, when difficult lines started to be put up on the eight-thousanders. That year a British team led by Chris Bonington climbed the great South Face of Annapurna. Dougal Haston and Don Whillans were the pair to reach the summit after a handful of climbers had spent a month fixing ropes up the difficult rock and steep, sometimes overhanging, ice passages, and ferrying up all the necessary equipment. The route they traced up the face was twice as high as the notorious Eiger Wall.

In the same year, the Rupal Face of Nanga Parbat was climbed for the first time during the course of an international expedition comprising German, Austrian and South Tyrolean climbers. My brother Günther and I were both members of that expedition; we were totally dedicated to this massive face, thinking of it as 'our problem'. This was my first experience of a big Himalayan mountain, and with it began a new era in my life.

The Himalaya are not only vastly bigger than the Alps, but for me, at that time, they were also more mysterious. The range extends more than 2,500 kilometres, from the knee of the Indus in the west to the knee of the Brahmaputra in the east, from Nanga Parbat to Namcha Barwa (which to this day has still not been climbed). The Alps had grown too small for me. In the Himalaya, mountains began where in the Alps they left off. The top of the Matterhorn, for example, which is about 4,500 metres, in the Himalaya would lie somewhere in the region of the Base Camp. And it is exactly because the eight-thousanders reach almost into the stratosphere, into that region where the air is so thin that man can hardly survive, that they pose such a particular problem to climbers.

Before I went to the Himalaya I had climbed many of the big faces in the Alps. In doing so, my object was not so much to gain the summits, but to dis-

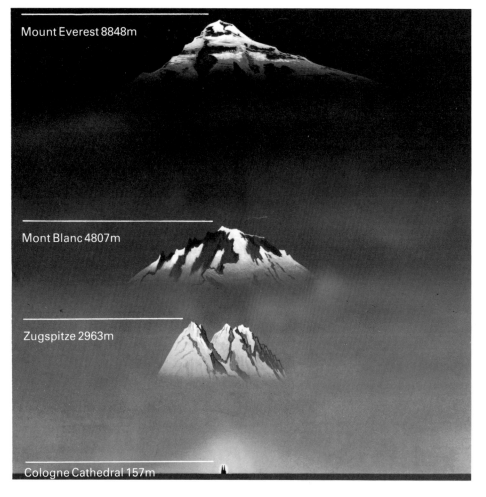

Mount Everest 8848m

Mont Blanc 4807m

Zugspitze 2963m

Cologne Cathedral 157m

cover in how little time and with how little technical aid it was possible to make the various climbs – as well as to put up some new routes, climbs that had not been possible till then. No sort of geographical conquest was involved, just the expansion of my own capabilities. I now wanted to transfer the same principle to the Himalaya. A man ought to be able to grow on these mountains, with their faces and ridges – and dangers. The impetus came not from idealism nor heroism, but a desire to express myself. To climb to a summit by the easiest route has never held much excitement for me.

At that time I regarded the eight-thousanders more or less as mythical mountains, inaccessible, incomprehensible, powerful in some curious way that could not be measured on the same scale as the Alps. However, when I finally came to stand at the foot of Nanga Parbat, I remarked that the differences in scale were not that immense. Visually, Himalayan mountains give the impression of being smaller than they really can be. Beginning where Alpine mountains leave off, means that from base to summit they are twice, perhaps three times, as high as an Alpine peak.

Of course, eight-thousanders are an arbitrary accident, although that was not yet clear to me. For English and Americans who measure in feet rather than metres, most of the eight-thousanders are more than 26,000 feet high. So they talk of a 27,000er. Not so catchy a figure! If Napoleon had made the metre a little longer, we would have had less than fourteen eight-thousanders; a little shorter and we would perhaps even have had a nine-thousander.

I am not completely sure there are fourteen eight-thousanders, yet this is what geographers assert. They have counted fourteen. But this only takes free-standing mountain masses into account, not the innumerable subsidiary summits (many as yet unclimbed)

that you find on Kangchenjunga, Broad Peak and, if you are honest, on almost all the eight-thousanders. Whoever sees Kangchenjunga from a distance gains the distinct impression of a single, massive mountain – its subsidiary summits seem scarcely important. It is right that they are seen as such and not as individual eight-thousanders. But the same cannot be said of Lhotse. It is the South Summit of Mount Everest (which is what the name means in Tibetan) and perhaps it should never have been counted as an independent eight-thousander at all.

Most of the eight-thousanders were measured by the Survey of India in the middle of the nineteenth century, when it was still a British colony. The highest peak in the world was named in honour of one of the surveyor-generals, Sir George Everest, although it was already known to the Nepalese as *Sagarmatha* and to the Tibetans as *Chomolungma*, names which are still used today. I would like people to go back to the original names for mountains. Take for instance K2, the second highest mountain in the world: K2 signifies nothing more nor less than a surveying reference, the second Karakoram summit from the left. To the people who live there, the peak is *Chogori*, the great mountain.

The question also arises to what extent the survey data of that time is accurate. The Himalaya are still rising, and the summit snow cover varies at different times of the year. If more precise measuring becomes possible in the future I am sure corrections will have to be made, perhaps so significant as to elevate one of the high seven-thousanders into the 8,000-metre category, or, equally possible, one of today's fourteen eight-thousanders may need to be demoted.

To climb an eight-thousander, you have first to secure a permit. In Nepal, Pakistan or China, where the fourteen highest summits in the world are to be found, it is not possible to climb without

permission. In Nepal you used to obtain permits from the Foreign Ministry, now you must direct your enquiries to the Ministry of Tourism. The same applies to Pakistan; a similar organisation, the Chinese Mountaineering Association, handles permits within China and Tibet.

These permits cost a lot of money, some more than others, but in any case several thousand dollars. That was always a great problem for us. In the 1960s, when I and others first embraced the idea of opening up the hardest faces on the eight-thousanders, we had plenty of new ideas. What we didn't have was money, or connections, nor was our idealism nationally motivated.

The business of getting a permit for the mountain you wanted was also difficult. Many mountain faces were not available to expeditions. Some mountains were considered holy and for that reason were struck off the list of permitted peaks; others were considered 'fully booked'. Compared to today, the chance of obtaining sanction to climb an eight-thousander in 1975 stood at around 100:1.

That was one reason why so few expeditions set out, financial difficulties were another. In the first phase of summit conquest, between 1950 and 1964, there was national interest in claiming the highest peaks for England, or for France, or Italy. Whole nations wanted their mountaineers to get there first. Americans, Japanese, Italians, Germans, French, British, all so to speak invested their best technology, their strongest men in 'conquering' an eight-thousander, on behalf of their people.

We were through with that sort of ideology, but at the same time it meant that money no longer poured into such expeditions. We had to find other ways to finance our dreams. Luckily, in the mean time industry and the Press had begun to show interest in big mountain climbs. Given the right approach and a lot of tenacity, it was possible to finance an expedition on the open market. To me this seemed more appropriate anyway than drawing on the taxpayers' money.

The approach march to a mountain seemed not unlike a long walk in the Alps. We needed those weeks to acclimatise, and in this respect things still haven't changed much. True, today, one or two members might travel by helicopter for that part of the journey from the capital to the last major settlement before base camp, but most go on foot as they have always done. Launching yourself into base camp by helicopter or plane is risky. If the intention is to go high, that initial, slow, even, acclimatisation is vitally important for the body; survival can depend on it. I have changed nothing in my walk-in procedure since 1970, not in the way of tactics, pace, nor my relationship with the local porters who help carry all the equipment to the base of the mountain and of whom, over the course of sixteen years, I have grown increasingly fond.

In 1970, when I first went to the Himalaya, everything was done in time-honoured fashion. On Nanga Parbat we worked in standard, unwieldy expedition-style. We fixed ropes, reconnoitred every stage of the route by going up and down it several times, then built up the camps and stocked them with food. Supported by a strong back-up team, we climbed as far as the summit region. From there, first alone and then with my brother, I made a bid for the top.

It was another five years before I had the skill and imagination to completely alter this style of climbing. At the beginning of my career, as a South Tyrolean I found it difficult to tap money from industry or the Press, so I was compelled to organise cheaper expeditions. Clearly, therefore, something had to change, and I was forced to rethink the accepted pattern of expeditioning. This led me back to a brand of 'Renunciation Alpinism' I had already practised in the Alps. If you reject oxygen apparatus and fixed high camps,

then you do not need high-level porters either. And if you do not have high-level porters, then you do not have the responsibility of supervising or caring for them, so can work more efficiently.

This was the style I devised. Unconsciously, it had already long been clear to me that I could only develop further if I forswore all props. Limited means forced me to get rid of all superfluities. As with a business operation, I had increasingly to dispense with 'indispensable aids'. Also, to me it seemed fairer than 'Technological Alpinism'.

All my eight-thousanders were climbed without oxygen masks – in the same way as I have never in my life used an expansion bolt. That was a rule I imposed on myself in the Alps when I first began extreme climbing. Expansion bolts make it theoretically possible to eliminate uncertainty, the very element that gives climbing its excitement. It is precisely this 'perhaps it's not possible?' that is so important. I would have felt cheated if, from the outset, I had cancelled that out with some technical device. In 1978 I knew I could climb to 8,500 metres using oxygen, but I did not want to. Instead, I wanted to know how far, using my own strength and notwithstanding any hang-ups or uncertainties I might have, I was capable of pushing into this 'perhaps it's not possible?' territory. As a man, and not as a man-machine.

Today, when I look back over my sixteen Himalayan years, I do not forget those moments when I wanted to give it all up, when the very thought of eight-thousanders terrified me. I was prey to all manner of doubts. How often I questioned whether I should go on or not. Sixteen years in the Himalaya represents sixteen long years of training and sweat. To abide by the discipline of risk – which you must to assure survival – demands concentration and endurance. Sixteen years of repeated failure and fresh starts – that was my key to success.

I did not 'collect' eight-thousanders,

as has often been suggested. Not even in 1982 when I succeeded in climbing three in a single season. But it was after this first eight-thousander hat trick that I took the decision to climb all fourteen of them. It was not simply to bring the list to an end. In 1984 I undertook a double traverse of two eight-thousanders and this, to me, was more important than all fourteen. I had been up both these mountains before, Gasherbrum I and Gasherbrum II, so they were of no significance to my 'collection'. The purpose of all my eight-thousand metre climbs, even the last two, has been to work through an idea. For reasons of time, I climbed Makalu and Lhotse by their normal routes, but that too was a record: it was the first time two climbers, Hans Kammerlander and I, had managed to scale two high Nepalese eight-thousanders in a single season. Several other climbers had attempted it, but none had been successful.

In all, I have been to the top of eight-thousanders eighteen times; four, I have climbed twice. On 16 October 1986 in terms of the 'race' for the eight-thousanders (as it was exaggeratedly seen by some people) I was further ahead of the other 'competitors' than ever before.

When my association with big mountains started in 1970, there was only one living Alpinist, Kurt Diemberger, who had climbed two eight-thousanders. Hermann Buhl, the first western mountaineer with two eight-thousanders, had been killed in 1957. In 1975, having climbed Nanga Parbat, Manaslu and Hidden Peak, I became the first man to have accomplished three. Since then, I have always been one place ahead on that accursed and ever-more-frequently published list, 'Who has the most Eight-thousanders?' On 16 October 1986 the Polish mountaineer, Jerzy Kukuczka, for whom I have the greatest respect, had been to the top of an eight-thousander twelve times (eleven different summits, two ascents of Broad Peak); I had stood atop an eight-thousander eighteen times. So the ratio was 3:2.

Luckily, climbing is not capable of being expressed either in terms of records or by numbers. It certainly cannot be measured in seconds, metres of height, or grades. I was lucky, the Gods were kind to me. I wish the same to all the others who are enthralled by the eight-thousanders – Kukuczka, Loretan, Ozaki . . . We all need luck, for the mountains are infinitely bigger than us. Mere men can never 'vanquish' them. 'Lhagyelo', the Tibetans say whenever they venture up a mountain or a high pass, and I say it too: 'The Gods have won'.

I am not proud of this 'collection', which I do not regard as such. I am not proud of the success, though I had sought it for a long time. But I am proud to have survived.

All the eight-thousanders – and survived

Granted, to outsiders and the average Alpine punter, Lhotse represented the finishing-tape of an unusual, spectacular and dangerous race around the highest mountains of the world. Only

Günter Sturm

it was not a race – maybe to those who were behind him, but not to Reinhold Messner.

Reinhold Messner was after more than that, much more. To demonstrate to the broad public by what margin Messner leads the field and dominates 'the White Arena', you have to consider the difficulty of the individual climbs he has done.

For sixteen years Reinhold Messner has been a shaping force in Himalayan climbing. Sixteen years of expedition climbing, that is sixteen years of being lonely, being constantly confronted by danger, anxiety and doubt. Extreme situations don't just bring happiness.

Critical moments, extraordinary moments: Reinhold Messner has come through them all. What is it that has enabled this man to survive? Experience? 'There's no such thing as experience. A man can do a thing badly all his life.' (Kurt Tucholsky)

Many experienced mountaineers have lost their lives in the Himalaya. Messner does have more experience and knowledge than other people, that is undeniable, but is not sufficient reason in itself to explain his success. What marks Messner out from the rest is his physical and mental skills, which, though inborn, he sharpens further with strict training discipline. Add to that an instinct, highly developed over the years, particularly when facing extreme life-threatening situations, for always making the right decision and acting upon it.

Messner's absolute uniqueness as a mountaineer is demonstrated in his art of climbing, his style. His success leaves no doubt of his talent. You feel he enjoys climbing mountains, enjoys the greatest challenges in the Himalaya, enjoys being under way. The mountain is no adversary, the climbing no struggle.

He also has a highly developed sense of when, where and how a major enterprise should be tackled, and by assessing all the risks is thus able to carry it through.

The biggest challenge Reinhold Messner set himself, the solo ascent of Nanga Parbat, took him six years from his first attempt to eventual victory. Six years, but then he did it faultlessly. Reinhold Messner is envied for his success. But it is not the success one should envy, it is his style.

Günter Sturm
(Climber of four eight-thousanders)

1 1953 Nanga Parbat 8,125m/26,660ft

The Naked Mountain

Historical Highlights

Geographical Position: Punjab Himalaya
Lat. 35°14′ N, Long. 74°35′ E

1895 After a reconnaissance of the mountain's Rupal Flank, British mountaineer A.F. Mummery reaches a height of around 6,000m on the Diamir side, but later disappears with his two porters when trying to cross into the Rakhiot Valley.

1932 A German–American expedition under the leadership of W. Merkl visits the north side of the mountain. They climb Rakhiot Peak and reach the East Ridge before being beaten by lack of Himalayan experience.

1934 Five German climbers and eleven Sherpas, again under W. Merkl, push the route reconnoitred in 1932 as far as the Silver Plateau. P. Aschenbrenner and E. Schneider attain a height of around 7,800m. The mountain is mapped by expedition scientists. U. Wieland, W. Welzenbach, W. Merkl and six Sherpas perish in a blizzard. A. Drexel had died earlier.

1937 In the course of another German attempt, led this time by K. Wien, all seven sahibs with their nine high-level porters are lost when Camp 4 is overwhelmed by avalanche. The same year P. Bauer organises a recovery mission.

1938 P. Bauer leads a strong team to the mountain's north side.

1939 A reconnaissance expedition, led by P. Aufschnaiter, attempts two lines on the Diamir Face, each time reaching around 6,000m.

1953 On 3 July H. Buhl makes the first ascent of Nanga Parbat in the course of the German–Austrian Willy Merkl Memorial Expedition. (The leaders K.M. Herrligkoffer and P. Aschenbrenner having previously ordered a retreat, Buhl, W. Frauenberger and H. Ertl take responsibility for the summit bid.) Buhl solos the last 1,300 vertical metres; Ertl produces a documentary film.

1962 Another Herrligkoffer expedition makes the second ascent of the mountain, this time from the Diamir side and by a route on the right-hand side of the North Summit, reconnoitred the previous year. In places it is extremely difficult. The summit is reached by T. Kinshofer, A. Mannhardt and S. Löw. Löw falls to his death during the descent.

1970 Siegi Löw Memorial Expedition. G. and R. Messner (27 June) and F. Kuen and P. Scholz (28 June) climb the Rupal Flank to the summit. The Messner brothers are forced to descend by the West Face, thus inadvertently making the first traverse of the mountain. G. Messner is killed by avalanche at the foot of the face. (Third ascent).

1971 A Czechoslovakian expedition under the leadership of I. Galfy makes the fourth ascent of Nanga Parbat, the second from the north side.

1976 Austrian mountaineer H. Schell organises a modest 4-man expedition to attempt the route on left-hand side of the Rupal Face, explored by T. Kinshofer. All four reach the top. This route remains the simplest way to the summit.

1978 On 9 August, climbing the Diamir Face, R. Messner succeeds in making the first solo ascent of Nanga Parbat – indeed of any eight-thousander. A small Austrian expedition repeats the difficult 1962-Kinshofer route. Five of the six members get to the top; above the Bazhin Basin the route differs in places and is easier than that of 1962.

1982 K.M. Herrligkoffer leads a new 12 person expedition to Nanga Parbat. Swiss climber U. Bühler makes first ascent of the Southeast Spur to the South Summit, the final stage solo.

1985 In bad weather conditions, W. Rutkiewicz and four other Polish women reach summit by the Kinshofer Route.

Reinhold Messner has opened three new routes on the Diamir flank of Nanga Parbat. In 1970, with his brother Günther, he descended the face from just above the Mummery Rib (two bivouacs). On his solo ascent of 1978 he climbed to the right of the huge band of seracs; and came down to their left.

With eight different routes, Nanga Parbat is well explored. The Kinshofer Route (1962) goes left through a series of cracks and snow-fields into the basin to the left of the trapezoid summit; from here several possibilities exist for the final climb to the top.

NANGA PARBAT 8125 m

O B₁ 1970

O B₃ B₄ 1978

O B₂ 1970

O B₂ 1978

B₁ 1978 O

Previous double page: The Mazeno Ridge and Nanga Parbat from the south. The Rupal Face (right half of picture) now has three routes: on the curving spur to the left, the Schell route (1976) which joins the ridge to the right of the Mazeno Gap and finishes on the Diamir side. The Messner (1970) route goes up the centre of the face, then to the left, crossing three ice-fields into the marked gulley below the South Summit, which is seen here as the highest point. To the right of the summit fall-line, keeping mostly to the Southeast Pillar, is a route that was first completed by a Polish expedition in 1985, although Uli Bühler had already reached the South Summit this way in 1982.

Above: New snow in the Diamir Valley. It was down here that Reinhold Messner struggled on frost-bitten feet after his tragic traverse of Nanga Parbat in 1970. Local farmers in these villages near the top of the Diamir Gorge came to his assistance.

Left: Upper part of the Rupal Valley with the eastern outliers of Nanga Parbat. Since 1970 Reinhold Messner has returned here many times.

Top right: In 1970 this young farmer carried Reinhold Messner on his back for many hours along the steep paths and rocky passages of the upper Diamir Gorge. Messner returned to thank him the following year. When he revisited him in 1973, he found the young man married; in 1978 Messner took this picture of him with his small son.

Right: Three of the men who helped Messner in 1970, carrying loads through the narrow Diamir Gorge in 1973 prior to his first solo attempt on Nanga Parbat.

Reinhold Messner on the lower section of the Diamir Race during his 1978 solo climb. He had to move fast up this snow gully between two icefalls, the most dangerous part of the whole climb. It took less than an hour to put it behind him (7 August 1978).

Right: Back in Base Camp at the foot of Nanga Parbat, Reinhold Messner tells Austrians Willi Bauer and Alfred Imitzer of his solo ascent. Imitzer died on K2 in 1986; Bauer, badly frost-bitten, managed to fight his way down through blizzards back to Base Camp.

The summit block of Nanga Parbat, seen from the west in the last light of evening. The actual summit is clearly visible to the right of the long, even ridge. In 1970, having reached it from the south, the Messner brothers climbed over the ridge and down the rocks directly into the gap (the big snow basin, right of summit), where they bivouacked without protection. They began their descent of the unknown Diamir face the next day, 28 June. In 1978 Reinhold Messner set up his bivouac tent on the flat surface of the icefall below the summit and on 9 August climbed straight up the rounded rock ridge to the top.

Nanga Parbat
Heaven, Hell, Himalaya

The true goal is not to reach the
uttermost limits, but to discover a
completeness that knows no boundaries.
Rabindranath Tagore

Is it not a fact that the best climbs are
done by the famous before they become
famous? Obviously this must be so, if
'Fame is the perfume of heroic deeds.'
Doug Scott in *Mountain*

Nanga Parbat from the west, the Diamir Flank.
A huge ice avalanche comes down the middle of
this almost 4,000m high face. Part of the
Kinshofer route is visible to the extreme left of
the picture. In the centre, to the right of the
avalanche, is the upper section of the Mummery
Rib. Reinhold Messner came down to the right of
this in 1978. Extreme right, his 1978 solo ascent
route (with part of the big detour to the right out
of shot). On the upper half of the face, the route
goes diagonally left to the highest point.

Until 1969 I was a fanatical Alpine climber. All summer long I lived only to climb. Any money I needed I earned working as a mountain guide. Occasionally I would give a lecture. But every free moment would be spent either training or on some serious Alpine wall or other.

Then in 1968, when a German expedition failed to climb the Rupal Face of Nanga Parbat, I was fired for the first time with enthusiasm for this eight-thousander. In 1969 I successfully completed the most difficult route in the Eastern Alps, the celebrated Philipp/Flamm on the Civetta; I climbed it alone and during a storm. I also solo free-climbed the hardest face in the Western Alps, the North Wall of the Droites. The Alps had become too small for me. This was not mere arrogance on my part: behind it lay the natural curiosity of a young and in many ways inexperienced man, impatient to stretch his limits. How much further could I go?

Back in the summer of 1970 the Rupal Face of Nanga Parbat occupied Number One place on my list of mountaineering aspirations, but I did not know if I would ever be able to go there. I was unlikely to be approached by any national expedition – as a South Tyrolean I was neither German, nor Austrian, nor even Italian. It's true that in the spring of 1969 I had been invited to the Andes by a North Tyrol expedition under the leadership of Otti Wiedmann, but that was because someone else had dropped out, and for the time being I saw no possibility of getting to an eight-thousander.

Nor did I have the financial means to put an expedition of my own together. Around this time I secured my first advertising contract from the French firm Millet; it came with a year's fee, but that wasn't enough to finance me, let alone an expedition. In those days I had to work quite a lot.

Fortunately there were models: climbers who partly financed themselves by advertising contracts. One such was Walter Bonatti. I took advantage of his experience when it came to drawing up the terms of my first contract. And when Bonatti dedicated *The Great Days*, his final climbing book, to me with words: 'For Reinhold Messner, last youthful hope of the great tradition of mountaineering', my self-confidence received an enormous boost. As a South Tyrolean, there was not normally much to be expected in the way of moral support, either. It was very important for us young climbers to be able to learn practical lessons from people like Bonatti.

The Himalaya seemed to me at that time like a dream, a kind of mountaineer's heaven. For that reason, I was sceptical to the point of astonishment when in the autumn of 1969 I received an invitation from the German expedition organiser, Dr Karl M. Herrligkoffer, to take part in his Nanga Parbat South Face Expedition. It was to be called the Siegi Löw Memorial Expedition. My sole regret was that my brother Günther, who had shared most of my first ascents in the Alps, would not be going as well. Later, however, when Sepp Mayerl and Peter Habeler, two of the original members, dropped out, Günther, too, was made a member of the team.

It was quite a large expedition of experienced German and Austrian climbers, and for about forty days throughout May and June 1970, with interruptions, Günther and I climbed on the South Face. Mostly we were out in front. We achieved a position at the foot of the Merkl Crack, where no one had been before. Several times, bad weather and avalanche danger had forced us back down to Base Camp. Once, Günther and I spent more than a week snowed-in in the middle of the face. Elmar Raab, Werner Heim, Gerhard Baur, Peter Vogler were our most frequent companions.

Several times we believed the expedition was doomed to failure. Finally, after long discussions with the expedition leader, one last all-out attempt was decided upon. Günther, Gerhard Baur and I climbed again to the top camp, where Felix Kuen and Peter Scholz had set up a tent at around 7,400 metres. From there, on 27 July, first climbing separately and then together, Günther and I reached the summit of Nanga Parbat. The Rupal Face, the highest rock and ice wall in the world, was climbed. During the final stages of effort both of us were at the limits of our endurance. In our youthful enthusiasm we were prepared to push things further than ever I would now.

It was late when we reached the summit. My brother was extremely tired and exhibiting the first signs of altitude sickness. I could see that he wasn't going to be able to go much further. In that condition it would have been irresponsible, not to say impossible, to try and shepherd him back down the Rupal Face. Especially as we did not have a rope with us. There was no way of safeguarding Günther. He would almost certainly have fallen somewhere on the way down.

Late that afternoon, in gathering cloud, I decided we should retreat down the West Face as far as the notch above the Merkl Gully. It was a short-term measure; I believed we would be able to get back on to the Rupal Face from there the next morning, and hoped that by then there would be other climbers coming up who could assist us. Thus, we waited out the long and dreadful night. We were at a height of 8,000 metres and had no bivouac equipment: no down jackets, no oxygen, nothing to eat or drink. It was a night that undermined us totally, physically and psychologically.

The next morning I could see we were in no fit state to go anywhere, certainly not all they way down the mountain. And when, after waiting till about 10 o'clock, we were forced to accept that Peter Scholz and Felix Kuen were not on their way to help us but were going for the summit themselves, we began, in desperation, to descend the Diamir side of Nanga Parbat. I was nearly out of my mind, and it was at this point that I fell down and felt my spirit leave my body. In a perfectly detached fashion I watched

myself roll down the mountain. Then, summoning up one last surge of effort, I forced myself back into my body; I had to get my brother down to safety.

The Diamir side is less steep than the Rupal Face. From above it looked feasible and offered the only solution to our predicament, albeit a slim and transitory one. I could not bear the idea of dying in inactivity. We would at least make a last, desperate attempt to get down. We struggled on until after midnight. I kept having to wait for Günther,

to guide him through seracs and down the rocks of the Mummery Rib.

By the third day of this nerve-racking descent we were well down, where the glacier levels off. I was out in front, scouting the route, and Günther failed to catch me up. When I went back and saw that a huge avalanche had come down since I'd passed that way, I knew immediately that Günther must be buried beneath it, that I was alone. But I couldn't accept that he was dead. He had been with me on hundreds of difficult

Left: Rupal Face direct route, Nanga Parbat. Several attempts between 1963 and 1968 having failed, the brothers Reinhold and Günther Messner became the first to reach the summit by this route in 1970, with five established high camps (C). After a bivouac in the Merkl Gap (B1), they were obliged to descend the opposite side of the mountain (Diamir Flank).

Nanga Parbat from the southwest, taken in 1938 by the Bauer Expedition (Photo: Deutsche Himalaja-Stiftung). The Messner brothers' bivouac between the Rupal Face (right, in cloud) and the Diamir Flank (left), was on the second (small) step on the ridge below the summit. The experience of that night is one which has most profoundly affected Reinhold Messner.

routes, it was unthinkable that we would never be together again! With him, I had always had the feeling that we were bound together, inviolately. How could he leave me here alone among these high valleys, these rocks and icefalls?

A whole day and night I looked for him. In the frozen rubble of this glacier world, parched, with frost-bitten hands and feet, I made my first acquaintance with madness. I no longer knew nor cared where I was, nor what I did. I could

barely walk. Even so, I stumbled on, painfully slowly. It was only when I met some wood-cutters who showed me the way to the valley, that I woke from the limbo where death had been walking a few steps ahead of me.

It took many years to get over this experience and the death of my brother, to accommodate his death as part of my life. I had first to learn to live with the tragedy. In the autumn of 1970 I had six toes and the tips of several fingers amputated in the University Clinic in

Innsbruck. At that time, I never believed I would be able to go back to the mountains. Nor did I want to. The distress of my parents and brothers and sister made me realise just how much of a burden climbers inflict upon those who love them. My mother begged me never to go to an eight-thousand metre peak again.

Until that year, 1970, I had lived just to climb mountains – with considerable ambition, with the resolve to employ as little in the way of technical aid as

27

Mathias Rebitsch

Survived – the traverse of Nanga Parbat

A new climbing star has been shining over the Dolomites in recent years, attracting increasing attention. The 'Reinhold' is now a standard. His rock climbs have become ever more audacious. He has climbed the very hardest routes solo; put up new direct routes of the most extreme difficulty, on the smoothest of walls, at the very top end of the range; has joined other climbers in making first winter ascents of Grade Six faces.

His exploits have surpassed all previous achievement, he has undercut all normal climbing times. Complete mastery of free-climbing technique, a calm in the face of danger, foresighted planning and deliberate execution mark him out. For Reinhold Messner rock would appear to present no further problems. A climbing genius – or perhaps only a rock acrobat . . . ?

Messner came to the Western Alps and there, too, he stood everything on its head with the swiftest ascent times. In so doing, he has demonstrated that he is as much at home on steep ice and mixed ground as on rock. His toughness and driving force are exceptional, as are his almost inexhaustible reserves of strength.

His brother Günther accompanied him on several serious ventures and also proved an excellent rock and ice man with remarkable staying power, but eclipsed perhaps by his big brother's shadow.

Messner had yet to demonstrate his worth on expeditions to the world's big mountains. This he did in 1970, when he climbed the Rupal face of Nanga Parbat!

Reinhold Messner has burst through the existing limits of Alpine knowledge and redefined standards. A towering phenomenon, yet by no means a robust, muscular woodcutter type. Sensitive, rather, slim, fine-limbed, but conditioned to the last fibre. In build he is not dissimilar to the late Hermann Buhl. He, too, is driven by inner fire, drawing the strength for his undertakings more from psychological reserves.

The essential key to his almost unbelievable ability to pull off what he sets out to do, the way he copes with altitude, really lies in his systematic autogenous training, in the yoga-type exercises he practises to maintain conscious control over his body. A climbing yogi! Rational expenditure of strength directed by sharp intellect.

The Rupal face of Nanga Parbat, the highest big wall in the world. In 1938 I saw it daily from the snow ridge leading to the Silver Saddle. Viewed in profile this 4,500m-high buttress of snow and ice is unbelievably huge. We saw it as the epitome of 'unclimbability'. At that time I was

representing the Tyrol as a member of Paul Bauer's expedition to the Rakhiot Face, organised by the *Deutschen Himalaja Stiftung*. A group from our team went afterwards to have a look at the Diamir side, and the rest of us took a flight around Nanga, sweeping past the South Face into the Diamir Valley. We saw the legendary Mummery Rib below us, almost near enough to touch. Back home we studied the pictures taken on the flight and laid plans for an expedition in 1940. But World War II put paid to our proposals.

The ascent of the Rupal Face is the boldest climb ever done and may well be the hardest on any eight-thousander . . .

Having made a first ascent of its most difficult face, Reinhold and Günther Messner came down on the other side of the mountain, down 3,500 metres of unknown ice and snow, into a strange, uninhabited glacier valley. They had to rely solely on their own resources; there was no chain of camps, nor could they expect any help from friends. A pioneering act such as has never been seen in the history of the Himalaya!

Mathias Rebitsch in the *Tiroler Tageszeitung* of 5.9.70 (member of 1938 expedition to Nanga Parbat)

The Diamir Flank of Nanga Parbat in profile. The Kinshofer route (1962) roughly takes the line of the left-hand edge of the picture. Reinhold Messner, on his solo climb in 1978, described a huge right-hand arc (extreme right, centre) on his way from valley floor to summit. Alone on a big mountain, his quest for perfection had found expression.

possible, with the notion of pushing beyond all the accepted limits of the time. I had been going my own way. From a study of Alpine history, I had extracted my own philosophies. The loss of my brother shocked me into real consciousness of just how closely mountaineering is linked with death, how dangerous it is. I hadn't really thought about it before. A climber who does not understand that death is a possible outcome of any serious climb is a fool. I learned, too, that there was nothing I could do to reverse the tragedy on Nanga Parbat.

After six months I began serious climbing again – from scratch. I was no longer so good on rock following the amputations, so I directed all my energies towards big mountains where there is top quality ice. In 1971 I went back to Nanga Parbat to search for my brother. In Base Camp, half-asleep, I dreamt he came out of the glacier and crawled down to join me in the tent. I had still not worked the tragedy out of my system.

Two years later I again returned to Nanga Parbat. This time I planned to climb it solo. I wanted to give my climbing a new direction. I wanted to climb a difficult route on an eight-thousand metre peak, by myself and without any technical assistance. I failed.

In 1977, during a personal crisis, I came to Nanga Parbat for the fourth time, again with the idea of making a solo attempt. And again, I failed. Partly through my own weakness, partly out of fear that somewhere up there, I would freak out and be unable to cope.

Only in 1978, after I'd learned that life can be borne alone and that man is an individual, after I had given up thinking in terms of pairs, only then did I have the courage to take this greatest leap forward in my climbing career. Alone, I climbed a new route on the Diamir Face, with no 'technical aids' apart from my crampons, axe, tent and sleeping bag, and I returned from summit to Base Camp by a different new route.

This solo climb began in the Upper Diamir Valley, almost from the very spot where, distraught, I had waited for my brother at the edge of the glacier in 1970. I set off up the mountain on 7 August 1978, at 5 a.m. In a few hours I had put the lower half of the face behind me and reached a small ledge at around 6,400 metres, where, under an overhanging bulge of ice, I set up my camp. It was only a tiny tent, which I'd had made specially for this expedition. I crawled inside into my sleeping bag, and melted snow to get enough to drink. I enjoyed being on my own like this, not answerable to anyone. I took it easy for a whole day inside that tent, and recovered well.

At exactly 5.02 the next morning, when I was already sitting up in my sleeping bag making tea, there was a sudden tremor and within seconds a loud cracking and rumbling all around me. I ripped open the tent door and, looking out, saw that on all sides, left, right, above and beneath me, huge masses of snow were tumbling down into the valley. Lower down, these snow masses were gathering together into a single avalanche. Several kilometres wide, it swamped the Diamir Valley.

It was only later I learned that an earthquake had triggered the avalanches. The narrow tongue of ice I had followed the previous day to scale the middle section of the face was gone completely. It had peeled off and plunged to the bottom of the mountain. Clearly, I would not be able to go back the same way. But it was no good worrying about that yet, and a day later I continued on up.

Despite the fact that my retreat had been cut off, I was in good spirits. I was aware it had only been luck that saved me, but pressed on as if luck itself bred more luck. I felt as though I were a spirit, immune from harm. I no longer had any fear at all. There was no going back, only forwards. In a state of exaltation, I climbed on. The sky above Nanga Parbat seemed like black eternity. With every upward step it opened ever wider, interrupted only by that wedge, white against the dark background, of the summit soaring above me.

This state of merging into infinity is a sensation I have frequently experienced on big mountains, and it always seems to accentuate the existential problems of man. Why are we here? Where do we come from? Where are we going? I have not discovered any answers, and if you discount religion, there are no answers, only that the state of being active within life activates the fundamental questions of Life. Up there, I didn't question what I was doing, why I was there. The climbing, the concentration, the struggle to push myself forward, those were the answers. I was my own answer, the question was cancelled out.

On the third day, 9 August, I finally reached the summit. Towards the end I was wallowing through deep snow, and clambering over the occasional rock. I left a piece of paper with my signature and the date to show that I had been up there. Out of concern that I had not taken enough pictures to be able to prove this solo ascent to the many sceptics – being hampered by a broken camera, and clouds over the surrounding peaks – I fastened an aluminium capsule with the document inside to a peg which I hammered into the summit rocks. It's the only time I have ever done this on an eight-thousander. Afterwards it never seemed necessary; before, it hadn't been possible.

I climbed back down to the top bivouac the same day. The little tent stood at 7,400 metres in a snowy hollow. The next day brought snow-drifts and cloud. Descent was impossible. New snow covered everything. All day long I waited. In my rucksack I had food and gas for a week. I didn't need to feel hassled by bad weather, but mentally, the waiting was even more difficult to endure than the climbing. I worried constantly over every conceivable danger. It was the inactivity in the tent that first led me to doubt whether or not I would survive. What if it kept on snowing, if the avalanche danger below me became impossible to predict?

On the second day of bad weather, I

View from the summit of Nanga Parbat, looking south. Footprints in the snow, evidence of human passing, will be filled in by wind and snow within hours – as if no one had been there. Mountains endure; not so, people.

took advantage of a short clearing in the cloud below me to get my bearings. Then I climbed down blind. In thick mist, without knowing where I was going, I took a line straight down. I knew only that the flat glacier floor lay 3,000 metres below. That was enough. I was no longer gripped by fear, only the will to hang on remained. In a few hours I had climbed down the complete Diamir Face. By midday I was on the glacier. I could hardly believe it myself, that so short a time before I had been high above, in serious danger of my life. The mountain was still shrouded in cloud. Higher up it was snowing.

Arriving back at Base Camp, a deep feeling of happiness came over me. As a climber, I had now achieved everything – more than I ever dreamed. Two Austrian climbers, Alfred Imitzer and Willi Bauer, were at Base Camp, and I related the events of my climb and descent to them. I pointed out my route. I talked, and talked, and talked.

At that time, out of necessity, I had begun publishing my experiences, my climbing tactics, my theories, how to finance an expedition, my instinct, how to survive dangerous situations. I wrote my first articles and books to expound my theories, and, if I'm honest, with an eye to getting known. I also needed to earn some money. Now, I had a story I wanted to tell: I had experienced so much. Although, from a climbing point of view, I was completely satisfied, I was not ready to give up serious mountaineering. I was a young man. The desire to keep in the game was still strong.

Since making my successful solo ascent of Nanga Parbat, I don't pursue mountaineering with the same animal earnestness that I did; I no longer have the ambition of a young rock climber, who wants to climb the hardest walls in the Dolomites without ropes. To me was given the good fortune to turn my boldest dream into reality: one man, one eight-thousander. From now on, mountains, for me, should be places that offer opportunities for performance; they should be a natural theatre where I can express all my skill, my craft, and my instincts.

On my first expedition to Nanga Parbat I experienced 'hell'. My second ascent, solo, brought me to 'heaven'. Now I knew the Himalaya.

The Holy Mountain

Historical Highlights

Geographical Position: Nepal Himalaya, Gurkha Himal
Lat. 28°33′ N, Long. 84°33′ E

1950 – 1955 After initial optical reconnaissance by Britons, four Japanese expeditions, one after the other, explore climbing possibilities from the north side as well as via the East Ridge.

1956 A Japanese team, under the leadership of Y. Maki, makes the first ascent of Manaslu from the northeast side, by what later becomes the normal route. The summit is reached on 9 May by T. Imanishi and Sherpa Gyalzen Norbu, and on 11 May by K. Kato and M. Higeta.

1971 A Japanese expedition from the Tokyo Metropolitan Mountaineering Federation under A. Takahashi succeeds in making the second ascent during the spring by a hard new route on the Northwest Face.

1972 A Tyrolean expedition led by W. Nairz has the South Face of Manaslu as its objective, and on 25 April by this route R. Messner reaches the summit. F. Jäger and A. Schlick die in a blizzard. Concurrently, a South Korean expedition, led by K. Jung-Sup, makes an unsuccessful attempt on the normal route. At 6,950m four Koreans, a Japanese and ten Sherpas are buried in an avalanche.

1973 The fourth ascent is made by a German expedition under G. Schmatz. S. Hupfauer and Sherpa Urkien Tshering reach the summit by the normal route.

1974 A Japanese women's expedition attempts the mountain by two routes. On the East Ridge they reach 6,000m, and by the normal route N. Nakaseko, M. Uchida, M. Mori and Sherpa Janbu make it to the summit. This is the first time women have climbed an eight-thousander. One woman member dies.

1975 Spanish climbers under J. Garcia Orts make the sixth ascent following the normal route.

1976 In the autumn a joint Persian–Japanese group under Brig. Gen. M. Khakbiz climb the normal route to the summit.

1980 South Korean climbers under Li In-Jung climb the normal route in the pre-monsoon period to claim the eighth ascent.

1981 A trekking expedition organised by Sport-Eiselin of Zurich, under the leadership of H. v. Kaenel, climbs the normal route and successfully puts 13 sahibs (German, Austrian and Swiss) on the summit. J. Millinger and P. Wörgötter make a ski descent from 8,125m. In the autumn of the same year, French climbers under P. Beghin open a new variant on the West Face, which in its second half follows the line of Messner's ascent. Even later, a Japanese group under Y. Kato successfully climbs the normal route.

1983 Attempting a first ascent of the South Ridge, two members of a Yugoslav expedition are lost in an avalanche. A Korean solos the normal route in the autumn. A German group led by G. Harter reaches the summit via the South Face, making the first complete repeat of the 1972 Tyrolean route.

1983/4 A Polish expedition under the leadership of L. Korniszewski makes the first winter ascent, following the Tyrolean route.

1984 In the spring, Yugoslav climbers under A. Kunaver reach the summit from the south side. During the autumn of the same year Polish climbers climb South Ridge and Southeast Face to the summit.

1986 A Polish-Mexican expedition under J. Kukuczka opens a new route on Manaslu during the autumn: they climb up the East Ridge and descend the Northeast Face.

Manaslu from the south. This route, first climbed by Reinhold Messner in 1972, has been repeated several times, even in winter. The right-hand ridge (South Ridge) has also been climbed. A direct line up the summit wall would be a logical objective and feasible, too, once the route had been prepared from Advanced Base Camp up the rocky pillar and across the icefall (between camps C1 and C2) into Butterfly Valley. The last part of the route from bivouac (B1) to summit runs across the featureless summit plateau and is not visible. Today the climber can choose between half a dozen different routes on Manaslu, as well as variations.

MANASLU 8163 m

B_1

C_3

C_2

C_1

ABC

BC

Right: Karki, our liaison officer, crossing one of the wood-and-bamboo bridges in the Marsyandi Khola with the porters. Karki later disappeared without trace. His death could never be properly explained. During the expedition he would frequently leave Base Camp to go down to the valley, and it is assumed he must have been killed in some local dispute.

Below: Porters from the Marsyandi Valley, men and women, resting on the way to Manaslu Base Camp. The route to the South Face was still unknown in 1972, and an advance party with bush-knives and compass had to go ahead to make it passable for the local valley porters.

Far right: Base Camp on the Thulagi Glacier. On the right, the lower section of Peak 29, West Face. Just left of centre, the rock pillar which affords safe passage between the calving icefall (left) and avalanche gullies (right).

Far left: Andi Schlick leads a group of Sherpa porters up the difficult rock pillar at the start of Manaslu South Face. Franz Jäger (in red pullover) brings up the rear.

Above: View of the upper half of Manaslu South Face from the so-called Butterfly Valley. On account of avalanche danger, the 1972 Tyrolean expedition made a wide detour to the left around this face.

Left: Horst Fankhauser on the pillar, Manaslu South Face. Expedition leader Wolfgang Nairz and his team had not foreseen such major obstacles and were forced to rely on improvised protection devices. A ladder was fabricated from bits of wood and rope to make the way safe for our Sherpas.

Previous double page: Emergency bivouac in which Horst Fankhauser and Reinhold Messner survived the first night of storm in Butterfly Valley (9–10 April 1972). That same night on the opposite side of the mountain ten Sherpas and five Korean climbers were killed in one of the worst avalanche disasters in Himalayan climbing history.

1972

Manaslu
Two Failed to Return

How often, when you have found the courage to do what you want, along comes someone else with his damned moralising.

Max Frisch

In my opinion, Reinhold Messner must accept blame for the tragedy. There are no circumstances under which a companion should be left to go back alone in a summit storm. The region between 5,000 and 8,000 metres is so inherently dangerous that a climber in poor condition, physically or mentally, rarely survives. Even if Franz Jäger had urged him to go on alone, Messner ought still to have accompanied him back down.

Hannes Gasser in *Kurier*

View from the upper section of Manaslu South Face (The Ramp), looking northwest. The peaks in the background belong to the Annapurna group.

After climbing the Rupal Face on Nanga Parbat, I was convinced that even harder faces should be possible. So, in 1972, I accepted an invitation from Wolfgang Nairz to join him and a few Tyrolean climbing guides on a trip to Kangchenjunga. Unfortunately, permission for that mountain did not materialise and at the last moment we had to look for an alternative objective. We found it in the South Face of Manaslu, a face which had never before been attempted. Not even a photograph of it was known to exist.

Our advance team, comprising Josl Knoll, Andi Schlick, Frank Jäger, Hans Hofer, Hansjörg Hochfilzer and Urkien, a well-known Sherpa Sirdar from Khumjung in the Solo Khumbu, was already on its way to Base Camp when the rest of us set off – Wolfgang Nairz, Horst Fankhauser, Dr Oswald Oelz and I. I had first met and got to know Oswald Oelz in 1970, in the Innsbruck Clinic after my Nanga Parbat trip; he used to come and visit his friend Gert Judmaier, who had sustained a bad fall on Mount Kenya. Oelz is known to everyone as *Bulle*, The Bull. Manaslu was the first mountain we were on together and it marked the start of a long friendship. After that, *Bulle* frequently came away on expeditions with me.

When we arrived at the foot of Manaslu and had our first real look at the South Face, we were so intimidated by its obvious dangers that we seriously considered turning back, there and then. The lower part of the face was nothing but icefalls and vertical flights of rock. It appeared to offer no safe passage to the big valley that clearly separated the first half of the wall from the second. We called this 6 kilometre-long interruption in the face between 5,800 and 6,600 metres Butterfly Valley. The summit wall above was a problem in itself, but first we had to reach it.

After observing the avalanche patterns to the right and left of the vertical rock pillars at the foot of the mountain, we came to the conclusion that it ought to be possible to find a route up the right-hand

buttress. With ladders and a lot of rope, and the installation of two camps, it was conceivable that by the climbing standards of the day, we could reach Butterfly Valley.

Right from the beginning we were a happy team. The five Tyrolean guides, who with Wolfgang Nairz formed the hub of the expedition, were as fine a bunch of men as you could hope to find anywhere. Full of enthusiasm and spirit, they were supremely confident we would make it to the summit. All had done major winter expeditions and some first ascents. They were approaching the Himalaya in the same spirit that had served them so well in the Alps for ten years and more.

We were going to need a fair amount of time to fix ropes up the rock buttress at the start of the climb, and to make the route safe for the Sherpas who were to help stock our high camps with food and equipment. For this reason, we established rather more camps than we would normally have done.

When Horst Fankhauser and I first entered the Butterfly Valley, it was immediately obvious that the only way to get safely on to the flat summit plateau and avoid the constant danger of avalanches was through this valley and up the ridge immediately behind it. Both of the successful expeditions to Manaslu before 1972 had finished over the vast summit plateau; it ought to be possible for us, too, to find a way across it.

We made the decision to bivouac in the Butterfly Valley and look for a safer campsite at our leisure the next day, but no sooner were we settled in than it began to snow. In fact, so much snow came down that night, it nearly finished us off. Luckily, out of some kind of presentiment, we had pitched our tent against a rock wall. Beneath its overhang, we were to some degree protected from storm and avalanche. Even so, the tent caved in on several occasions during the night from the blast of the many avalanches cascading on all sides.

We feared suffocation, cold, storm.

Our sleeping bags were soaked through. We didn't have a working stove. We kept thinking, 'We'll never survive this night.' In the morning snow lay more than chest-deep, and we waded back down to our second high camp. From there, we roped into Base Camp through further falls of fresh snow.

This set-back was not the only one to hit the expedition. Several more times we were forced to break off the climb and retreat. Our hopes of reaching the summit dwindled. But we did not give up, and at the end of April there at last seemed a chance of going for the summit.

At that stage, Horst Fankhauser, without doubt the strongest member of the expedition, fell sick and had to retire to Base Camp; Franz Jäger offered to take his place as my partner for the summit climb. Franz was a good-humoured young man, always bubbling with enthusiasm, yet at the same time very self-composed. Perhaps he was less ambitious than the others, but none of us were in any doubt that he had the strength and condition to make the climb.

The other members would support us on our way to the summit: from the third camp, now established at the upper end of Butterfly Valley at a height of 6,600 metres, we would climb a huge ice-ramp to 7,400 metres, and from there, cross the plateau on its north side to reach the highest point. We would leave our bivouac tent erected at the edge of this gigantic summit snow-field, between the South Face and the north side, so that the others could follow.

We completed the climb to the plateau, but not in a single day as originally planned. We were forced to bivouac on the way. However, on the night of 24–25 April, our tiny tent was tucked immediately under the ridge, still on the south side, between plateau and wall. We slept badly, not knowing how far we still had to go, how strenuous it would be, nor if the weather would hold. We were tired from the two days' climbing, which had included a lot of load-hauling and some route preparation.

In the morning we set off early. Our equipment was cumbersome. In those days we did not have down salopettes. Climbing in thick *loden* breeches and triple leather boots, which only kept the cold out for a short time, we moved slowly and awkwardly. The heavy axe and crampons were help and hindrance at the same time. Initially, we only moved at a snail's pace for the snow surface was crusted and broken. Higher up, we found harder snow. Everything seemed endlessly long. We were not able to gauge the distance between us and the summit ridge, as the topmost point was still hidden in cloud.

We planned the first summit attempt to the minutest detail and fixed it for 25 April. All the members of the expedition were spread between Camps 2 (5,850m) and 4 (7,400m). A long period of settled weather had been essential in putting them in position for us to make a bid for the summit. And it showed every sign of holding.

At 6 o'clock on the morning of the 25th, Reinhold Messner and Franz Jäger set off in good weather in the direction of the summit. At the same time Horst Fankhauser and Andi Schlick left for Camp 4 in support. Hansjörg Hochfilzer and Hans Hofer, who had performed extremely well in setting up the chain of camps, went back down to Base Camp for a rest. Wolfgang Nairz, Josl Knoll and the Sherpa Sirdar Urkien turned back towards Camp 3.

Horst Fankhauser/Hannes Gasser
in the *Tiroler Tageszeitung*

After a few hours, Franz Jäger began to indicate – first with gestures, then in words – that he would prefer to go back. It was not that he was tired or sick; just that he could not see any possibility, with these sort of distances, of reaching

the summit in a day. He didn't want to stop me; I would make better progress on my own. He simply didn't think he had a chance, and so he turned back.

The stretch between us and the last camp was technically easy. There were no crevasses, no danger of snowslides. Neither of us foresaw any difficulty for Franz making his own way back while I kept going. It was a perfectly logical decision for us to take.

Now I had to break trail on my own, had to husband my strength. After toiling over two interminable snow humps, I reached the ridge which stretched away to the east. I really believed I could now reach the summit fairly quickly, but in this I was again deceived. The ridge was quite difficult. It was already afternoon by the time I finally stood on the summit of Manaslu, stood on the pinnacle which juts up from the ridge. It is composed of two types of stone, and in it were two old, rusty pitons.

I only remained on top for a short time. The weather was changing and it was a long way back. A huge bank of cloud had begun rolling in from the south. Gusts of wind were sweeping the summit. I knocked out one of the pegs, put it in my pocket, and having climbed back over the sharp summit ridge, headed down towards the valley. The wind bearing the cloud bank was growing stronger and had already reached me. Thick mist blanketed everything and the snow began to drift.

So far, I felt no alarm, no misgivings that anything untoward could happen. I pressed on down, my strength holding out well. I was sure I could reach the tent within one, or at most two, hours. It was only when I noticed this stretch seemed to be taking far longer than it should that I began to wonder if perhaps I'd gone wrong in the mist. Was I lost? It was certainly a long time since I had seen any of my upward tracks, but that could just be because they had blown away. Visibility by now had dropped to about ten metres; there was no longer any hope of getting bearings from

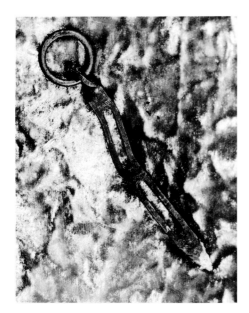

The piton which Reinhold Messner retrieved from the summit rocks of Manaslu. A Japanese climber had left it there after the mountain's first ascent in 1956. There being no photographs of Messner on the summit, this was the only proof he had been there. Later he presented it to expedition leader, Wolfgang Nairz.

distinctive rock or ice features. Panic seized me. I believed I was simply following a straight line, but what if I was going round in circles?

I first asked myself this question after it had grown dark and I realised I would not be able to survive a night out in these drifts, not at a height of 7,500 metres. I felt utterly helpless and alone. Then I heard Franz calling me, quite clearly. He's come to give me directions, I thought.

After going round in circles a couple more times, I knew my only hope was to stumble across the tent quickly. It was as if Franz's voice was making a fool of me. The 100 square metres that bounded my vision, became the biggest ice desert in the world. I was lost! It was impossible in this stormy inferno to recognise a single landmark.

Then, suddenly, I knew what to do! The storm was coming in from the south: I had seen that from the summit. I was somewhere on the plateau. Therefore, I had to go against the wind, because the plateau is to the north of the ridge on which our tent stood. So I headed into the storm; it was the only way of finding my direction. Step by step, I fought against its strength. Soon I came to the fairly prominent ridge separating the plateau from the South Face of Manaslu. But there was no tent standing there. So I went first along the ridge to the left, upwards: and then downwards. Finally, I saw a little, dark speck, a small, slightly darker patch in the snow-drifts of the night. 'Franz!' I called. I was so relieved I burst into tears.

I wanted to rush into the tent, but my legs stuck in the snow: I fell in through the door. Inside, it wasn't Franz, as I'd expected, but Horst Fankhauser and Andi Schlick. Where was Franz? I heard him calling my name. I had been sure he was calling because he knew of the danger I was in. Wasn't it his cries from the tent that had helped me find it?

Franz was not there. Nor had he been there when Horst and Andi arrived. Safe at last in the tent with the others, my

terror subsided. There was someone to put an arm round my shoulders and give me a hug. But if one nightmare had gone, another was quick to take its place – alarm for Franz Jäger. The other two were astonished when I said he'd been shouting for ages, that I knew he was around here somewhere. He could not be anywhere else, for he had come down a long while ahead of me. No, he had not been with me to the summit. Yes, it was his own idea not to go for the top, perhaps because he didn't want to hold me up.

Horst went outside the tent. When he came back a short time later, he confirmed what I'd said: Franz Jäger was out in the snow-drifts, calling for help. Horst and Andi were already tired from their climb, constant buffeting from the storm had really taken its toll. Yet without hesitation, they turned out once more in the belief that they could quickly find Franz and bring him back to the tent. Only one of them was to return.

Chilled to the bone, I remained alone in the tent, in my sleeping bag, my whole body shivering violently. With my hands between my thighs, and my head tucked right in, I lay there listening to the noises of the storm. The tent groaned, gusts of wind smashed against the rocks. Was that footsteps? Did someone shout? Hallucinating from cold, tiredness and worry, I waited for the others to come back, feeling so helpless in the face of tragedy and death. The wind was forcing snow through the fabric of the tent, so that now ten centimetres of snow covered my sleeping bag. I could not get warm. I was too exhausted to light the stove, and too anxious and edgy to think of eating or drinking, anyway.

The whole night was spent in this wretched condition, alone in the tent. Now and then, over the radio, I would report back to Wolfgang Nairz or *Bulle*, who were waiting for news in the lower camps. By now everyone was extremely worried, not just for Franz Jäger, but for Horst Fankhauser and Andi Schlick as

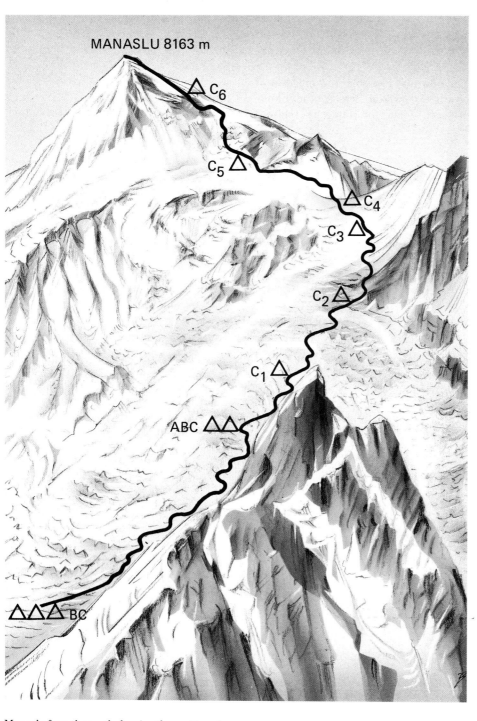

MANASLU 8163 m

C6
C5
C4
C3
C2
C1
ABC
BC

Manaslu from the north showing the position of camps used during the first ascent (1956). The mountain's third ascent was made from the south; Reinhold Messner emerged on to the great summit plateau just below the site marked for Camp 6. Coming down from the top, he missed his way in a snowstorm. During the night of 25–26 April Andi Schlick and Franz Jäger both died high on the mountain.

well. I couldn't think what had happened to them. Where were they? Why hadn't they come back?

Although they were never more than a few hundred metres from the tent, neither of them could find it again that night. The weather made it impossible to pick up any bearings. Next morning Horst returned alone. He was at the very end of his strength, physically and mentally, and told in a few words what had happened. I understood immediately Andi Schlick must have lost his grasp on reality, confused and exhausted as he was, and sapped by the cold. All we know is he went out and did not come back. Horst could find no trace of him; his shouts went unheard. The storm had swallowed Andi as well as Franz.

That morning Horst and I searched desperately for our comrades, but again, without success. More than a metre of new snow had come down over everything – perhaps two, we couldn't tell exactly; up there, snow, wind and cloud form a single, indeterminate mass. For a short while the weather improved. Despite feeling absolutely exhausted, Horst and I went up on to the plateau again, to search together. We were both played out, but we refused to believe that our two friends were not there any more, that we would never find them. We kept hoping they would somehow appear, that we should see them crawling towards the tent. But they didn't come. There was no sign, not a sound, not a movement on the whole plateau; only the wind riffling the snow crystals, only wisps of mist. Common sense told us that neither of them could have survived a night in the open, but it was not something we could grasp. Inwardly, we rejected so terrible a rationalisation. If they had to be dead, at least, we prayed, let us find their bodies.

And so we kept looking, with never a chance of finding anything. Nor did we think of our own position, which was becoming increasingly risky the longer we delayed going back to Camp 3. Up there, at 7,500 metres our blood would

Horst Fankhauser

Survived – but marked

Horst Fankhauser and Andi Schlick wandered so far from the camp they could not find it again in the storm and gathering darkness. Reinhold Messner, who had stayed behind in the tent at Camp 4 while the others made superhuman efforts to find their missing comrade Jäger, was ready to guide them back when the time came with torch signals.

For Fankhauser and Schlick, unable to relocate the tent, the only chance of surviving the night was to dig a snow hole to obtain some protection from the cold and storm. In this improvised bivouac they huddled together. Even though it was now dark, Schlick kept urging that they again go out and look for Jäger, whose pathetic cries for help had been heard in the vicinity of Camp 4 for five hours now. Fankhauser agreed; he also

hoped to find the tent, but after a short while could see that the situation was hopeless. The first snow hole was now lost too, so a new one had to be dug, in which Schlick and Fankhauser hoped for some protection. Weakened by effort and cold, they cowered in their snow hole, Fankhauser massaging Schlick to keep his circulation going. After a short while, Schlick again pressed to renew the search.

Suddenly Schlick left the snow hole – perhaps only to see what the weather was doing. But when after a short while he had not returned, Fankhauser grew uneasy and went outside to find out what had happened. He shouted several times but Schlick had disappeared. Devastated, Fankhauser crawled back into the hole and waited for morning.

At first light Fankhauser was able to orientate himself and struggled down through deep snow to Camp 4. It took him four hours. During the night's storm the tent had been completely buried by snow. When Fankhauser had recovered, he and Messner went out again in search of Schlick and Jäger, but they were soon forced to accept the hopelessness of the situation. Andi Schlick and Franz Jäger could not possibly have survived a night of storm at 7,500 metres and 30 degrees below.

Horst Fankhauser/Hannes Gasser in the
Tiroler Tageszeitung
(Expedition members on Manaslu)

soon thicken if we were not able to eat or drink anything. We were chilled through. Already our fingers and toes were showing signs of frost-bite, and it was getting worse. Yet, this, too, we ignored. We wanted proof that Franz and Andi were no longer alive.

Finally, in the afternoon, we abandoned the search, and retreated down. From below, no one was able to come up and meet us: the avalanche danger between them and us was too great. All we could hope was that no avalanches would come down as Horst and I waded our way down the great ramp between the plateau and Butterfly Valley.

The descent took hours. Every time we felt the slightest tremor from the slope, we held our breath. We looked back up to the bivouac tent as the sun came in and out of the clouds and the plumes of blown snow from the summit plateau chased over the ridge. There was nothing to see. Then, once more, a gloomy, grey nothingness washed over us.

An air of depression hung over everyone in Base Camp. Wolfgang Nairz did his best to comfort us. At that moment, I little guessed how all the self-righteous critics back at home would brand us as murderers – me especially. At that moment, all I saw were the two empty sleeping bags, and I felt unutterably sad. There were two empty places at our primitive stone table in the mess tent, where for four weeks we had all lived and eaten together. We had lost two friends, and we missed their voices, their company.

Manaslu was my second eight-thousander, and a second tragedy. For the second time, I lost the will to go back – but only briefly. I was devastated by the loss of my friends and the renewed frost-bite, and did not believe I could bear the agony of going up an eight-thousander a third time – and coming back alive.

When we returned home, I read the first of the articles criticising our expedition, articles written by people who had never themselves climbed an eight-

Descent of the pillar on the lower section of Manaslu South Face. After his summit climb Reinhold Messner had to rope down here while suffering from frost-bite.

thousander and were unlikely ever to do so. What could they know about what it means to climb at such great heights? To stay alive in hurricane winds of 100km an hour? What it means to fall over in the snow thirty times; not to believe in yourself any more? What it's like to have no strength left at all; to repeatedly pull yourself together, get back on to your feet and go on searching? How long it took to find that tent, that little space of 2 square metres under its protective awning, where someone could survive such a night?

A lot of people blame me for this tragedy and have been quite vitriolic in their condemnation. It has been very wounding, but I have not given in to it. I have stood accused of treading over the bodies of my companions. When I was going for the summit of Manaslu, there was not the remotest intimation of possible tragedy. The weather conditions were good; Franz Jäger was in fine shape when he left me. It was only when I was coming back down that the storm suddenly broke; and it was in that moment, just as suddenly, that tragedy became uncheckable.

Today I believe it possible that Franz Jäger did reach the tent before Horst Fankhauser and Andi Schlick arrived there, but left again to come and guide me back when the snowstorm started. On the plateau, in that indeterminate 'hell', no one could find their way. He hoped, by calling out, to direct me to the tent. Like Horst Fankhauser and Andi Schlick a few hours later, Franz Jäger became disoriented up there and was unable to find his way back to the sanctuary of the tent.

He helped me; he wanted to save my life. When the time came, I was no longer in a position to do the same for him. Nor could Horst Fankhauser and Andi Schlick, who gave everything they had, risked their lives to find their friend. And in doing so, Andi sacrificed his own life.

After this experience on Manaslu, I decided not to go on expeditions with

Survived – the snowstorm

'. . . The adventure of braving the world's worst glaciers, steepest slopes and highest altitudes demands an exceptional bodily fitness and power of endurance which many do not possess. The small amount of oxygen in the air at these altitudes renders every breath an effort and every step an exertion . . . [Yet] there is a spiritual value plus a spiritual significance in these repeated challenges to Himalaya. Anyone who voluntarily sets out to explore its face and permits no limit of height to daunt him, must surely possess qualities which belong also to the noviciate of a diviner life. He is ready to part with his dearest property, his right to exist, in the risk of his high enterprise . . .'

The writer of these lines, Paul Brunton (in *A Hermit in the Himalayas*), did not know Reinhold Messner. At the time of the first attempts to climb Mount Everest, Brunton was on a pilgrimage through the Himalaya. He was wrong on one point: certainly today no one – and this applies to Reinhold Messner more than anyone – is prepared to 'part with his dearest property, his right to exist, in the risk of his high enterprise.' And yet in another sense Brunton was correct when he said that whoever climbs up there and survives must possess special qualities!

I remember exactly how Reinhold, on Everest in 1978 when he was stranded on the South Col in a storm of hurricane proportions, radioed down to Camp 2: 'Don't worry. I'm not frightened, we'll come through it somehow. Surviving is my great art!' The art of survival cannot be learned. To think calmly in critical situations, without panic, is a fine art that Reinhold has mastered.

The situation on the summit plateau of Manaslu, between 7,500 and

Wolfgang Nairz with his Lhasa Apso.

8,000 metres, was worse than hellish. Franz Jäger had turned back hours before – he must surely have reached the safety of the tent. The storm grew stronger and thick cloud made route-finding impossible for Reinhold, who was trying to find his way down after going to the summit alone.

In this inferno Reinhold had to think clearly and make the right decision if he wanted to survive. And he did: the storm came from the south, and that, also, was the direction where the shelter of the tent was to be found. With strong will and superhuman strength Reinhold battled against the storm, step by step, and finally reached the tent.

We returned home together after this dramatic and tragic time. It was very difficult for Reinhold. This was his first expedition since the Nanga Parbat climb when he had lost his brother, and once more he had to come back as the 'survivor'. The mental strain on him was terrible. Despite all the cruel accusations, the expedition team members remained as close-knit and friendly afterwards as they were when they set off. A chain of unfortunate circumstances had led to the Manaslu tragedy; and if

Reinhold had not done all he did to survive, it would have been very much worse.

This gift he has of being able to make clear-headed decisions at critical moments, has often amazed me. He also has great sensitivity, and it is this, along with his physical and mental strength, that has enabled him to climb all of the fourteen eight-thousanders.

I am very pleased with and for him in this great success!

Wolfgang Nairz
(Expedition leader, Everest climber)

other people again. If I wanted to go, I told myself six months later after I had recovered to some extent, then I must go alone.

But in the years 1972–74 I was not strong enough to carry through a major solo climb – I didn't have the mental resources for it. Nor was I exclusively committed to it: the world around still clamoured too loud for me to tolerate being alone with silence. There were habits and dependencies that I still had to shake off if I was to venture this next step further.

The Hidden Eight-Thousander

Historical Highlights

Geographical Position: Karakoram
Baltoro Mustagh
Lat. 35°43′ N, Long. 76°42′ E

1861, 1887 Lt. H.H. Godwin Austen and Lt. F. Younghusband (respectively) make first references to Gasherbrum I.

1889–1929 Early in the history of Himalaya–Karakoram development, Gasherbrum I is measured and photographed by British and Italian explorers. M. Conway coins the name Hidden Peak for this shapely pyramid, to distinguish it from Gasherbrum II.

1934 An international expedition under the leadership of Swiss mountaineer, G.O. Dyhrenfurth, undertakes a large-scale reconnaissance of Gasherbrum I. H. Ertl and A. Roch climb the Southwest Spur to a height of around 6,300m.

1936 Transport problems and porter strikes impede the progress of a French expedition under H. de Segogne. It climbs the South Spur to a height of around 6,900m.

1958 An American expedition led by N. Clinch and P. Schoening succeeds in making the first ascent of Gasherbrum I. The summit is reached by P. Schoening and A. Kauffman on 4 July by a route following the Southeast Ridge and the Urdok Comb; the final stages of the climb are hampered by extreme cold and very deep snow, which leaves members wishing they had brought skis and snowshoes.

1975 As a 2-man expedition, employing 12 porters as far as Base Camp only, R. Messner and the Tyrolean climber P. Habeler on 10 August climb Gasherbrum I by its North Face. The ascent is made in classic Alpine style and without the use of artificial oxygen. (This is the second ascent of the mountain.) A day later three Austrians stand on the summit – R. Schauer, H. Schell and H. Zefferer. They have followed the line of the first ascent over the Southeast Ridge.

1977 The fourth ascent of Gasherbrum I is made by the 2-man partnership of A. Stremfelz and N. Zaplotnik (Yugoslavs); they are first to reach the summit by the Southwest Ridge. D. Bregar disappears while attempting the summit alone.

1980 A French expedition claims the fifth ascent, and at the same time the first ascent of the South Ridge.

1981 The sixth ascent of Gasherbrum I goes to a Japanese expedition.

1982 Under the leadership of G. Sturm, the German Karakoram Expedition sets out for Gasherbrum I. Following a new North Face route, G. Sturm, M. Dacher and S. Hupfauer reach the summit. From a Franco-Swiss expedition, led by S. Saudan, five members, among them Saudan and his wife, reach the summit (first female ascent). Saudan skis from summit back to Base Camp (first complete ski descent of an eight-thousander).

1983 A Swiss expedition succeeds in climbing three adjacent eight-thousanders in succession – Gasherbrum II, Gasherbrum I and Broad Peak. From a total of nine members, E. Loretan, M. Ruedi and J. C. Sonnenwyl climb all three peaks in two weeks alone in Alpine style, including a new route on Gasherbrum I over the North Ridge. During the same summer the two Poles J. Kukuczka and W. Kurtyka make the first ascent of the Southwest Face of Gasherbrum I Alpine style. A Spanish party under J. Escartin, climbs the mountain by its Southwest Face and Southeast Ridge (with a ski descent, but their planned subsequent ascent of Gasherbrum II is aborted).

1984 In the space of a week R. Messner and his fellow South Tyrolean H. Kammerlander succeed in June, in making the first traverse of two eight-thousanders – Gasherbrums I and II. No camps are positioned in advance and they do not return to base during the climb.

Hidden Peak (Gasherbrum I) was the first eight-thousander to be climbed in Alpine style: Peter Habeler and Reinhold Messner made the first ascent of its Northwest Face over three days in 1975 (bivouacking twice on the way up, twice on the way down). In 1984, in the course of their traverse of the two Gasherbrum 8,000m peaks, Hans Kammerlander and Reinhold Messner opened another ascent route on the same face. Having traversed the summit, they descended partly by way of the Yugoslav route. There are now more than half a dozen different routes on Gasherbrum I, and as many variations.

HIDDEN PEAK 8068 m

1984 B₅

B₂ 1975

B₆ 1984

1984 B₄

1975 B₁

Above left: At the time of Reinhold Messner's 1975 expedition to Hidden Peak (Gasherbrum I), equipment was still fairly 'primitive'. His idea to reduce what he took to the absolute minimum was a new and revolutionary one. Shown here, the bivouac tent at around 7,100 metres.

Left: Some of the climbing equipment in front of the tent (last bivouac, 9 August 1975). Boots were made of leather, ice-axes were cumbersome. Almost everything weighed twice as much as the corresponding items today. Even so, by eliminating most of what was considered necessary, it was possible to climb light.

Above: Base Camp 1984 for the Gasherbrum traverse. In the space of ten years, tents have become lighter and stronger, and capable of being erected in storm conditions. Messner has collaborated in the development of boots, tents, crampons and clothing.

Right: Reinhold Messner in 1975 on the Northwest Face of Hidden Peak. In 1984 scaling this mountain was only part of the undertaking. For a traverse to be successful, still less equipment had to be taken. Rather than look for new climbing aids, Messner learned to do without practically everything.

Above: Hans Kammerlander climbing to the Gasherbrum La (25 June 1984). After traversing Gasherbrum II, Messner and Kammerlander embarked on crossing a second eight-thousander.

Previous double page: Reinhold Messner on the summit ridge of Gasherbrum I, a few metres below the top (28 June 1984). In a snowstorm, without a rope, this corniced ridge demanded the utmost caution.

Left: Reinhold Messner taking a rest on the upper section of the northwest side of Gasherbrum I (28 June 1984). As in 1975, he carried a 16mm camera to the summit.

Above: Hans Kammerlander on the steep wall above the Gasherbrum La (27 June 1984). Despite the broken rock, Messner and Kammerlander used no protection.

Hidden Peak
An Old Style as a New Idea

If you do not like the word 'obsession', call it drive or enthusiasm. But remembering you cannot even do nothing by halves, I would go further and say that true enthusiasm means fanaticism.

Max Stirner

After climbing Broad Peak in 1957, Fritz Wintersteller and I wanted to go to Everest. We wanted to climb it as a twosome, without oxygen, and of course without the help of high level porters. A variety of reasons – family, business and financial – prevented us from doing so. To this day, it's something I still sometimes secretly regret.

Marcus Schmuck

Hidden Peak (Gasherbrum I) seen from the upper Abruzzi Glacier. Voytek Kurtyka and Jerzy Kukuczka were the first to climb this concave hanging glacier (1983). The northwest flank, to the left, is not visible in this picture.

With the ascent of Manaslu, I had now climbed two eight-thousanders. Only one living European had achieved that before: Kurt Diemberger. I did not see myself in 'competition' with him in any way, particularly since Diemberger's two eight-thousanders – Broad Peak and Dhaulagiri – were both first ascents, and claimed at a time when these peaks were far less visited and less-known than now, fifteen years later. But, quite naturally, I was tempted by the idea of being the first person to climb *three* eight-thousanders. However, what was far more important to me around that time, was to initiate an alternative method of financing high altitude mountaineering.

In the first place, I wanted any future expeditions of mine to be independently organised. With a few chosen companions I planned to do what till then had only been attempted by large expeditions. To climb eight-thousanders alone, or as one of a pair, became a fixed idea in my mind. If I was going to renounce porters, then I had to also manage without a chain of high camps or fixed ropes. Oxygen was naturally out as well, but then I had not used it on either of my other two summits.

But what about money? There was no way I could finance my expeditions from what I earned. It is true that various South Tyrolean concerns had supported me on my earlier trips, but not with the sort of amounts I would need to put an entire expedition on its feet. In 1970, and again in 1972, it had taken a whole year's income to enable me to go on an expedition – and during the months I was away climbing in the Himalaya, I was of course not earning anything. I was going to have to come up with something that I could *sell* when I got back: pictures, films, ideas for better items of equipment.

Any success I have enjoyed as a climber has come because I climbed with complete dedication. I planned to use this same dedication to finance my ideas and to be my own expedition leader. If I cut down the technical aid I took on trips, I would not need to hire so many porters in Nepal or Pakistan, and the projects would become cheaper.

In those days, there was no hope of balancing the books. When some money came in, then I could pay for the travel, or the equipment, or the food. I did not then believe that an expedition had to be self-supporting. Today it is different – I only set out once an expedition is fully financed. Otherwise it is impossible to climb for any length of time – unless you are very rich. It used to take me one or two years, in the pauses between expeditions, to earn enough money for one of my special projects. So I became head of a climbing school, a lecturer, and an author. As long as I had a chance, however small, of recouping the money afterwards, I felt all right about setting off on a trip.

If I am successful in a *commercial* sense today, it is because I am now reaping the 'interest' from those days. It was a different matter in the early 1970s, when hardly anyone thought I had the remotest hope of success with what I was doing . 'Freelance mountaineer' was scarcely a recognised profession. It is true that people like Walter Bonatti and René Desmaison partly financed themselves by advertising, but neither had tried to organise a cost-intensive expedition to the Himalaya singlehanded. Alpine skills were no longer enough, I had to become an administrator as well to put new ideas into practice from year to year. If I didn't want to be a member of someone else's party, then I had to become financially independent. By doing this, I have now achieved a position that allows me to go off and climb mountains, and for the trips to be self-financing.

Today thousands of young climbers have entered the same 'profession'. I hope they find something in the books I write and in my life-style to help and encourage them. The prospects are good: anyone who has the enthusiasm and willingness to put heart and soul into both the 'fun' side and the 'work' side will be successful.

When it comes to realising dreams, the most important prerequisite is the courage to think in a revolutionary manner. If I had an idea I wanted to develop, I would think it right through carefully, and only then seek permission for it.

'Alpine style' was the first of these ideas. This is the traditional way of climbing mountains. Alpine style incorporates every tactic and development that has been employed in the Alps since the beginning of climbing there two hundred years ago. Starting from the foot of a climb, you go up – with or without bivouacs – to the summit, and then back. You carry your own equipment. Route preparation is not necessary. What I wanted to find out was whether such a style could be extended to climbing the highest mountains of all.

It was an old concept, therefore, but the reason it had never been adopted in the Himalaya was simply because most mountaineers have a preconception that you have to lay siege to eight-thousanders, and this involves installing chains of camps, fixing ropes, and engaging columns of high-level porters. This is a cumbersome business, and one which is costly in time and money. There had been lightweight expeditions before, to Cho Oyu (1954) and Broad Peak (1957), but they were a long way from being true 'Alpine style' undertakings.

The best hope of success for a climb of an eight-thousand metre peak in true Alpine style seemed to me to be offered by one of the Gasherbrum peaks in Pakistan. I was delighted in April 1975 to receive permission for a trip to Hidden Peak (Gasherbrum I); here at last was the opportunity to put my ideas into practice. The Karakoram had been closed to mountaineers for several years when the Pakistani Government made both the Concordia and Abruzzi glaciers forbidden areas. Now the first expeditions were being allowed back in, and I was among them. My request for a permit had been in for some time. With it now safely in

my pocket, I invited Peter Habeler to come with me.

As the idea was already several years old, I had been able to think it out very carefully. I was sure it could work. Peter found someone in the Tyrol prepared to sponsor him, and ZDF agreed to let me make a television film of the climb. The fee for that, together with some private donations, made up our expedition kitty. If we earned anything after we got home, at least there would be no debts that needed paying off first, as there had been after the 1972 Manaslu expedition. So it was, in June 1975, we travelled to Pakistan.

I came straight from Nepal, where I had been attempting the South Face of Lhotse with a large Italian team in traditional expedition style. We had been unsuccessful. Could it have been done differently? My curiosity was intense. I wanted to show how absurd expedition style was.

Peter and I had only a small amount of equipment. We set off from Europe with 200kg. A dozen good porters were to see us up the Baltoro Glacier and into Base Camp. We could have made do with half that number if we had not been obliged to take a liaison officer with us. Like all other expeditions, we were required by the authorities to accept a man nominated by the government to accompany us as far as Base Camp. He had to be fed and kitted out by us, and his job was to keep an eye on us. He would be held responsible if we became involved in any dispute with the local people.

With so few porters, we experienced no problems and our little troop made swift progress. The young Balti lads were easy to supervise and we had no objection to paying them well. It was only right that we should.

In that first year after the reopening of the Karakoram, several visiting groups experienced difficulties with local people. One large American expedition to K2, for instance, was unsuccessful simply because it was unable to get along with its porters. Recognising how dependent

the sahibs were on them, and playing on the power this gave them, the Baltis demanded far too much from the climbers, under the general impression that they were all multimillionaires.

We succeeded in reaching Base Camp from Skardu in less than two weeks and there paid off our porters so that they could return home.

My strategy was first to do a training climb in the Gasherbrum Valley; that would give us the opportunity of having a good look at the Northwest Face of Hidden Peak, which until then, I had only seen in photographs. Then we would return to Base Camp and make a final decision about which route and style to adopt. If the Face looked possible, we wanted to climb it in a single push, from Base Camp to summit and back with all equipment and food on our backs. That initial climb would also help build up our acclimatisation, already begun with the long, steadily-ascending approach up the Baltoro and Abruzzi Glaciers.

When we saw the Northwest Face and the summit for the first time our determination wavered. Looking across from 5,900 metres we wondered whether we really did have the strength to carry everything we needed for a week up its steep slopes. Were we that good? How many days were we going to need? The Face, similar in many respects to the North Face of the Matterhorn, was very broken and in many places iced over. It had never been attempted before.

On 8 August we went up to our first camp. The next morning in brilliant weather we continued through the Gasherbrum Valley then climbed the whole middle section of the Northwest Face, the hardest part of the climb. We reached as high as 7,100 metres that day, where we spent the night, setting up our tiny tent on a shoulder. On the third day we climbed steadily towards the summit. Although I carried the 16mm camera the whole time, Peter and I took it in turns to break trail. When we reached the summit ridge, I settled

Peter Habeler on the summit of Hidden Peak. He has tied a flag to his ice-axe, the pennant of his home town. Messner's camera was defective. He used Habeler's camera to snap him on top, as well as filming him with a heavy Bell & Howell (16mm). These pictures prove only that Messner was 'working hard' up there, not that Habeler got to the top first.

myself in the snow and filmed Peter as he climbed the last bit to the top. Then I followed him. My camera wasn't working; I photographed Peter with his. My hand was not steady enough to take proper pictures; all the shots were blurred.

We had succeeded in making the second ascent of Hidden Peak and in a style that was to revolutionise mountaineering.

Technically, the Northwest Face was easier than we expected, easier indeed than a lot we had done in the Alps. All the same it demanded our complete concentration. Going down we had to be even more careful, for, though it was less strenuous, the danger of falling was infinitely greater. Most of the accidents on eight-thousand metre peaks occur on the way down. We climbed unroped, without support, and without being able to rely on the usual 'fixed' sections. We dared not let ourselves burn out too soon. At the bottom of the Face, we would still have the descent of the Gasherbrum Valley ahead of us. We needed to maintain this acute concentration until the end. We were tired when we returned from the summit to our top bivouac, exhausted even, but not at the end of our resources.

With hindsight, there is no great art to climbing an eight-thousander in Alpine style. But once something has been done, it always seems easy. This kind of climbing really is the simplest you can imagine. It is only that you must take everything into account, all the foreseeables – and the unforseeables, too – otherwise you will not live long.

That last bivouac night was very stormy; our tent was *kaputt* by morning and we were forced to make an early start. Still in the morning shadow, we climbed back down the face, following the same route we had taken on the way up. On the last part, well under the rocks, we threw our rucksacks down to the bottom. That was one way of conserving our strength. We watched them go, bouncing down the face, right to the foot of the slope. They stopped just short of the Gasherbrum Valley.

There was no really critical moment on this expedition. It had shown us that this type of venture, the first of its kind, was perfectly feasible. All the same, we were fully stretched continuously, with a tension like that of a wild animal about to spring. We were employing every one of our senses the whole time, had to keep in mind the various possibilities, and not make a single mistake.

Before we set off, the few really experienced high altitude climbers who had commented upon our proposals had been sceptical, without exception. A lot of other people had laughed outright. An eight-thousander from bottom to top without pre-placed camps, seemed impossible to almost everyone at that time. Only after we had done it, did it suddenly become perfectly feasible!

Now, even earlier pioneer ascents were being hailed as Alpine style climbs. Herbert Tichy's ascent of Cho Oyu, for instance, in 1954, with Sepp Jochler and Pasang Dawa Lama. They did not have many high-level porters and only four high camps, so it was a really small expedition. Even so, it was still traditional in the sense that there was a chain of camps and Sherpa support. Hermann Buhl on Broad Peak deliberately went a stage further than Tichy on Cho Oyu. Both men were meticulously accurate in describing what they did. It was only later that some imprecision crept in among chroniclers. On Broad Peak in 1957, Markus Schmuck, Kurt Diemberger, Fritz Wintersteller and Hermann Buhl actually dispensed with high-level porters and carried all their own loads up from the foot of the face. But they then installed a line of camps and some fixed rope before making their final assault on the summit. This was a lightweight and exemplary expedition, yet still a long way from what we would today call a true Alpine style ascent.

When Peter and I got back to Base Camp, Polish climbers were the first to congratulate us. A Polish womens' expedition – which, however, included a few men – was making an attempt on

two other Gasherbrum summits, Gasherbrum II and Gasherbrum III. That was when I first got to know Wanda Rutkiewicz, who today is internationally recognised as the most successful woman climber. Polish climbers had just discovered the Himalaya and Karakoram. Their skill and, above all, their team spirit were impressive. At that time they were gathering the experience which in ten years would make them and their students the most proficient high altitude climbers in the world.

With my ascent of Hidden Peak, I was now the first person to have climbed three of the fourteen highest summits in the world. And at the same time, I had transposed traditional expedition style with the still older Alpine style. Climbs of eight-thousanders had become simpler, and with more modest resources, possible and accessible to all. With this success, too, it had been possible to break through an ideological barrier; a taboo was lifted. Future expeditions could be organised differently.

I paid for this success dearly. Old friends suddenly regarded me with suspicion. I had become too famous for them, no longer belonged to them as I did before. Because of my publicity exposure in the Press and on radio and television, they felt 'betrayed'.

In the many interviews and discussions that were prompted by the criticism we received, I defended this style of expedition as a wonderful opportunity for mountaineering. Several questions taking me to task over this or that, I must have answered a thousand times. Becoming better known gave me better chances of financing my expeditions; but it left me with less time than before – less time for new ideas, and less time for my friends. People believed I had become self-important and aloof, when really exactly the opposite was the case. It is true I was possessed with a desire to do more; but the need for friends, for acceptance by them, and for the opportunity of exchanging ideas, these were greater than ever.

Gasherbrum III, Broad Peak (small, in background), Gasherbrum II, K2 (large, behind), the shoulder of Gasherbrum II and Hidden Peak (right). On their Gasherbrum traverse in 1984, Hans Kammerlander and Reinhold Messner, after climbing Gasherbrum II by the normal route, descended the right-hand icefall between the Shoulder and the normal route, to be in position for the traverse of Gasherbrum I. The complete tour was a massive 'horseshoe'.

Having proved my tactics could work without disaster, I was convinced that I could climb more eight-thousanders in the same manner. I was not going to be stopped by the criticism, nor even by the failure of my marriage which it precipitated. At no other time did a challenge appear as logical to me, as when I juxtaposed the existence of an eight-thousander with my fantasies. It was ludicrous to suggest I climbed only for profit. I was a dreamer and have stayed a dreamer. I have never ceased to put new ideas into practice and will give up my activities only when they hold nothing more for me, not just when there is nothing more to be earned from them.

In 1984, after almost ten years, I went back to Hidden Peak, to Gasherbrum I. There was, though, a different motive for this expedition than for the first. We – that is, Hans Kammerlander and I – also planned to climb in pure Alpine style, just the two of us without support, but this time we wanted to make a

traverse of the mountain together with that of Gasherbrum II. We intended to climb up the Northwest Face of Hidden Peak, following a line to the left of my route of 1975, and then from the summit down the West Ridge to Base Camp. We wanted to make this traverse *after* having already traversed Gasherbrum II – climbing that by the normal route and descending by what is known as the Suicide Route, further to the right.

It was a completely new idea and one I would not have considered possible in 1975; it had only become so as the result of a change in my attitude towards the mountain, and towards myself. In common with most other mountaineers, I used to think that when you reached 40 years old, you were only fit for the scrapheap. Now I know that endurance and will-power remain fairly constant between the ages of 20 and 50. Walter Bonatti gave up climbing too soon. In 1965 he was only 35, an age which for the eight-thousanders gives the very best

prerequisites: adaptability to altitude and staying power. An ideal age, too, as far as sponsors are concerned.

So here I was in 1984, ready to take another step forward into what was considered 'impossible' in high altitude climbing. I was still the taboo-breaker!

In the Gasherbrum Valley, having come down from climbing Gasherbrum II, Hans and I were still as fresh as we had been at Base Camp on other expeditions. We had conserved our energies well, not climbed a wasted metre and remained conscious of the fact we needed to pace ourselves. So we did not hesitate, and on the morning of our fourth climbing day went up to the saddle between Gasherbrum II and Gasherbrum I.

There, on the Gasherbrum-La, we erected our bivouac tent. After a peaceful night there, we climbed next morning to the left of the German–American route opened up in the early 1980s, up to the spot where Peter Habeler and I had bivouacked in 1975. But we were not intending to stop there. No sooner had we arrived than the weather began to change. In rising wind, we pushed on as far as a shoulder at around 7,400 metres above sea level, and made our bivouac there.

The bad weather front had now properly reached us and we found ourselves in a serious situation. The storm was hammering against the tent and we could not see a thing outside. We heaved a few rocks against the tent to anchor it down; we did not want the wind carrying us away in the night.

Cut off up there, surrounded by nothing but snow, both of us suffered from hallucinations. It would have been wiser to call off our traverse attempt, but at the same time it was obvious that we would never be able to get this far again, certainly not on this trip. Perhaps never in our lifetime would we come so close to making a Himalayan traverse.

We had all the equipment and food we needed, had already carried it up the first mountain and down again, and now, just under the highest point of the second mountain, it looked as if the weather was going to put paid to all our efforts. Damnation!

Throughout the storm-battered night in the bivouac, we kept telling ourselves the traverse was over, and that the sensible thing was to give up; nevertheless, we went on climbing! There was still enough rogue ambition left next morning to urge us on; that, after all, had been what led us to the idea in the first place.

Despite the stormy weather we reached the summit of Hidden Peak on 28 June. We had made it! After coming all that way, taking it in turns to be out in front, we did not linger on top, but just kept going, knowing we had the difficult descent of the West Ridge ahead of us.

We literally groped our way down. Often losing sight of each other, often believing we hadn't a chance in hell, we slowly descended the ridge, which was knife-sharp in places. It was cloud, storm and snow-drifts all the way. The

knowledge – why shouldn't I say it, pride – that we had achieved something new, gave us the extra boost to keep going. Luckily, from time to time, we came across bits of old fixed rope left when the Yugoslavs climbed the ridge a few years before.

On the seventh climbing day we were back in the Gasherbrum Valley. We were played right out, our nerves stretched to the limit, *kaputt*. We were so overtired and so over-stimulated that at first we found it impossible to sleep. So we decided to keep going and try to get down to Base Camp that same day. That was a big mistake.

It was a wonder, and more thanks to luck than judgement, that we did not tumble into one of the many crevasses or get wiped out by falling stones on the way down. Perhaps what saved us was that animal instinct that grows from constantly putting yourself into dangerous situations, as you do if you have been climbing over many tens of years. If you have been alert to danger for months, when it comes to a question of survival, you instinctively make the right move.

The traverse of Gasherbrum I was much harder than my first climb with Peter Habeler. Not only did it require double the energy because we were climbing two eight-thousanders, it required far more self-confidence and experience. But without the 1975 experience, without adopting the bold resolution to throw traditional practices overboard, to reject the 'self-evident' and to try out a new style in the Himalaya, then the second proposition would never have been conceivable, much less realisable. Putting together the traverses of two eight-thousanders, involving four different routes, without outside support, without previously established supply-dumps, without anyone else having been on either of the long stretches, is something that to date no one has been able to repeat.

In the meantime, such an expedition becomes less and less possible, because the governments of Pakistan, Nepal and

'Babu' Klasmann (camera) and Werner Herzog were the film crew for the Gasherbrum traverse. They made a documentary, *Dark Shimmer of the Shining Mountains*, which went more deeply into the soul of a mountaineer than any other had done before. It could not be called a climbing film; Werner Herzog drew a portrait of Reinhold Messner. Two obsessives face to face.

Survived – just to be devoured by publicity?

A life at Reinhold's side has absolutely nothing to do with the *dolce vita*, as many people (especially women) seem to think. In fact, it is quite the reverse. Travel is our freedom, but we have to pay dearly for it.

I know Reinhold needs publicity to be able to achieve his style of life, And indirectly, he needs it emotionally as a confirmation of his total commitment to success. Celebrity, fame, is something that everyone wants or thinks about at one time or another – I did too, as a teenager. Yet how different is the reality from the dream.

It is true you get many advantages, especially material ones, yet you have to give up so much for them, like your personal freedom. It becomes difficult to do anything spontaneous together, or to find privacy when everyone knows you.

Emotionally, Reinhold's life is like alternating hot and cold baths: hot when he is being showered with compliments and good wishes and everyone wants to know him; cold when he has to endure the spiteful attacks. To be obliged to keep justifying yourself over things that are taken for granted in other people is not only wearing, but over any length of time is discriminatory.

I am still fairly young, but I have learned some important lessons from this: being famous is not all roses, it is a very hard condition, a difficult burden. Reinhold communicates to people an aspect of life to which they themselves have no entry. For that he receives instant recognition and, indirectly, money. That means being careful. Without inner reserves and a sense of his own worth, he could very easily be consumed. Nobody makes concessions to a VIP. But everyone

Sabine Stehle

wants what he can get out of him.

As fame spreads, so the number of admirers grows, as do the grudgers and those 'friends' who very quickly are no friends at all. Who would not become careful and mistrustful in such circumstances?

It seems to me to balance out like this: you trade in your freedom in your early life against pressures later; and earlier restrictions against current opportunities, according to how you look at it. The danger that Reinhold could have lost his personality under the pressure of publicity was great. He has come through it, as he has through avalanches and storms – until now, at least.

Sabine Stehle
(to Base Camp on three eight-thousander expeditions)

China now issue so many permits that these mountains are usually overrun by climbers attempting several different routes at the same time. Whether you want to or not, somewhere you are bound to bump into a series of camps or the fixed ropes of other climbers. The very fact that there are other people there, that help can be requested in an emergency, diminishes this form of adventure. Also, the knowledge that if you had to, somewhere you could fall back on the equipment, food or gas of other people, erodes the potential of the game.

Mass-climbing has opened up to everyone the possibility of practising this 'sport', it is true, but the few who seek real adventure have often been robbed of the chance of finding it. We were able to indulge our traverse idea without restriction. We were lucky.

4 1953 Mount Everest 8,848m/29,028ft

The Highest Mountain in the World

Historical Highlights

Geographical Position: Mahalangur Himal, (Khumbu Himal), East Nepal/ Tibet
Lat. 27°59′ N, Long. 86°55′ E

1921–1938 Several British expeditions attempt to reach the summit of Mount Everest (Chomolungma) from the north. They follow the Tibetan route from the East Rongbuk Glacier over the North Col and Northeast Ridge.

1952 Two Swiss expeditions under E. Wyss-Dunant and G. Chevalley: on the first the South Col is reached via the Geneva Spur and the Southeast Ridge climbed to a height of around 8,595m. The second establishes a route over the Lhotse Face to the South Col which has since become the classic route.

1953 In the course of the tenth British Everest expedition under J. Hunt, E. Hillary and Sherpa Tensing Norgay make the first ascent of the highest peak in the world on 29 May. T. Bourdillon and C. Evans are first to climb the 8,760m South Summit.

1956 Swiss expedition under A. Eggler makes the second ascent: the summit is reached by E. Schmied/J. Marmet and A. Reist/H. von Gunten.

1963 W. Unsoeld and T. Hornbein make the first traverse of Everest during the course of an American expedition under the leadership of N. Dyhrenfurth. They climb the West Ridge and descend by the Southeast Ridge. The expedition also makes two summit climbs by the Southeast Ridge, those of J. Whittaker/ Nawang Gombu and B. Bishop/ L.Jerstad.

1975 In the course of a Japanese womens' expedition led by E. Hisana, J. Tabei becomes the first woman to climb Everest when she reaches the summit with Sherpa Sirdar Ang Tsering. A large Chinese expedition on the north side provides the second when the Tibetan Phantog reaches the top together with eight men. In the autumn a British expedition led by C. Bonington makes the first ascent of the Southwest Face. D. Haston/D. Scott and later P. Boardman/ Sherpa Pertemba reach the summit; M. Burke is lost in the summit area.

1978 R. Messner and the North Tyrolean climber P. Habeler climb to the summit on 8 May without the aid of artificial oxygen. It is the fifteenth ascent and they follow the normal route. With them on the mountain is an Austrian expedition led by W. Nairz, from which six members reach the top, including R. Karl, the first German to do so.

1979 A Yugoslavian expedition makes the first complete ascent of the West Ridge, the hardest route to date.

1980 Polish climbers achieve the first winter ascent. Despite terrible conditions, L. Cichy and K. Wielicki reach the summit in February by the Southeast Ridge. A Japanese expedition in the Rongbuk divides into two groups, one of which makes the first complete climb of the North Face; the second repeats the classic route up the North and Northeast Ridges. Y. Kato becomes the first non-Sherpa to climb the mountain a second time.

A Polish expedition makes the first ascent of the South Pillar. On 20 August R. Messner makes the first solo ascent of Everest, climbing without oxygen, over the North Col and following a partly new route across the North Face to the summit.

1982 A British Expedition under C. Bonington attempts a new route over the East-Northeast Ridge, picking up the Mallory Route to the summit. P. Boardman and J. Tasker are last seen around 8,000m. Also in the spring season, a Soviet expedition under J. Tamm lays siege to the Southwest Pillar. Altogether eleven men in five summit climbs reach the top by this new and difficult route. A Japanese winter expedition suffers two dead: Y. Kato (after reaching the summit) and T. Kobayashi.

1983 On one day in October several ropes reach Everest summit: Americans after an East Face climb, and Japanese up the South Pillar. They are followed by another Japanese rope which has climbed the Southeast Ridge, and a second American East Face group.

1986 E. Loretan of Switzerland and J. Troillet of France make a swift ascent in August of the Hornbein Couloir on the North Face.

Today, with variations, there are more than a dozen routes on Mount Everest. The mountain is overrun with people and ought to be 'closed' in the 1990s.

64

MOUNT EVEREST 8848 m

B$_2$ 1980

B$_1$ 1980

C$_4$ 1978

C$_3$ 1978

C$_2$ 1978

C$_1$ 1978

Left: Josl Knoll leads a group of Sherpas through the lower part of the Khumbu Icefall. The ladders and poles were used higher up to make a passage through the labyrinth of crevasses.

Right: Oswald Oelz, using oxygen, leaves the South Col Camp (10 May 1978).

Below: Prayer flags in Everest Base Camp. Left, the Khumbu Icefall; to the right, above, Nuptse.

Previous double page: Reinhold Messner (centre) just above the North Col on his solo climb (18 August 1980).

Left: Mount Everest and Lhotse (with the South Col between) from the top of the Khumbu Icefall.

Right: Reinhold Messner and Peter Habeler left a short length of rope and the camera batteries used to film their ascent without artificial oxygen tied to the summit tripod. The tripod was erected by Chinese climbers in 1975 and remained visible until 1980.

Below: Nena Hòlguin going up to Advanced Base Camp on the north side of Mount Everest.

Below right: Reinhold Messner prepares for his first bivouac on the North Ridge (18 August 1980).

Chomolungma
The Last Step

*Only the unknown frightens men. But
once a man has faced the unknown, that
terror becomes the known.*

Antoine de Saint-Exupéry

*You think you know a man down on the
flat, and then after spending 14 or 20
days with him in the mountains, or a
month, you realise you knew nothing
about him at all.*

Marie-Jose Vallencot

*Truth does not make a man free. It only
makes him unpopular.*

Sol Stein

Second high camp (about 6,400m) in the
Western Cwm on the south side of Mount
Everest (1978). Above, the Southwest Face,
climbed in 1975 by British mountaineers (the
route runs diagonally from right to left, top half
of picture, then back to the South Summit on the
right of the summit ridge). In 1982 Soviet
mountaineers opened a difficult route on the
Southwest Pillar to the left of the British route
(from the camp it runs right towards the marked
pillar left of the summit fall-line, and up this to
the West Ridge).

To go a step further than your predecessors in mountaineering is a kind of quantum leap. How often I have pushed against the limit – that imaginary limit that for the moment is considered to mark the edge of the possible, but which is in fact movable. The limit at any given time is really only a taboo which can be shifted, so that we slowly move towards what is absolutely impossible, something nobody can reach, but which is the magic point that keeps adventure and uncertainty alive. Gradually, I learned, through expeditions to the 8,000 metre peaks, just how much more it is possible to do, and how better to do it. But before I could do that, I had to know what could be simplified in the doing, and what eliminated. My final step was to be a solo climb to the summit of Mount Everest.

That this last step depended on the first wasn't just something I read in René Daumal's *Mount Analogue*, it is a truth I have learned for myself by experience. On all my big first ascents and expeditions, I have paid special attention to the summit area and the starting-point. When I first conceived the unlikely idea to climb Mount Everest alone and without an oxygen mask – that is, not just for the first time without oxygen, but climbing from the very foot of the mountain to the highest point on earth on my own – my thoughts circled around one question more than any other: how could I make the last 300 metres safely?

I knew that Colonel E. F. Norton on Everest in 1924 got just about as far as the 8,600-metre barrier. And I knew that George Mallory, who was obsessed with the idea of getting to the top, made a last-minute decision to use oxygen to give him a better chance of success. He no longer believed that anyone could gain the summit without a mask, and so reached out for a climbing aid that in the bottom of his heart he disapproved of. I knew, too, that almost all doctors and most climbers were convinced that it was physiologically impossible without

this 'English air', as the Nepalese call it, to get to the top of any of the five highest mountains in the world.

During the 1950s and 1960s, special apparatus was developed which gave the opportunity of carrying compressed air in sufficient quantity to compensate for the reduced oxygen content in the air above 8,000 metres, to make this height bearable for the human body. Putting on the masks, in fact, had the effect of bringing the height down from 8,800 metres to the much more tolerable level of around 6,400 metres. What interested me, however, was not what it was like to climb at 6,400 or 7,000 metres, but what it would be like at 8,800 metres. I had already been without oxygen to the top of three peaks above 8,000 metres. I wanted to find out whether the top of Mount Everest could be reached in the same way.

With the object, therefore, of climbing the world's highest mountain 'by fair means', I busied myself with the preparations. For this reason I attached myself to an Austrian expedition, which Wolfgang Nairz, Dr Oswald Oelz and I had been planning since Manaslu in 1972. We had waited years for a permit, before finally getting the OK for spring 1978. I had decided to invite Peter Habeler on this Everest venture, which would be financed solely by me. I contributed a substantial amount into Wolfgang Nairz's expedition kitty, to allow us to use his Base Camp and to share the route, which we, with our Austrian friends and with Reinhard Karl, the sole German member of this expedition, would prepare collectively.

Peter and I, however, wanted to operate separately from the others. Originally our idea was to climb the South Pillar, a new route between the Southeast Ridge, which was first climbed by Hillary and Tensing in 1953, and the Southwest Face on which Chris Bonington's expedition enjoyed success in 1975. Once on the mountain, however, we soon saw that because of its extreme steepness and the bad ice conditions, this route would prove too much, as it was two steps in one – that is, a difficult first ascent and at the same time doing without oxygen. We decided therefore to stay on the route of the original ascent, to enable us to keep to the same tracks as the Austrians.

Naturally, besides climbing Mount Everest, I wanted to get to know the area of the Solo Khumbu better, which has been home to the Sherpas for around 300 years, and which has suffered more ecologically than any other Himalayan region because of the many expeditions and the trekking industry.

So long as we were fit, Peter and I helped set up the camps. Our relationship with the other expedition members was good. A British team under Leo Dickinson was making a film about our climb, but I was going to have to carry a camera to the summit to document the last stage of the climb. The sale of the film rights had gone a long way to covering the expenses of our attempt.

Before we left for Everest, when word came out that I wanted to climb it without oxygen, there was even more opposition to my ideas and to me than before. Pundits appeared on television, at great press conferences, saying that we might just possibly reach the summit of Everest without masks, but we certainly would not make it back down again. And if we did, it would be as mental vegetables. Naturally all this talk and doubt and aggression had its effect on us. Our enthusiasm was dampened a bit. All the same we still wanted to try it, against all premonition.

Swimming against the tide like this raised doubts, but at the same time, I found that the constant battle with the many outside critics served in a way to strengthen my resolve; not only so far as mountains were concerned, but in the rest of my life, too. It was not just out of pigheadedness that I wanted to prove to these people that I was right: I wanted to submit my conviction that it ought to be possible to climb even Everest without bottled oxygen to serious test.

Peter and I, therefore, went to Base Camp in the spring of 1978 with the Austrian Mount Everest expedition. There was still a lot of snow about and it was icy cold, even at 5,400 metres. Towards 5 o'clock each night, the cold would seep through our sleeping bags, chilling us from head to toe and making it impossible to get warm again. At that time, in the growing atmosphere of uncertainty at the foot of this huge mountain, listening to the constant cracking of the icefall, I did not believe our strength would be up to struggling higher against the cold and the lack of oxygen, and against the anxiety. But I had no fears for my life. It was not unusual for me to experience faint-heartedness at the start of a two-month expedition, given the prospect of all the suffering and exertion ahead. The feeling evaporated as the weeks went by.

By the end of April, I was already on the North Col. Peter was unwell and I thought I might try for the summit alone. With me on the Col were two Sherpas, Ang Dorje and Mingma. A tremendous blizzard blew in and we

Sir Edmund Hillary and Reinhold Messner. With the first ascent of Everest in 1953, Hillary solved the greatest problem in all mountaineering history, and at the same time became the most celebrated mountaineer in the world. Almost exactly 25 years later, Reinhold Messner proved it was possible to do the climb without resorting to oxygen masks. Two great unknowns had thus been resolved within the space of a quarter of a century.

74

were trapped up there for two days and two nights. For the first time, I was experiencing what it meant to have to live at 8,000 metres without oxygen. All I wanted was to get down safely. Despite this, I grew stronger in my conviction that given good weather, it should be possible to climb much higher than the South Col camp.

On 8 May, after Wolfgang Nairz, with Robert Schauer, our Sirdar Ang Phu and the cameraman Horst Bergmann, had been to the summit, Peter and I finally got our chance. We went as far as the South Col with the Welsh cameraman Eric Jones, tucked ourselves snugly into one of the tents there, and the next morning set off at the crack of dawn, paying no regard to the stormy weather.

We had deliberately chosen the South Col as our starting place to minimise the time we had to spend above 8,000 metres. We did not want to expose ourselves to a bivouac without oxygen at 8,500 metres. This tactic was certainly one of the factors in our success. Had we, like practically all other expeditions before us, divided the climb into two halves – from the Col to 8,500 metres, bivouac, then on to the summit and back – I am positive we would not have made it. Instead, climbing at our usual pace, the short time we spent high up meant that the danger of suffering altitude damage was much reduced.

It took us about eight hours from the South Col to the summit. I led the last bit and filmed Peter. As he climbed over the Hillary Step and up to the summit, I was able to capture the historic moment on film. When I look at those pictures today, they immediately recreate that final moment when we sat, dazed, upon the highest point. We had focused our attentions for so long on getting here, we were for a while incapable of doing anything more.

The descent was dramatic. Peter hurried ahead and slid a good way down to the South Col on the seat of his pants. I stayed on top a bit longer – to film, to look at the view and to say a few words

Doug Scott

Destruction of the environment and local culture

Except on the walk-up to Everest, K2, and maybe around the Annapurna sanctuary, there is very little evidence that tourists have affected the local environment to any significant degree. There may well be tin cans and paper, but to the local people that's exactly what they are, tin cans and paper, not litter: litter is a Western concept, litter is inevitable as the local people move imperceptibly nearer to the consumer economy.

Even on the approach to Everest there is only one structure built by a foreign enterprise, the Japanese hotel, which is now struggling to survive and may well close. The Himalaya are never going to be exploited in the same way as the Alps have been by the tourist industry. The lack of one very basic necessity – oxygen – will prevent facilities being introduced to cater for short stay tourists.

In 1975 I visited the Japanese hotel just as a party of elderly ladies arrived from Seattle. They had been flown into Kathmandu airport, transferred to a helicopter, whisked up to the nearby hotel airstrip where they were put on oxygen, and carried on yaks along a made-up stone path to the hotel. There they sat with their oxygen masks looking for Everest, which failed to emerge from the dense mist. For 10 dollars a night extra they slept on oxygen. Next morning they staggered off down the track, back to the helicopter and their onward flight to Thailand, mumbling, 'Gee, if only I'd known it was going to be like this, I'd never have come.' They had never walked on Khumbu soil, nor hardly breathed the air.

The first mistake many people make is to stereotype the Sherpas as some sub-species incapable of making decisions on their own. Elaine Brooke and Tom Laird have both rightly reminded us that the Buddhist religion plays a central role in the life of a Sherpa. Going on the mountains may bring them into conflict with their beliefs and the Buddhist hierarchy, but when you get down under the dogma, as with all of us, there are as many religious paths to 'the One' as there are people. The Sherpas in particular jealously guard their rights as individuals. This applies to all the people of the Himalaya.

Doug Scott in *Mountain*

75

into my recorder. With these memory aids I hoped to transport the summit experience more exactly back to Base Camp. Nothing is more deceptive than memory.

When I followed him down, I could see Peter as a little black dot already far below me. I did not hurry. By the time I reached the South Col, I could feel a terrible burning in my eyes. I had been taking off my goggles all day to see better as I was filming, and now had developed such snow-blindness that in the tent that night it was agony. The pain was so bad that for a lot of the time I could only bear it with tears in my eyes – weeping took the edge off the soreness.

Next day, the weather was still stormy. Going down proved a nightmare, as I could only make out outlines. Peter climbed on ahead while I groped my way down, clutching the fixed ropes. He waited for me in Camp 3, where we rested for a short while. Then he was off again and I climbed down alone to the foot of the Lhotse Face, where, luckily, he was again waiting. Like me, he was in need of help, as he had sprained an ankle sliding down from the South Summit and was no longer sure on his feet. It was two invalids that returned to Camp 2, but at the same time we were immensely proud of what we had done. Against all warnings and predictions from those who supposedly knew best, we had been to the top of Everest without artificial oxygen!

As always, there were still a few who cast doubt on our achievement. We had proof of what we had done, but the wicked tongues really only stopped after other people had also climbed Everest without using oxygen, when this form of climbing an eight-thousander had become self-evident.

In 1980, two years after the first Everest climb without oxygen, I made the first solo ascent. This second Everest expedition was not undertaken to give additional proof to the first, nor to show that I was capable of climbing Everest without the help of Peter Habeler, but

because I now believed it possible to go a stage further than in 1978. For one thing, I had in the meantime begun a new game, that of getting to know the eight-thousanders at all possible times of the year; for another, I had never yet been to Tibet. I had been to the Himalaya in spring, in summer, in the autumn, but never during the monsoon or in the winter.

When the Chinese authorities 'opened' Tibet to climbing expeditions, I immediately applied for a permit. The idea of Tibet fascinated me at least as much as the eight-thousanders. Besides, the north side of Mount Everest was for me one of the most historic and interesting places of all. I looked forward to this expedition with far more excitement than any other, before or since. How lucky I had been to get this permit when I was in Peking. In July 1980 I would be on the Rongbuk side of Mount Everest. It was the side of the mountain to which all

Peter Habeler in the icefall on Mount Everest. Though in perfect accord on the mountain, after the climb Habeler and Messner went separate ways. Differences between them arose under the strain of intense media scrutiny. Messner came in for harsh criticism when he challenged Habeler's version of events. It made him more unpopular than ever.

the pioneering British expeditions of the 1920s and 1930s had come.

This time, the only person to come with me was my friend Nena Holguin, although we were obliged to take a liaison officer and a translator as far as Base Camp. It was therefore very much a mini-expedition, yet it cost far more money than anything I had undertaken before; more money than I could ever earn back from it, either from lecturing about it, or from my book *Der gläserne Horizont*, or from industrial contracts. Even so, I went, because Tibet and the Everest-solo were so important to me. When I am completely hooked on an idea, the cost is immaterial – I go.

Once on Everest, it soon became apparent that the climb would only be possible if the monsoon let up for a few days. I could not afford the time to make trail through deep, new snow. I needed good snow conditions. A first attempt to get on to the North Col was successful in as much as I made it, but it also showed me how dangerous this climb was in deep sodden snow. I returned to Base Camp

and went off walking and exploring in the West of Tibet and did not come back until August.

Now at last there were a few days of fine weather. I hesitated a bit longer because I did not know whether this was a real break in the monsoon or not, then we moved up from Base Camp to our Advanced Base at 6,500 metres. This is as far as the yaks can go. I made one trip higher to dump some gear and was back in camp with Nena a few hours later. The next day I went straight up to the North Col and on to 7,800 metres.

I knew I needed to move fast on Everest – I had learnt that on Nanga Parbat when I soloed my first eight-thousander. The style was forced upon me. Since I was carrying everything myself, I had to be frugal – on gear, on food, on luxuries, and also on time.

I made good height that first day, but not high enough to be able to climb the mountain in two days. On the second day, I discovered it would not be possible to go the way I originally planned, nor by the Mallory route, because the hollow

beneath the Northeast Ridge was filled with deep snow. So I traversed out to the right, and took a line I had observed from Base Camp. Here, too, on the North Side of Everest, I had taken care I knew the beginning and end of the climb, before venturing ahead: 'The first step depends upon the last, the last on the first.'

On the second day, 19 August, I crossed the entire North Face. On 20 August I reached the great Norton Couloir, climbed this – it is not particularly steep, but is still dangerous – up to where it flattens out, and expected then to be soon on top. But that last section of the summit ridge seemed to go on for ever. My tempo had become so slow that I despaired of ever making it. I could not manage the last few metres – I crawled on hands and knees.

It was continual agony; I have never in my whole life been so tired as on the summit of Mount Everest that day. I just sat and sat there, oblivious to everything. For a long time I could not go down, nor did I want to. Finally, I forced

Reinhold Messner preparing to bivouac on the north side of Mount Everest (1980). The badge on his jacket is the manufacturer's logo. Messner has always refused to let himself be used as a living billboard. He will not wear labels on his clothes that are unrelated to the product. Also, he has a certain image he likes to maintain, his personal style.

Mount Everest and Lhotse from the south. These two eight-thousanders offer the boldest opportunities for the future. Several traverse possibilities suggest themselves (from north to south; the 'horseshoe' starting from Nuptse; southeast to northwest – the 'Big S', etc.). The fact that two of the world's four highest mountains are involved makes the length of time spent over 8,000m a critical factor. Success can only be guaranteed by speed; that is, if one is not to take a step backwards in style, such as using oxygen equipment or installing depots. Only on these two mountains will it be possible to surpass Messner's 'Limits'.

Survived – solo on Mount Everest

Reinhold Messner's unique success in his mountaineering career is epitomised in what is probably his finest achievement of all – his solo ascent of Everest. He combines a mixture of pioneering boldness, tackling the seemingly impossible, with a sound realism which enables him to analyse the many factors for any particular project and then overcome them in an effective way.

We can see this in Reinhold's approach to Everest. The concept of climbing the highest mountain on earth, solo, in a single push was so colossal that he needed to approach it in a series of creative stages. His ascent with Peter Habeler, without oxygen, by the South Col route – in itself a huge step into the unknown – was a necessary step also in ascertaining that the human body could attain the height of 29,028 feet without the aid of oxygen.

He also needed to acclimatise himself to the loneliness of the Himalayan giants. In this respect his solo ascent of Nanga Parbat gave him the reassurance that he could cope with the immense mental and physical stress of facing a Himalayan peak on his own. In bringing together his experience on Everest without oxygen and his self-reliance on Nanga Parbat, he could then realistically face what must have been his ultimate challenge. The very speed, sureness and efficiency of his ascent of the world's highest mountain masks the size of the barrier through which he was breaking.

Chris Bonington
(Expedition leader and Mount Everest climber)

Chris Bonington

myself to begin the descent. I knew I was physically at the end of my tether.

My solo ascent of Everest was not all that risky. True, on the first day, shortly after I had left Advanced Base Camp – it was still dark – I fell about 8 metres into a crevasse just under the North Col. My life was in danger then, but with a bit of luck and skill I was able to get myself out. I immediately put it out of my mind.

On my way down from the North Col to Base Camp, soft snow gave me a lot of trouble; I slid and fell more than I climbed down. It was not all that dangerous, because I fell like a cat. Luckily, I have good co-ordination and am able to dodge stones and crevasses quite neatly.

It was only when I reached the foot of the mountain and the ordeal was over, when I no longer had to worry about falling, or dying of exhaustion, or freezing to death, that I collapsed. I no longer had to grope forwards in the mist; no longer summon my whole will to take another step forward – and with that, all will left me. As long as there was danger, I had been able to keep going, as long as I was going up or coming down, but in the instant it was all behind me, I was finished.

After my second climb of Mount Everest, and knowing I had pushed my physical potential to its limit, several of my friends and my mother, too, advised me to give up extreme mountaineering. Yet, I did not. I was in the middle of my life, feeling strong. One thing above all else that this Everest climb had made crystal clear to me was that by employing the same methods, I could climb smaller mountains in next to no time. And I knew that by tackling more difficult things, even if on smaller mountains, I would still have the opportunity to discover new limits.

Mountain of Mountains

Historical Highlights

Geographical Position: Karakoram
Baltoro Mustagh
Lat. 35°53′ N, Long. 76°31′ E

1856 German explorer Adolf Schlagintweit climbs the East Mustagh Pass. In the same year British survey officer Capt. T. G. Montgomerie sees from a distance of 200km 'a cluster of high peaks on the horizon', the inner Karakoram. He numbers the highest among them K1, K2 etc, 'K' standing for Karakoram. Only much later is it learned that the local name for K2 is Chogori; this never attains international usage, however.

1861 British colonel H.H. Godwin-Austen explores large tracts of the Western Karakoram. He produces the first general map of area (1:500 000), as well as the first description of the approaches to K2.

1892 The British mountaineer W.M. (later Lord) Conway makes a reconnaissance expedition to the foot of K2.

1902 An international expedition, led by O. Eckenstein, attempts to climb K2 by its Northeast Ridge. The upper Godwin-Austen glacier is opened up and the Windy Gap reached. Probable high point on K2 – 6,200 m.

1909 Duke Luigi Amedeo of Savoy (Duke of the Abruzzi) leads an Italian expedition to K2. He recognises the Southeast Ridge, later known as Abruzzi Rib or Ridge, as the most promising route to the summit. His party reach around 6,000m.

1929 Duke Aimone di Savoia-Aosta (Duke of Spoleto) comes not with mountaineering objectives, but to carry out scientific work in the Baltoro.

1938 A small American expedition under C. Houston climbs Southeast/Abruzzi Ridge to a point between the Shoulder and the 'Black Pyramid', thereby for the first time overcoming the key difficulties of the route.

1939 A second American expedition arrives, this time led by German/American F. Wiessner. In a summit bid (without oxygen), Wiessner comes within few hundred metres of the top of K2. One member and three Sherpas die on the descent.

1953 C. Houston leads another American expedition to K2. The weather turns against them after they have climbed to just above 7500m. A. Gilkey is taken ill. In an attempt to rope him down, there is a mass fall, miraculously checked by P. Schoening when two ropes snag. Gilkey disappears without trace.

1954 A large Italian expedition under A. Desio makes the first ascent. After a slow build-up of camps, L. Lacedelli and A. Compagnoni reach the summit on 31 July by the Abruzzi Ridge.

1977 A mammoth Japanese expedition under I. Yoshizawa – altogether 42 climbers – ascends K2 by the Abruzzi Ridge. Two parties, including a local Hunza porter, reach the summit.

1978 For the first time the Pakistani authorities grant two permits for K2. A British team led by C. Bonington abandons its attempt on the virgin West Ridge after death of N. Estcourt in an avalanche. Americans, led by J. Whittaker, successfully climb the Northeast Ridge, two ropes reaching the summit.

1979 The summit of K2 reached for the first time by a small expedition. R. Messner abandons original plan to attempt the 'Magic Line' on the South Spur, and instead climbs to the summit by the Abruzzi Ridge with M. Dacher on 12 July (4th ascent). A large French expedition fails on the South Spur.

1982 A Japanese team makes the first successful ascent of the West Ridge.

1986 This summer sees eleven expeditions operating on K2. First ascents are made of the 'Magic Line', the South Face, and a Secondary Rib on the right-hand side of the South Face. Three women stand on the summit (including W. Rutkiewicz). The mountain claims 13 victims.

K2 is truly the most beautiful eight-thousander, perhaps also the most difficult if you compare the easiest routes on the highest mountains and suppose a self-supporting expedition team. In 1979 Reinhold Messner repeated the route of the first ascent (the Abruzzi Ridge, 1954) after abandoning an exploratory climb on the south face. Six different routes now exist on K2, along with a few variations. The west, north and east faces all offer further opportunities for first ascents.

Right: Dancing Balti porters about to set off for K2 (1979).

Above: Renato Casarotto at his morning toilette. Reinhold Messner invited him to take part in his 1979 expedition, but at that time this dedicated mountaineer was not quite ready for the mountain. He climbed almost to the summit in 1986, only to be killed on the way down when he fell into a crevasse just above Base Camp.

Right: Column of porters in the Braldo Gorge, where the threat of stonefall is ever-present.

Far right: Rest stop for the porters at Concordia on the way to K2. The climber in the blue jacket is Michl Dacher. Mitre Peak rises behind.

Previous double page: Last camp on the way to K2, 1979 (at the foot of the Angelus). Alessandro Gogna and Jochen Hoelzgen stand by the tents; by the containers, Friedl Mutschlechner and Michl Dacher.

Right: Reinhold Messner with radio on the summit of K2 (12 July 1979).

Below: On K2, Michl Dacher climbs through deep snow to the Shoulder. Looking northeast.

Right: K2 from the south. On the extreme left, the West Ridge (first climbed by the Japanese in 1981). Next, the Southwest Pillar or 'Magic Line', which starts from the Negrotto Saddle diagonally left of the summit; first attempted in 1979, it was finally climbed in 1986 by a number of expeditions operating in parallel. The South Face (centre) was reconnoitred in 1979 by Friedl Mutschlechner and Reinhold Messner as far as the big serac, and climbed in its entirety in 1986 by the Poles Jerzy Kukuczka and Tadeusz Piotrowski. Piotrowski was then killed descending the Abruzzi Ridge (right-hand skyline, route of the mountain's first ascent). Between these two routes, the Cesen-Variation (Yugoslav, 1986) takes the line of the pillar as far as the Shoulder.

Below right: Friedl Mutschlechner at the bivouac on K2 South Face (1979). Behind, left, Chogolisa.

1979

Chogori
Lonely Summit

K2 from the southwest. The 1981 Japanese route follows the left-hand ridge, then goes around the summit block in a large right-hand arc (snowfields). The upper section of the 'Magic Line' is to be seen on the right skyline. There are still problems waiting to be solved on this face as well as the West Face (out of sight, left).

In 1979, a year after I climbed Everest without oxygen, I went to K2 – or Chogori, as it is known to the local Baltis. It was not just that I wanted to make an oxygenless ascent of this eight-thousander as well, but that I felt ready to take another of my 'steps' forward. My new plan was to attempt the world's second highest mountain with a small team and by a difficult route. And for this, I had selected the South Pillar, that ridge which plunges from the summit straight down to the Godwin-Austen glacier, and which we had christened the 'Magic Line'.

'Drawing a line' like this on a big mountain to reveal a hitherto-unconsidered ascent possibility, is not merely a technical process, it is an act of creativity, and one which has fascinated me for many years. You cannot see the line, of course, but it is there all the same. Once conceived, it remains a 'living line' for all time – the nothing becoming something because it has been thought to exist; the route forcing itself to become a climb.

With me on this K2 climb were Italian climbers Renato Casarotto and Alessandro Gogna, the South Tyrolean Friedl Mutschlechner, German Michl Dacher and Austrian Robert Schauer. Our liaison officer was Mohammed Tahir, and Joachim Hoelzgen, a journalist with the current affairs magazine *Der Spiegel,* also came along.

We lost a lot of time on the journey. In those days you could not travel in by bus or jeep from Rawalpindi, but had to take a plane from the Pakistani capital to Skardu, the starting-point of the expedition proper. This involved a lot of hanging about, but then, when we did eventually reach the Baltoro Glacier at the beginning of June, it was only to find it covered in deep snow. We were very much later than we planned by the time we arrived at the foot of the mountain.

Our original idea was to go around to the west of K2 and establish Base Camp behind the Angelus, one of the subsidiary summits on that side of the mountain. From there, we hoped to cross the Savoia and Negrotto glaciers to the saddle between the Angelus and K2, the actual start of the South Pillar.

We set up an interim camp on the Godwin-Austen Glacier in much the same place as in 1954, 25 years before us, the large Italian expedition camped when making the first ascent of K2. Moving up from this 'southern base' to our proposed real Base Camp, one of our porters was killed in an accident.

I had stipulated when we set out that morning that none of the men should leave the prepared trail, because I knew this last stretch of the route was very dangerous. There were crevasses left and right of the path. I was out in front looking for a safe passage through when one porter, disregarding the warning, wandered a little off route and fell into one of the crevasses. We were all there, to hand, and immediately got a rescue attempt under way. Robert Schauer abseiled down to the man, but he was already dead. The fall must have killed him outright.

It is often suggested that expeditions should be abandoned when a member dies. This is not something I have ever done, partly because those accidents I have been involved with – on Nanga Parbat in 1970 and Manaslu in 1972 – occurred towards the end when withdrawal was only a matter of time anyway. In any case, I do not believe it is of any benefit to the victim for an expedition to break up after his death. There are some teams who would give up if a sahib – one of their European members – met with an accident, but who would think nothing of carrying on after the death of a porter. I have never been able to understand such anachronisms.

The death of our porter shocked us all. We broke the news to his relatives and reported the accident to the appropriate authorities in Rawalpindi. I immediately took the decision to call everyone off the Negrotto Glacier, back to our southern Base Camp. There, for the time being, we would be safe from further danger.

K2 is the second highest mountain in the world, but it is perhaps the hardest. We realised we would have to abandon our plan to climb the 'Magic Line', if we did not want to be beaten before we began. There was no longer enough time left for all the preparation work needed; and the spot from where we had hoped to launch our attempt proved not to be a good one. Moreover, we knew that a French expedition was due to arrive in a few weeks with a similar objective in view. Their budget was ten times bigger than ours, and they had many more climbers. If, having only got part of the way up the South Pillar, we were then forced off to make way for them, all we should have done would simply have been to prepare the ground for them. I did not relish the idea of sharing a first

ascent in that way. I would rather relinquish the route.

With the exception of Renato Casarotto, who wanted to stay with our original plan even though at that time he was the weakest among us, the others agreed we should transfer our attention to the Abruzzi Ridge, the route of the first ascent. We would still have the chance of trying something new: K2 had never been climbed by so small a team as ours.

In places on the ridge we found ropes left by a Japanese expedition two years before, but most of the protection had to be put in again. We erected three small high camps, and fixed ropes as far as the top of the Black Pyramid at 7,400 metres, so that we would be able to find our way down even in the fiercest storm. From there, on 11 and 12 July, in the

The summit pyramid of K2. The ice mushroom, left of centre, divides the 'Magic Line' (Southwest Pillar route) into two halves. The Abruzzi Ridge runs behind the line of the horizon, right. Between them the South Face (1986).

first fine weather period, and in otherwise pure Alpine style, Michl Dacher and I climbed to the summit of K2, with one bivouac en route.

This bivouac was above the big shoulder, not far from the spot where in 1954 Walter Bonatti and the Hunza-porter Mhadi spent a night in the open, huddled together, after carrying up oxygen supplies for the final push of the self-elected summit team.

The night was bitterly cold, but the morning brought splendid weather. Michl and I left the tent and climbed the avalanche-prone slopes leading up into the Bottleneck. This narrow passage between a vertical ice bulge and steep rock forced us to climb out to the left until we reached the foot of the huge snow-covered summit pyramid.

It took us hours to toil up. It was a brilliant day, with not a cloud anywhere. Like a black and white picture, the mountains and valleys lay beneath us. There was no green, no red and no yellow, only the blue of the sky. The higher we climbed, the darker blue it became, until it was nearly black. But where was the summit? When we had given up hope of ever reaching it, suddenly, we saw we were almost there, on a ridge leading across flatter ground. The summit ridge! A little later we were both standing on the highest point in the evening sunshine.

We didn't stay up there long. Before it was dark, we had climbed back down the same route to our last bivouac. The next day we plodded on, down through deep drifts and thick cloud in the direction of Camp 3. On the way, we bumped into Gogna, Schauer and Mutschlechner who were waiting for us. They had hoped to be able to go for the summit themselves, but had given up the idea when the weather turned bad. Together we descended to Base Camp.

The section from our bivouac down to Camp 3 had proved the most critical of the expedition. Michl and I could so easily have gone astray in the mist. We were under constant threat from avalanches

Last bivouac above the Shoulder on the Abruzzi Ridge. Above that, the 'Bottleneck' and large overhanging seracs. As high as this, one no longer questions 'Why?' The intensity of the moment removes any search for meaning.

and strong gusts of wind tugged at us as we inched our way down. We were extremely relieved finally to hear our friends calling and realise we must be getting close to the camp. They led us back to the tent. There is only this one way down on to the Black Pyramid, but it is not easy to find.

We had come down from top to bottom of the Abruzzi Ridge in a single day, and soon we were back at the foot of the mountain. This last section, protected in many places by fixed ropes, gave us no further problem. Even though our tracks had all gone, we found our way down the partly well-worn route all right. We then crossed the glacier without mishap and by evening were back in Base Camp.

K2 is a most beautiful mountain, but it is also a very dangerous one. The reasons for some of the many tragedies that have occurred there remain a mystery. To get a lot of climbers off the mountain safely requires a lot of luck.

Being such a small team meant we could climb K2 very quickly. To climb the upper section in Alpine style, as we did, was something of a try-out. At that time, I had still not put my ideas of climbing one of the bigger eight-thousanders by this lightweight method to the test, but now it appeared realisable.

The K2 expedition was the fourth trip I had organised to an eight-thousander (coming as it did after Hidden Peak, Dhaulagiri and the Nanga Parbat solo). At first, it had not been easy to finance these expeditions on the open market, but now I was getting more experienced at it. Also my track record was making a difference.

After success on Everest, media and sponsors were prepared to place even greater trust in me. Then, provided I obtained a press contract for each trip, along with support from my equipment firms, it proved possible to set several expeditions on their feet year by year. The people who came with me paid only a fraction of what it cost to bring them – or nothing at all. That made it simpler

Alessandro Gogna

Survived – descent in the mist

What is left after seven years? What has remained in my mind after so long a period? And suppose I multiplied what I remember of this experience by fourteen – how would that change things? It does amaze me just how many times Reinhold, solely in order to be able to live according to his philosophies, has willingly put himself in situations in which survival was extraordinarily difficult; and I try to recreate the one time when I was there too. Subjective experience is the only thing that counts.

I recall our climb in the storm on K2. We were at 7,500 metres. Irresolution prevented us from turning back to Camp 3. We wanted to get higher or to meet up with the other two who had been to the summit, then bivouacked at Camp 4, and who may by now be in need of assistance. We

climbed without speaking, from time to time pausing to draw breath or exchange glances. We were worried. Although we kept calling the others, the wind offered as little chance of hearing them as the mist did of being able to see them.

As I climbed I tried to push common sense to the back of my mind, focusing my attention instead on the undisturbed snow in front of my feet, or the hollow footprints of the others. Suddenly I noticed a few small blobs of snow rolling down past me. I stopped and looked up. Other little snow-slides were coming down. 'Here – we're here! Reinhold! Michl! Reinhold!' No one answered. But the snowballs were getting bigger all the time, and finally we were able to make out two dark shapes coming towards us.

They had heard us and were hurrying down in the direction of the sound. I couldn't have been more pleased to see them if it had been the other way round, me coming back from the summit. I was delighted that the expedition had been a success, and more than delighted to be feeling no bitterness about not having been in the summit team myself.

The night before, I remember, when the summit had suddenly broken into view, I had been almost transfixed. Until that moment I had worked for the good of the team without particular personal ambition. But then I felt I had to put myself first in future, work for myself. It had been an instinctive reaction. Now here we were, faced with escorting Reinhold and Michl back to Base Camp in the snowstorm, and I did not mind. I was worried for them. After all their efforts, it was Reinhold and Michl who were at risk; we were still fresh.

Seven years later, in the summer of 1986, everyone followed with horror the dreadful events on K2: thirteen dead. In almost all cases, their grave errors had been made in the appraisal of real survival possibilities. Two Alpinists among the dead were on K2 when we were up there.

I do not believe it had anything to do with individual lack of experience. A lack of luck, certainly, but more than that, it had to do with general attitude. Attitudes towards the mountain have changed greatly since our day. The mountain seems to have lost its real meaning, as indeed have all the Himalaya. It used to be a case of man versus the forces of nature – now it tends to be much more the pitting of one man against other men. The resulting competition is abrasive. If by storming a mountain, you reduce its value to nil – which is what you do do – then you are also converting your respect for that mountain to nil, and the instinctive relationship, the balance between climber and mountain, gradually disappears. The removal of all taboos and the general under-appreciation of the mountain as a natural force, naturally diminishes your appreciation of mental and physical limitations as well. Catastrophe is an ultimate result of such diminution.

This may seem too harsh an analysis, but it embodies my own experience.

I have still not concluded my descent in the mist. How much further I have to go down, I do not know. Today I ask myself whether fourteen eight-thousanders have saved Reinhold from the business of having eternally to climb down through this symbolic mist, mist in which for one moment of our lives we found ourselves together.

Alessandro Gogna
(Member of K2 Expedition, 1979)

than when everyone had to contribute his share. I was now able to raise the bulk of all the expedition costs myself.

In an ideal world, I would prefer not to have to be burdened with responsibility on an expedition. I would rather be in a group that did everything together; have a manager to take care of all the organisation and finance; choose a goal that was equally important to everyone; grant everyone absolute freedom to undertake publicity assignments (films, photos, reporting), and a democratic vote when it came to climbing decisions.

A lot has changed in the Karakoram since 1979, not only on K2, but also on the lesser eight-thousanders. As a result of underlying competition among many Alpinists and very often an inflated opinion of their own importance, a hectic state has come about that I find nauseating. Nevertheless, high-level success is still not quantifiable, and certainly not qualifiable. The quality of climbing depends on the man/mountain relationship. Quantity is what many people today hope to find in their relationship with competition. Fast times, and the 'climb-under-any-circumstances,' mentality assume overriding importance. The risk-factor grows. The accidents on K2 in the summer of 1986 demonstrate this.

The increase in the number of expeditions to 8,000-metre peaks is no guarantee that this sort of climbing will get any safer. With many groups climbing the same route concurrently, all are more than likely to be thrust into situations that are potentially more dangerous, more life-threatening. If climbers who are not at their best as far as condition and endurance are concerned, find themselves in such situations, the possibility of their being killed increases dramatically. Looking back at all the accidents which took place on K2 during 1986, I would not want to cast any individual blame. But I remain convinced – and my experiences on Lhotse certainly did nothing to change my mind on this – that anybody who wants to

climb an eight-thousander should be responsible for preparing his own route. Whoever has humped up his own camps, installed his own fixed ropes, achieves a far more intimate feel for the mountain. He does not need to be told what increased risks he is taking. The difficulty of the mountain, the height, our own personal limitations do not permit us to go up into areas beyond our capabilities without outside help.

But if the route has already been prepared, from bottom to top, and there are enough tents and stores on the way, it could induce the less experienced, the weaker climbers, up into the death zone too. That this happens literally on the backs of the others is of little concern. As a 'parasite', you need exert yourself less to climb high. If the weather then suddenly changes, however, if strength fails, then that climber is charging blindly towards disaster.

There are half a dozen different routes now on K2; it is even being climbed from the Chinese side. Why do most people still, therefore, go up the normal route? It is true some new routes often have several expeditions attempting them at the same time – as did the South Pillar, the 'Magic Line', in 1986 – while other possibilities remain untried. It was a great tragedy that the 'Magic Line' should have been tried by overlapping expeditions. True it was climbed for the first time, but not by one, rather by three parallel groups. Renato Casarotto was among them. He died, one of 13 climbers who were killed on K2 that dark summer.

I had invited Casarotto to come on my expedition in 1979, because I felt him to be at the time one of the strongest classical climbers in Europe. He had made bold first ascents in the Alps and in South America. But on our expedition he proved so slow as to be something of a liability; that was one of the reasons why I gave up the idea of climbing the South Pillar. It did not seem I would be able to count on him.

In 1986 Casarotto went back to the

K2 from the west. This face is a great problem. It tempts Reinhold Messner in the same way as does a traverse of Everest and Lhotse, but he intends to abide by the promise he made to his mother not to attempt any more eight-thousanders. 'I will investigate other possibilities of adventure.' After repeated experiences in the vertical, and at great height, he wants to explore the wide and horizontal world.

South Pillar of K2. Whether he wanted to settle an old account or whether from the start it had been important to him to make the first ascent of the 'Magic Line', I do not know. I only know that he died. Renato Casarotto, for whom I had the greatest respect, fell into a crevasse on the way down, not far above Base Camp, and was killed. It was sad occasion for all of us who had spent two months on the same mountain with him seven years before.

After K2, I felt strongly – far more than after my earlier eight-thousanders – what it meant to stand on the summit. *Der Spiegel* reported the expedition and in discussions on television I got drawn into arguments about it. Being successful on so many summits brought me considerable popularity, but also hostility. In the mid-1970s, when I failed on Makalu, Lhotse and Dhaulagiri, the carping criticism died down a bit. It seemed people took some pleasure in the fact that I had apparently lost my knack for climbing eight-thousanders. But in 1978, when I climbed two eight-thousanders one after the other – Everest without oxygen and Nanga Parbat solo – the atmosphere grew cool again. And so did I.

In the summer of 1979, after K2, I experienced a fresh wave of antipathy; I felt more lonely on this pinnacle of celebrity than ever before. Even friends withdrew further from me. The Press reacted critically. Although K2 had never been climbed by so small a team before, nor as quickly, this expedition was interpreted as a 'deviation' from my usual style, even though we climbed without oxygen masks and placed no

94

camps or fixed rope on the upper sections, and even though we operated without Sherpas.

I have never sought to be a folk hero and was used to rejection. All the same, it was not always easy to cope with so much misunderstanding. I felt no great temptation to try and ingratiate myself with the critics; I thought it better to keep quiet. Recognition was less important than the need to remain true to myself, especially when swimming alone against the tide. These steps forward I take in mountaineering, must never be taken two at a time. If you want to push out limits, you have to do it slowly, stealthily, bit by bit. If you go too fast, and try to leap-frog stages, sooner or later you will stumble.

On Everest we had been a large and strong team. We built up a whole chain of camps before Peter Habeler and I, in our oxygenless attempt, were in a position to set off for the summit. On K2, we were not the first to reach the summit without oxygen – this had been done a year earlier by Jim Whittaker's American expedition, climbing the northeast side – but we were the first *small* party to operate without artificial oxygen. Today, K2 has been climbed in less than 24 hours; it has become a matter of course to charge from Base Camp to summit without a rucksack, up a route prepared and secured with ropes by other climbers. Our methods mean nothing to anybody any more.

What really annoys me, even more than this race for the eight-thousanders ('Who can get to the summit fastest?') is the fact that it leaves so little opportunity for young people with dreams and ability to put their ideas into practice. The eight-thousanders have now become so overrun that you can hardly find a route anywhere on which to be quite alone, where there are no residual fixed ropes, where no one has built a camp before, and no depots have been left behind. Every time you come across some item in place, it cuts back on your own experience, and in so doing, puts this personal experience at stake.

In this respect, all climbers have a great responsibility towards the subsequent generations. None of us has the right to tie up the eight-thousanders with fixed ropes, to put in high camps and then leave them untidily behind. Of course, we all have a right to climb, each where we will and on any conceivable route. But at the same time we have the duty to take back down the mountain everything we have carried up. We must learn to leave mountains as we find them. That is the only way they can remain thrilling and interesting places for the people following after, and continue to afford the fascinating challenge that we needed, and which future young mountaineers are going to need every bit as much.

Our generation, as I have often said, is not going to be measured by how many eight-thousanders we bagged and how fast we made the climbs; we will be remembered for how intact we leave these mountains as places of opportunity for the next generation. A South Pillar clean of pegs and ropes will still hold interest in later years; a Pillar heavy with protection is not merely boring, it is repellent.

When I think back to K2, there are one or two special moments that still strike a strong chord in me. Such as the time when, just going down from the summit, I saw out to the east the shadow of K2 cast across the mountain ranges beneath me. A huge dark form lying across the Karakoram mountains. And on the very top of this shadow I could make out a tiny dot. Was it me? Some years later my little daughter Layla asked me why I had not waited for the mountain to 'go to sleep' before climbing to the top. Her words immediately conjured in my imagination the silhouette of K2. She continued, 'Yes, then, when the mountain got up in the morning, you would have been on top.'

How simple it would be if mountains really laid down, or if we were blessed with the ability to project ourselves to the top of eight-thousanders on the wings of our imagination. With such unearthly powers, we would certainly reach the highest points without the effort and danger it costs us now. But so long as I am unable to step right outside this physical world, I find the greatest adventures do not take place in the head – that is only where they begin.

The Last Eight-Thousander

Historical Highlights

Geographical Position: Central Himalaya, Tibet
Lat. 28°21′ N, Long. 85°47′ E

1963 A group from Central China and Tibet reconnoitre this isolated peak, that previously had been better known by its Indian name, Gosainthan. At 8,046m, this counts as the smallest eight-thousander. They climb the north flank to a height of around 7,200m.

1964 Only a year after reconnaissance, Chinese and Tibetan climbers are successful in making a first ascent. On 2 May a total of ten climbers reach the top by the Northwest Face and North Ridge. A 3-man fall on the descent luckily results in no injury.

1980 Shisha Pangma becomes accessible to outsiders. In the course of a German expedition led by M. Abelein and G. Sturm, two ropes reach summit by the 1964 route during the pre-monsoon period. An attempt on the North Face fails at around 7,500m. In the autumn an Austrian group under H. Mautner is successful on the same route. The expedition doctor, Dr Alt, breaks both ankles during a solo climb and it is several days before he can be rescued, badly frost-bitten.

1981 In the spring a Japanese womens' expedition, led by J. Tabei, makes the fourth ascent.
On 28 May R. Messner and F. Mutschlechner stand on the summit in the worst possible weather conditions; they have opened a variant to the old route (5th ascent).

(Climbs are given here not by ropes, but by expeditions. R. Messner is of the opinion that when a team reaches the summit – even if there are several rope-parties that get there – it remains one ascent because the route has been prepared by all of them. Only when within a single expedition, different routes are climbed, are these climbs counted separately.)

1982 A year to the day later, British climbers under D. Scott open a new route. Without fixed ropes or intermediate camps Scott, A. MacIntyre, and R. Baxter-Jones climb the 3,000m South Face, descending by the Southeast Ridge. In the autumn all six members of a Japanese expedition under M. Hara repeat the Chinese route to the summit.

1983 In the spring, in the course of a German–Swiss expedition led by S. Hupfauer, three Germans reach the summit. At the same time the mountain claims its first victim – F. Luchsinger. (Aged 62 when he died, Luchsinger had climbed Dhaulagiri at the age of 59, and in 1956, had taken part in the first ascent of Lhotse.) An autumn expedition under G. Porzak brings 3 Americans to the summit.

1984 Another American group, this time under the leadership of J. Murphy, follows the Chinese route to the summit.

1985 Following the same route, a German–Austrian–Swiss expedition, led by M. Schmuck, enjoy greater success. 12 members stand on summit of Shisha Pangma. In the same spring an Italian also reaches the highest point. Three members of a Swiss expedition under M. Itten reach the top in the autumn.

1986 The mountain is visited by climbers of many nations: French, Japanese and Austrians climb the normal route to the top. The 'organised adventure' had become acceptable on the eight-thousanders as elsewhere. Young star climbers strive less for clean, independent routes; they are interested purely in speed (e.g. E. Escoffier).

Shisha Pangma, lying totally within Tibet, is one of the easiest eight-thousanders. Nevertheless, poor conditions, such as a lot of snow or cloud, can render the climb difficult, if not impossible. Previously there had only been two routes to the summit: one from the south (English route, 1982), and one from the north (Chinese, 1964), which Reinhold Messner and Friedl Mutschlechner also followed in 1981, but with the introduction of a new variation on the lower summit wall.

Several other logical possibilities suggest themselves (West Ridge, two variations on the north side of the summit wall, East Face and South Face).

SHISHA PANGMA 8046 m

c_2 △

△ c_1

△ △ ABC

Above left: Friedl Mutschlechner in the first camp on Shisha Pangma. The summit can be seen just behind the ridge in the foreground.

Left: Descent on skis from 7,200m. In the picture, Friedl Mutschlechner.

Previous double page: Base Camp with Shisha Pangma, Tibet (1981).

Above: View of summit ridge of Shisha Pangma, looking north across Tibet. There was such a severe snowstorm when Reinhold Messner and Friedl Mutschlechner made their summit climb that they were only able to snatch a single glimpse of the Tibetan plateau beneath them. In the autumn of 1985 Oswald Oelz reached the top in better weather, though he encountered far more snow.

Right: Friedl Mutschlechner coming down from the summit through drifting snow (28 May 1981).

Above: Advanced Base Camp on Shisha Pangma. From here Vanessa Oelz and Gerhard Baur, who were making a documentary film of the expedition, were able to follow the progress of Oswald Oelz, Friedl Mutschlechner and Reinhold Messner.

Above left: A yak caravan brought equipment from Base Camp to Advanced Base at the foot of the mountain, and back again at the end of the expedition. Some containers were dropped and valuable film material lost. Tape recorders and cameras were damaged.

Left: Yaks with their drivers, Tibetan farmers.

1981

Shisha Pangma
Mist Obscures View

A man is not 'called'; he has no 'mission', no 'true vocation', any more than a plant or an animal has a 'calling'.

Max Stirner

A large proportion of members on an expedition spend the best part of their time dreaming about their wives. But it has also to be said that many men – who are to be assumed both intelligent and well balanced – go to the mountains in order to get away from their wives.

Pierre Chapoutot

Shisha Pangma from the north. The summit can be seen left (south) of the long ridge behind the pointed peak. A British route runs up the South Face (1982); from the north, two variations are possible.

Shisha Pangma no longer counts as the smallest eight-thousander – latest surveys cast Gasherbrum II in that role. Seen from the north, standing completely alone, a solitary, somewhat alien extrusion rearing out of the earth-brown Tibetan plateau, Shisha Pangma, for me, is one of the most lovely eight-thousanders. An expressionistic apparition!

Our 1981 expedition comprised four male Alpinists and two not-very-extreme women climbers. It included Gerhard Baur as cameraman, and two of my most frequent companions on 8,000-metre climbs. Dr Oswald Oelz *(Bulle)* and Friedl Mutschlechner. We arrived at Base Camp on 10 May after a Japanese womens' expedition – which included Junko Tabei – had reached the summit of Shisha Pangma by its normal route.

Equipped with a permit from the CMA, the Chinese Mountaineering Association in Peking, we had come in through Peking, Chengdu and Lhasa. In the markets of Lhasa and in the mountain villages we noticed some small concessions had been made to the Tibetans by the Chinese since we were last here. From Lhasa we went to Shigatze where we visited the Tashilumpo, the monastery of the Panchen Lama. Finally we moved on to Tingri, which is situated in a hollow at about 4,400 metres above sea level, and spent around ten days there acclimatising. At the beginning of May we drove and walked across the Tibetan plateau to 5,000 metres, setting up Base Camp in a little basin by a stream which came directly off Shisha Pangma.

The North Face of Shisha Pangma, our objective, is about as high as the Matterhorn North Face. It rises high on the mountain, above the flat glacial valley used also by the normal route, that of the Chinese first ascent, then leads left on to the Northeast Face. The summit wall is crossed diagonally by a ramp, which in its steepness can be compared with the classic routes on the Brenva Face of Mont Blanc.

Naturally, I wanted to climb Shisha Pangma without oxygen apparatus, without fixed ropes or high-level porters. My plan was to take our equipment from Base Camp up to 5,800 metres by yak, the local form of cattle which are adept at climbing and tolerant of high altitude. There we would establish Advanced Base Camp. We would follow the Chinese route as far as the foot of the wall, setting up a small depot under the steep face at around 7,000 metres. Higher up a small bivouac would be necessary for our summit attempt.

Gerhard Baur suffered headaches, presumably altitude-induced. *Bulle* Oelz, Friedl Mutschlechner and I were in fine form, but the weather played havoc with our plans. The monsoon broke about two weeks earlier than it normally does. Nevertheless, Friedl pressed on. He was all set on making it to the summit. He knew how it felt to have to go home empty-handed from an eight-thousander climb. On 27 May, as soon as it began to grow light, he was urging us to get started. We toiled up the normal route. In a wind that whipped our breath away, we climbed 400 metres above the last bivouac.

There was no sense in going any higher. I had been saying that privately to myself for two hours already. Two weeks early or not, the monsoon was upon us. If we did not go down right away, it would be too late. Somebody some day would come across what was left of us, just as I had already stumbled across other victims: climbers mummified in their down suits, their bodies preserved in the eternal ice.

In a short time metre-deep snow would turn the descent route into an avalanche nightmare. If the snow-drifts became any deeper and the mists thickened, it would be impossible to get our bearings. Friedl, who was forging on ahead, stamping down the snow, was going like the clappers. He was the one who had egged us on in the morning, despite the storm which was brewing up, and he was the one who did not want to give up. For him, it was a point of honour

105

Tibet today

We were all very taken with the Tibetan plateau after travelling a good 1,000 kilometres across it. A few of us would have liked to have stayed there forever – provided of course that Tibet could be a free country once more, as it was for hundreds of years.

Anyone who has spent time in Tibet can never forget this country with its wave upon wave of hills and its shining, seemingly transparent horizon. How far away are those next mountains! You are lured on into the next valley, and on and on to the distant horizon. You yearn to explore the great rivers away to the north, to understand the complicated river system of this the greatest high plateau in the world.

No country I had visited before ever aroused in me so deep a longing to understand its secrets. I wanted to penetrate further and further into this seemingly barren land, which appeared to hold the answers to all the fundamental questions of life. This beloved landscape of so few colours is a never-ending panel, above which the white clouds scud from morning to night. White clouds that, seen from below, appear to have been chopped into pieces with a kitchen knife.

The village of Shekar (near Tingri). View from Shekar Dzong – a fortified monastery from the summit of which Chomolungma (Mount Everest) is visible. Behind, ranges of weathered mountains. Today most villages and towns in Tibet are divided into two: a cluster of the original traditional Tibetan buildings and, beyond them, accommodation for the occupying Chinese authorities, with straight streets, tin roofs and administration blocks.

to keep going to the top, which now rose before us. Two years earlier he had been forced to turn back shortly before the summit of K2. Once again, only a short distance separated him from his goal, Shisha Pangma, the first eight-thousander of his career. My goal, however, was a little tent, 1,200 metres below the summit, which we had left that morning and now had to get back to urgently if we were to survive.

I have never fooled myself about my expeditions to the highest summits of this earth. I have always known that something could go wrong, but at the same time I have prepared myself for conceivable dangers and planned in detail what to do in such circumstances. That is how I have been lucky enough to look down from the top of five different eight-thousanders, five of the fourteen that exist. Yet something was happening now that was unexpected. The monsoon had caught us by surprise, and no eight-thousander is easily won in a monsoon storm. Remembered snatches of other expeditions floated through my mind.

I thought about the world below, from which we had severed ourselves four days before. Thought of Uschi, my wife of six years, who was waiting down there at Base Camp 2,000 metres beneath us. Surely she and Vanessa, *Bulle's* wife, would be peering through our special telescope, trying to make us out. I doubted they would be able to see anything in this inferno; our own visibility was down to nothing.

I thought about Tibet, a land which had been closed to outsiders for so long after the Chinese took it over, but through which we had now been travelling for a month. We were one of the first groups to be allowed back in. We had been surprised and shocked to see how much had altered since the flight of the Dalai Lama in 1959 and the governmental take-over by Peking communists. Local people told us that of the 3,600 monasteries that had once been the religious strongholds of Tibet, only thirteen remain standing today. All the others

Friedl Mutschlechner coming down after the first attempt to reach the summit of Shisha Pangma by its normal route. In thick cloud and deep snow this was a dangerous retreat. Mutschlechner and Messner remained in their tent at around 7,000m; Oswald Oelz continued down to his bivouac.

Left: On the summit ridge of Shisha Pangma (28 May 1981). 'Above us only storm, below us cloud; of the outer world there was nothing to be seen, but within we had experience enough.'

Right: The flat U-shaped valley at the foot of the summit wall of Shisha Pangma (about 7,000m). 'The world is spread like an open book, and you stand at its centre with eyes of recognition. There is no need to seek further.'

were destroyed and many monks perished in Chinese work camps.

Down in the valley I had often asked myself how such a thing was possible; how could a country, so ideally protected by nature, be destroyed in this way? But I have also observed how the ordinary people have prevailed despite their sorrow and suffering. They have never yielded to their Chinese conquerors and so have retained some part of their freedom. Restrictions are gradually relaxing and they are now allowed to do some things that were forbidden for a long time. They can trade again, and what is more important for them, are permitted once more to practise their religion freely.

Peking has granted the Tibetans a freedom which in China itself would be unthinkable. Perhaps the party leaders recognised that only an autonomous Tibet could provide a bulwark against the major powers to their south and west.

Thoughts such as these were occupy-ing my mind as we battled on through the rising monsoon storm.

It was 8 o'clock in the morning when we came upon a small tent; it had been ripped open and the wind was filling it with powder snow which whirled about inside. We crawled in amongst the drifts and stopped up the hole with our rucksacks.

When *Bulle* fought his way up to us from a lower camp around midday, the position was hopeless. *Bulle* and I had been to the top of Everest as members of a shared expedition, and would have liked to have done the same here. But the situation grew more threatening as time went on, the steep slopes increasingly ready to avalanche. We had no choice but to leave the camp, this little tent at 7,500 metres, left behind by the Japanese, and climb back down to our own bivouac tent, set up the night before.

The storm tore at our tent all evening. We did not get a wink of sleep. At 2 o'clock it was still blowing. Friedl looked outside, 'The sky's clear,' he said 'It'll soon blow over!' Once more he was pressing for action. He was so sure we could make it, I got dressed. Though secretly I believed it was pointless, I said nothing, and at 5 o'clock we set off. This time without *Bulle*.

The storm dashed handfuls of stinging crystals into our faces. There really were stars in the sky. We noticed a gully above us, down which an avalanche had come in the night. That was a stroke of luck, as we were able to climb up its scoured confines and over steep rocks to reach the ridge.

It was hours before we were on easy ground. Meanwhile the storm had blown up again, wrapping us in dense cloud. We could see no more than a few metres ahead. This is craziness I told myself. To climb on a peak like this in the middle of the monsoon – utter craziness. But there was no going back.

The storm became so fierce, we had to keep taking shelter. Yet there was no holding Friedl. He wanted to go on, to go up. He wanted the summit. Twelve years' experience had taught me what a struggle

it is to climb at these heights without using oxygen. It is a tremendous effort – even without the monsoon whipping your every breath away. My hesitation, though, lasted no more than a moment. A single moment is all it took Friedl to inspire me to forget our exposed position, and forget this senseless exertion – for the moment, at least.

The cloud around us was like a fog in my head, stupefying. In it, it was easy to lose all sense of direction. Was that really a figure in front of me? Friedl? How could anyone keep going with no ground and no sky? Colourless, amorphous, heaven and earth blended together. We climbed on, eyes wide, in a grey nothingness of mist and snow. A bit further, a bit back, a few metres left, then right, compensating, cancelling. Perhaps you needed to do everything back to front up there.

I could see our trail about 10 metres behind us. The shadows helped pick it out. Further down it was already blown away. How slow we were! When your sense of space disappears, time goes with it. No tiredness, no anxiety, just this sense of being lost in space. I could not bear it. At least not with both feet in snow. Only when Friedl looked my way, was I able to adjust myself in time and space. He was obviously mirroring my world.

Neither of us spoke in those last metres. Like robots, we approached our goal. Then we were up. I embraced my taskmaster, my *doppelgänger*. It was his first eight-thousander – cause for celebration, but not here. I peered into the thick cloud. A window opened up through which I could see the high plateau of Tibet. What a long way away the world was down there, I thought. Three days later, we had returned to it.

The end of an expedition does not just mean being able to relax your guard, being safer. It also means loving and belonging. My need to give myself completely to someone else, my partner, was never stronger than after coming down off a big mountain. Danger past makes me crave new 'borderline' experiences, but I am also hungry for love and for death. Death is preceded by many 'little deaths'. Perhaps that explains my heightened need for love before and after experiences at the edge of human existence, explains why my longing is so great.

Originally we proposed to climb the North Face by the diagonal ramp running right to left from the big valley under the summit wall to the fore-summit, and thence to the main summit. It seemed a logical line, but because of the quantities of monsoon snow on the route, we were not able to try it. Instead, we followed a gully to the right of the normal route, regaining the normal route for the final stage of the climb. We thus approached the summit in the same way as all those before us.

In 1981, at the time of our Shisha Pangma expedition, high altitude climbing and in particular the exploitation of overseas mountaineering trips was becoming more professional – not just as far as I was concerned, but for many other

Survived – summit climb in a snowstorm

The monsoon storm tears at my little tent which is pitched on a flat bit of ice at 7,000 metres and anchored with ice screws and my climbing axe. Every time a huge gust catches it, I expect the walls to give way. I think about Reinhold and Friedl, who must also be sitting out the storm in their tent, a hundred metres above me.

Two days ago, when we first came up, I simply could not manage that last difficult pitch. We originally planned to go for the summit today, but this crazy storm has put paid to that. We had a go yesterday, when in the morning at least the weather was not so bad, and reached 7,400 metres before the monsoon winds and snowfall grew too strong. In thick cloud we had to make our way carefully back down the steep slopes to our tents, making use of the lulls in the wind.

Now I am just lying around, talking over the radio with Vanessa and waiting. We are going to have to give up and go home, leaving Shisha Pangma as unfinished business, if only this storm will ever let up.

It is 5 o'clock in the evening when, half-asleep, I hear my name being called above the howl of the wind. Two ice-encrusted figures arrive in front of the tent: Reinhold and Friedl, leaning on their ski sticks. Reinhold gasps, 'We've been to the top – in this! We left early this morning; Friedl was dead set on giving it a try. This was a big day for him. He broke trail most of the way – it was murder.'

It must have been. Their haggard faces appear almost green above icicled beards. In this incredible storm, they had to climb a thousand vertical metres to reach the summit. And they lived to tell the tale! Anyone else would be sitting in the snow somewhere by now, sleeping – perhaps for ever.

From somewhere Reinhold is able to summon up sufficient energy to press on, he wants us down in Advanced Base tonight. Without skis, he keeps sliding, then sitting in the snow, unable to stay on his feet. But he always gets up and goes on, so that towards 1 o'clock in the morning we stagger into camp.

An overwhelming urge to break taboos and climb in that border region between life and death has already led Reinhold into other critical situations, on Nanga Parbat and Manaslu, as well as on his two solo ascents of Nanga Parbat and Everest. It has made him into one of the few survivors of high altitude mountaineering.

When he started this game in 1970, Reinhold brought to it all the right physical prerequisites: he had grown up in the mountains, his body and mind had been toughened on many of the hardest tours in the Alps; he was the leading Alpinist of the late sixties.

Scientists and others have shown great interest in his psychological characteristics. Before his historic

Greetings card from Shisha Pangma. For a small sum it is possible to order a postcard from a forthcoming expedition; it will be stamped and franked in the country visited and bear signatures of all the expedition members.

Oswald *(Bulle)* Oelz

climb of Everest without oxygen, various university professors and pundits, believing they knew more about it than Reinhold did, declared that the attempt would fail, or at the very least would lead to severe brain damage. When no intellectual impairment could be discerned in either Messner or Habeler after their Everest adventure, the line was then taken that they must both be unusually able to take up oxygen and make economic use of it. However, studies I and others have made indicate that in all aspects of oxygen uptake and use, Reinhold, like other successful high altitude climbers we have tested, falls within the normal physiological limits of any athletes who engage in sports which require good staying power and who are in medium to good training.

The secret of Reinhold's mountaineering success, therefore, does not lie in any exceptional physical capabilities apart from his ability to assess a situation shrewdly. Rather it lies in his motivation and his capacity to endure hardship and pain, which allow him to overcome barriers that are rather more psychological than physiological. Messner has exploded other myths, as he did the one that man could not live above 8,500 metres without an oxygen mask. The impetus that drives him is an alert spirit, open to fantasies and readily ignited by taboos and barriers. The same aggressiveness and relentlessness which Reinhold displays when attacking real and imagined opponents or problems, he can also turn upon himself, whenever success or survival demand it.

Thus, he has become the principal player in the 'Sufferings Game', in that he has pushed his body and mind to the uttermost limits of endurance. This is something Nena saw on his return from his solo ascent of Everest; he was totally played out, drained to his very soul. And I, too, observed it when he and Friedl came down off Shisha Pangma. But exhausted as he was, Reinhold was still capable of drawing new strength from somewhere.

Oswald Oelz
(Climber of two eight-thousanders)

people as well. No one was actually paid to climb eight-thousanders, but it had become possible to finance such ventures.

If you look upon the economic side of these expeditions as a commercial enterprise, which of course in a way it is, you are talking about a system of financing. At one time it was only millionaires or scroungers who could afford expeditions. Today, anyone seeking to do something new, provided he has the ability to 'market' himself and his idea, can find the money for it. Of course, he has to be prepared to work hard. But then, by writing accounts of the trip, or delivering talks, or giving the equipment industry the benefit of his technical experience, it is possible to fund the next project if the previous one has captured the imagination. You can only succeed indefinitely if you are one of those people who keeps coming up with new ideas, a pioneer of one sort or another.

After I had been to Tibet, I saw my climbing differently. That was not just because of lamaism. The Tibetan rhythm of life, and the Tibetan attitude towards death had an influence on me. Solitude took on new meaning. To see life as a climb into your own mysteries seemed so logical in this landscape. The desire to lose myself, and no longer need to prove myself, became stronger than ambition to be best. Milarepa (1042–1123), who meditated on Everest, fascinated me, as did Gesar, a legendary Tibetan hero.

The Five Treasure-Houses of the Snows

Historical Highlights

Geographical Position: East Himalaya, Nepal/Sikkim/Tibet triangle
Lat. 27°42′ N, Long. 88°09′ E

1899   The Briton D.W. Freshfield and the Italian photographer V. Sella make a circuit of Kangchenjunga. (Kangchenjunga translated means 'five treasure–houses of the great snows'.) German-speaking mountaineers often shorten the name to *Kantsch*. The multi-topped massif comprises Main Summit (8,586m), Middle Summit (8,482m), South Summit (8,476m) and West Summit, or Yalung Kang (8,433m).

1929   German expedition led by P. Bauer reaches a height of around 7,400m on the Northeast Ridge.

1930   G.O. Dyhrenfurth leads an international expedition to the north flank. A Sherpa is killed in an ice avalanche attempting to reach the North Ridge. The group then turn their attention to the Northwest Ridge and reach a height of about 6,400m.

1931   P. Bauer leads another expedition to *Kantsch*. This time a height of about 7,700m is attained on the Northeast Spur. H. Schaller and a Sherpa are killed in a fall; the Sherpa Sirdar dies of sickness.

1955   In the course of a British expedition under the leadership of C. Evans, Kangchenjunga is climbed for the first time on 25 May by G. Band and J. Brown. The next day N. Hardie and T. Streather also reach the summit. Both ropes respect the mountaintop as sacred to local people and refrain from treading the actual summit snow – they stop a few metres below.

1973   First ascent of West Summit (Yalung Kang) by a Japanese team in the spring, following the Southwest Ridge.

1975   A German–Austrian expedition under the leadership of S. Aeberli and G. Sturm succeed in climbing the West Summit by a new route. Nine members in three groups reach the top of Yalung Kang.

1977   An Indian military expedition under Col. N. Kumar successfully reaches the Main Summit. Following the Northeast Spur and North Ridge one member and one Sherpa reach the top.

1978   First ascent of South and Middle Summits from the Southwest by a Polish group.

1979   Third ascent of the Main Summit, this time from the North, by a British expedition. D. Scott, P. Boardman and J. Tasker reach the highest point via the North Col in Alpine style and without artificial oxygen.

1980   In the course of a Japanese expedition, led by M. Konishi, two summit parties successfully reach the top during the spring, opening up an impressive Northwest Face route.

1982   R. Messner and the South Tyrolean F. Mutschlechner reach the summit on 6 May without oxygen masks and supported by only a few Sherpas. They climb a variation of the north flank route partly in Alpine style (10th ascent overall).

1983   The Austrian J. Bachler climbs solo from top camp to summit over the Southwest Face. P. Beghin (France) climbs same route to the summit, alone, without artificial oxygen, porters or intermediate camps.

1984   A Japanese party fails in its attempt to traverse the Main, South and West Summits, in two groups, one starting at either end. The South and Main Summits are both attained.

1986   Spanish are successful in climbing the Southwest Flank (first ascent route) during the autumn.

The route chosen by Reinhold Messner on the north side of Kangchenjunga was first proposed in 1930 by an international expedition led by G. Dyhrenfurth. It was only partly a new route in 1982, the British having found a route to the left of it and the Japanese to the right.

Four different routes now meet on the main summit of *Kantsch*, as well as a few variations. On the south and east sides possibilities exist for new routes. One extremely difficult face-route would be the east flank of the South Summit (involving some rock climbing).

KANGCHENDZÖNGA 8586 m

Above left: Reinhold Messner below the third serac step in the icefall. After climbing the vertical ice, it proved impossible to continue that way. Mutschlechner and Messner found an alternative passage through an ice chimney further to the left.

Left: Friedl Mutschlechner on the West Ridge of Kangchenjunga Main Summit, only a few rope-lengths from the top. Below, in cloud, the West Summit (Yalung Kang).

Previous double page: Evening in the first camp at the foot of Kangchenjunga North Face. As soon as the sun went down, the soft snow froze within minutes. In the morning the sun did not rise from behind *Kantsch* until late.

Above: Ang Dorje packs his rucksack at the last bivouac after the stormy night in which the tent was destroyed.

Left: Back at Camp 2, Ang Dorje, the Sherpa whose own desire it was to go to the summit. He was the only one of us to remain healthy and free from frost-bite.

Reinhold Messner and Friedl Mutschlechner on
the summit of Kangchenjunga (6 May 1982).
Ang Dorje's Nepalese flag is photographed on
the measuring post left by Indian
mountaineers in 1977.

Above: Ang Dorje and Friedl Mutschlechner climbing down over the Shoulder towards the North Ridge in a snowstorm.

Left: Critically ill and hallucinating, Reinhold Messner ropes down the North Face after going to the summit on Kangchenjunga.

1982

Kangchenjunga
Pinned Down by Storm

The person committed to 'experiencing life', in his intensity can easily forget to enjoy it.

Max Stirner

On a mountain, a man meets fear. The more he understands about what he is doing, the more fear he will experience. Because the abler he is then to recognise danger.

Yannick Seigneur

Kangchenjunga from the north, seen from Base Camp. The route taken by Messner and Mutschlechner leads out of the basin under the North Face, through the seracs (obscured by cloud), and left to the North Ridge. Along this, over the big shoulder, from where a right-hand traverse of the summit wall brought the pair on to the West Ridge and the summit.

In the summer of 1981, I was up in the Hintergrat Hut in the Ortler Group with Friedl Mutschlechner, who ran the ice section of my climbing school there. One evening he came up with an idea: since I had been successful in 1978 in climbing two eight-thousanders during a single summer, might it not be possible to do three in one season? A hat trick? Now that was something no one had tried before!

I found the idea compelling, but I knew it would not be easy to put together such an undertaking, financially or bureaucratically. It would be necessary to get three separate permits, phased to follow one another through the season, and to find the money effectively for three expeditions. Our hat trick would only work if we could get from one eight-thousander to the next without any hitches.

I was finally granted a pre-monsoon 1982 permit for Kangchenjunga, which I had wanted to climb by its North Face for a number of years, as well as one for Gasherbrum II and another for Broad Peak in Pakistan in June and July of the same year. It should be possible to climb these three eight-thousanders in sequence. Friedl and I agreed on a plan: in the spring of 1982, we would travel to Kangchenjunga to attempt the North Face, one of the most impressive walls in the Himalaya. The route we had in mind lay between two others – to the left of that of Doug Scott, Peter Boardman and Joe Tasker, and to the right of the Japanese route. It was an ideal line, first attempted as long ago as 1930 by the Dyhrenfurth expedition but never completed to the top. If we could pull off this first ascent, securing the first of our three summits, it would be a good prelude to the hat trick, a bold stroke.

We would then need to fly directly to Pakistan, trace the Baltoro Glacier up to Gasherbrum II and traverse that, going up by the virgin East Face and down the normal route. For our third and final eight-thousander, we would then make another traverse, this time of Broad Peak, starting from the foot of K2 and going over the North and Middle summits to the main one before descending by the normal route.

When, after a three-week approach march, we arrived at Kangchenjunga, there was still snow above the last village of Gunza. It was cold and windy. I was carrying my six-month-old daughter Layla on my back, but she showed no signs of altitude discomfort nor susceptibility to cold. She never complained. Doctors had assured me that children rarely experience any problems below 5,000 metres, as long as you take time building up to that level. Layla certainly enriched our expedition.

I do not hold with taking small children further than Base Camp. To carry them up on to the face would be ridiculous, offering little to child or parent. The altitude 'record' of 6,000 metres which Ozaki, the well-known Japanese climber, set up with his small son Makoto on Island Peak was something rather different. All you read in the papers about climbing children in the Himalaya – '3-year-old climbs Makalu', 'Infant to summit' – is mostly invention or mischievous reporting. It would be boring for the child, certainly.

Friedl Mutschlechner and I only spent a few days in Kangchenjunga Base Camp, just long enough to put up tents, build a kitchen out of drystone and a plastic sheet, and arrange for our post to be brought in every two weeks by two local runners.

The wind didn't let up at all. We left Layla with her mother, Nena Holguin, while Friedl and I and a handful of porters went up the glacier to the foot of the face. It took us two days to establish Camp 1, and we remained in it for a whole week.

Above Camp 1 the route was difficult. 200 metres above us a girdle of seracs hung across the face, virtually barring the way ahead. And below them, we made our first acquaintance with the dangers and difficulties of this North Flank. All the time, enormous chunks of overhanging ice would break off and thunder down the face. Tons of green, shiny ice fragments were lying in heaps at the bottom. It was not at all easy to find a way through this barrier of ice without exposing ourselves to extreme risk. At first it looked as if it would be impossible.

We made several attempts, sometimes managing only 50 metres a day. Often we were as good as beaten. Had we been too ambitious in our intentions? It was clear that two of us were not enough – we were not making any headway. Yet we could not push anybody else out for a stint in front, because there was no one else.

We certainly did not want to give up, whatever the difficulty. Inch by inch, we probed the smooth, overhanging ice above us until we had found a way into the middle of the seracs. But even from there, it did not seem as if we could go any further, left or right. A 20-metre thick ice wall blocked the way. Eventually, we discovered a narrow crevasse just wide enough to squeeze through. On the other side was a labyrinth of hard-snow rubble. Again, we found a way. It was exciting: we were climbing through an incredible vertical world of snow and ice, with formations stacked one on top of another. No fairy story ever had a more magical setting. Had it not been for the attendant dangers, we could really have enjoyed just being there.

At the beginning, we always climbed very hesitantly through this icefall. Later we grew accustomed to the strange noises from inside the ice, its groans and cracks; and to the snow avalanches which came down every time there was new snow. We grew accustomed to the constant danger.

We made good progress. At our second attempt, we managed to set up Camp 2 way above the seracs and believed then that we had the climb in our pocket. We had reached around 7,200 metres, just under the North Ridge, when we ran out of rope. The ice was so hard that it was too risky going on without fixing pro-

tection. We would never have been able to get back down again. All at once, defeat stared us in the face. We had been beaten by a shortage of equipment.

Coming down was desperate. It did not stop snowing and we were under continual threat from avalanches. The light powder snow built up on every incline and each half-hour or so would peel off from the blank ice underneath. These new-snow avalanches kept pouring over us, for hours on end.

Just above Camp 2, Friedl and I sat in a crevasse to gain some respite. It began to grow dark. Without bivouac equipment and in our wet clothes we were in danger of freezing to death in the night. Ought we to try and get down to the tent? We deliberated whether we should make use of a pause between avalanches and hurtle back to Camp 2, or whether, all told, it would be wiser to sit it out up here, even if there was a chance of being frozen. It took us hours to come to a decision, but we resolved to make a dash for it. We were lucky and got safely down to our camp.

Back in Gunza we managed to buy more ropes – rope that the local farmers

Friedl Mutschlechner abseils in deep snow in the crevasse above Camp 2. A few minutes later the first snow avalanche poured down over him and Messner, so that the pair had to wait for hours in this crevasse.

Critically ill

I must have picked up an amoebic infection on the march in to Kangchenjunga, probably from drinking polluted chang, the Tibetan rice beer. When we made our summit climb, I began feeling unwell immediately we left Base Camp. There was a strange stabbing pain somewhere in the region of my stomach or liver, and I was also having trouble with my breathing. This worried me and was affecting my climbing.

Shortly before we reached Camp 1, I told Friedl Mutschlechner, with whom I found myself no longer able to keep up, that I was sick and would probably have to turn back. He then climbed on ahead, and I endeavoured to keep going behind him, but with very little hope of getting far. It was only with considerable pain and effort that I reached camp that day.

The next morning, when it dawned fine and we set off full of optimism, I felt all right. It is true I was not going as strongly as on other expeditions, but I was anxious to continue and felt I could. I do not know if I was able to suppress the pain, or whether concentrating all thoughts on the summit lifted it. Whichever it was, I reached the final bivouac and from there, was in my usual form. Going to the summit I felt very good, and that is probably why I decided to risk it despite the stormy weather.

It was only on the way down that the pain came back. As the tension eased and as tiredness took over, I was unable to sleep for pain. Once back in Base Camp, I totally collapsed, I was critically ill.

Walking out, I kept feeling stabs of pain in my liver as if I had been shot, I was tired almost to death. It took as much effort puffing up all the little rising stretches as it had to the summit of Kangchenjunga itself. In Kathmandu an American doctor diagnosed an amoebic abscess on the liver.

Reinhold Messner breaks trail up the steep slope leading towards a small notch under the summit (about 8,400m). 'The deciding factor is not strength, but will. Will makes of the body, an arrow.'

had acquired from an earlier Japanese expedition. Then Friedl and I, together with the Sherpa Ang Dorje, climbed back up the face. This was to be our last attempt. The climb had to succeed this time.

We used the new rope to fix the section above where we turned back before. Our retreat was now secured. Then we climbed on towards the summit. Here and there we found remnants of rope from Doug Scott's small expedition which climbed Kangchenjunga from the North in 1979. We made our first bivouac in a shady recess on the North Ridge.

The next day we were too tired to go any further. After overnighting there again, we climbed to 8,000 metres, where we set up two little tents on the ridge. We were now at the point where the Northeast Spur and the North Ridge came together. Again, we bivouacked.

On 6 May we started out for the summit. It was windy, with hardly any warmth in the sun at all. A pale, inter-mittent shimmer hung in the thin air. It was like being in a dream world. The snow at times reached to our knees, but at other times it was only boot-deep. We had a fantastic bird's eye view! It was as though all the valleys and mountains were under a belljar that had been gently misted over by the breath of the world's spirit, and intensified as if under a magnifying glass.

On the North Ridge we climbed over some pinnacles, and laboured up through deep, drifted snow in a gully. Then, crossing right from the ridge to the deep col west of the main summit, progress became very slow. Approaching out of Tibet came a thin cloak of mist, driven by a strong northwest wind. The atmosphere – a conjunction of light, wind and, above everything, the haloed sun – became even more eerie. A smell of pulverised rock hung upon the air. The terrain was very exposed, with snow-fields between steep granite pillars. Here and there lay patches of soft snow crusted over with ice.

Our crampons would not always grip well. All the same we continued unroped, each going solo. We would not have been able to protect the whole stretch. We were already taking far too long, but more than that, it would have been too strenuous to fix rope all the way. It was not until we reached the notch between the south and west side of Kangchenjunga, already well above the West Summit, that the three of us roped together. The route continued up a series of cracks and gullies. We kept having to cross over to the right between granite slabs and snow patches. And so it was, we approached the summit dur-ing the afternoon.

The strong northwest wind immed-iately caught us full in the face; we had been protected from it for a short time as we climbed up the south side. We knew we had to turn back down quickly. All the same, we lingered. It was not that we were careless of our safety, just that we felt no particular sense of urgency. There were old oxygen bottles lying on the summit. A measuring pole left by Indian climbers stuck out of the snow. We took photos of each other. Then suddenly I came to my senses and urged the others on.

We set off back down to our bivouac tent as fast as we could go, before it was too late! With every metre we went down, the icy north wind gathered in strength. It was now battering us with full force. I put on my bulky down mittens and endeavoured to keep a grip on my iceaxe. Friedl hesitated a few minutes too long before putting down gloves on over his felt ones, and in consequence suffered severe frost-bite. He could not feel anything yet. His only concern was to descend carefully so as not to fall.

It was late in the evening when we reached camp and crawled into the tent. We couldn't be bothered to cook or drink; we just lay there, in the hope that we would manage to get back to safety the following day. It was essential to keep going down as fast as possible.

The frozen fingers on Friedl Mutschlechner's right hand after the *Kantsch* climb.

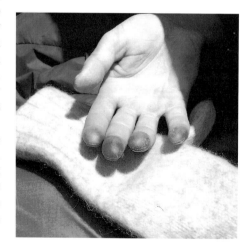

Friedl Mutschlechner

Survived – even though the tent ripped

On the way down the storm assumes hurricane proportions. It takes all our concentration to find the way and reach the security of the tent without mishap. Despite the euphoria, I feel tired and worn out. Each of us has given the climb his all, and for this reason the storm now seems to hit us harder.

All hell is let loose – driving snow lashes into our faces, so that we can't see a thing. Even so, we manage to get back to our tent before the onset of darkness. We leave our crampons outside and crawl into our icy sleeping bags with our boots on. The storm rages on with such ferocity it is impossible to cook anything, or to sleep – that would be the end. Sitting with our backs to the walls of the tent, we endeavour to withstand the force of the wind. We have pitifully little with which to counter its effects.

At some stage I notice my right hand has lost all feeling. The fingers are frozen stiff. I must not give up, on any account – I concentrate everything on this one thought. All sense of time is lost. Minutes become hours; hours, eternity.

We dare not make the slightest error. Vainly I shout outside for help, but even Reinhold, who is sitting beside me, cannot hear me over the noise of the storm. The tent-front rips on a pole. We look at each other, knowing what can happen. With my hands, I make a sign to Reinhold to brace himself more firmly against the side. He shouts, 'Tell those Canadians out there to stop throwing stones at our tent.' A shiver of fright passes through me. I can't help thinking of expedition reports, in which climbers go outside the tent and disappear. I fear the worst.

I speak all my thoughts aloud. That way I can maintain better control over myself. My concentration diminishes markedly. I wonder to what extent I am still thinking clearly. The thought of dying no longer frightens me. Death has become a tangible option; it would not be that bad, lying down and dying. The temptation to take that tiny step towards eternal sleep is enormous. That is when the tent rips, and suddenly we are lying in the open air. 'Lucky we left our boots on,' I think, but my thoughts come in slow motion. A last convulsion of strength allows me to put on my crampons. The wind keeps toppling me over as I do it. I notice Ang Dorje, our trusted Sherpa, is having the same trouble. We begin the climb down together.

Below the ridge I look for somewhere to shelter and wait for Reinhold. Obviously he is having more trouble putting on his crampons than Ang Dorje or I. I shout myself hoarse that he come on quickly, but the storm is too loud for him to hear. He keeps falling over. I would like to help him, but haven't the strength to climb back up, even that short distance. The only thing I can do is not leave him on his own. Each of us knows that in situations like this, you are your own responsibility, there is only strength for yourself.

All I can do is wait, helplessly, watching him struggle. It is a question of survival. It would come very hard if to save yourself, you were forced to leave a partner behind in such situations, but that is the reality. Each has the right, perhaps even the duty, to do just that. Reinhold's attitude of mind has helped him to survive many other big mountain adventures and I believe it will see him through this one. No one knows better than he that there's no one here that can help him.

I have no idea how long it takes before he is standing next to me. Without a word, we continue down. Only when the Sherpas in Camp 2 greet us with hot tea, do we know that we have survived.

Friedl Mutschlechner
(Climber of three eight-thousanders)

125

We were not able to sleep that night, and did not rest or recover at all. The storm tugged at the tent all the time. Suddenly it gave way with a loud rip. It was about 5 o'clock in the morning. My tiredness, the will to survive and the first hallucinations all combined to induce a kind of intoxication. I was less worried now – the first signs of losing grip on what was happening. A few minutes later, Ang Dorje's little tent, too, was ripped to shreds.

Muffled in our sleeping bags, all three of us were now exposed to the rising tempest without any kind of protection. Our clothes full of snow, our axes heaven knows where, we gazed up at this unreal world: only stars and snow above us as far as we could see. This and the deafening noise of the wind. But with it, suddenly, there was an easier, more comfortable feeling, not the slightest anxiety any more. Our gloves blew away – we would have the utmost difficulty gathering together our belongings. The storm,

blasting over the ridge at 100 kilometres an hour, threatened to engulf us.

Without a word Friedl stood up. Everyone then tried to get dressed, and protect himself as best he could. Friedl, although tired from the exertions of the previous day, was still in good shape and first to be ready. Ang Dorje, too, was all ready to go while I was still trying to fasten crampons to my boots. I could not do it. I was so clumsy and awkward. Shaking with cold, I had insufficient control over my hands.

All I wanted to do was remain sitting there. Friedl came back a few steps and told me not to hang about. When I had at last got my crampons on and was all set to go, I could not seem to make any headway. As much as I braced myself against the strength of the storm, it forced me back. Like a bird, I let myself fall into the wind – again to no avail. It is a strange feeling, to stand up and keep falling over like a drunk. I was growing more and more crazy. Only after several

attempts, and then only because Friedl was waiting for me, did I slowly make my way down, sideways to the wind. Friedl more or less forced me to move. It was perhaps only having him there, encouraging me with looks and hand-signals, that I went at all.

Once I had caught him up, it was much easier. We were no longer so exposed, the wind no longer as strong. We could climb on down together. Totally exhausted and plagued by hallucinations we got down as far as Camp 2 that day. Death was not all I kept at bay that day, but madness too. For the first time in my life, I knew what it meant to be crazy, to have clear trains of thought turned on their heads and all jumbled up. I talked in pictures, like in fevered dreams.

We reached Base Camp during the next night. We were both dead on our feet. Friedl had been so badly frost-bitten on his hands and feet that he could hardly move any more; I was suffering violent pain from somewhere

in the region of my kidneys. Whether I had suffered a lung oedema, or an amoebic abscess, I do not know. I only know I was critically ill.

The return march was frightful. I could not sleep, could not lie down for the pain. Nor did I have the strength to carry Layla; Nena had to do that. For Friedl it was even worse. In the warmth, his feet swelled, increasing his agony hour by hour. He had to struggle down from the mountain to the valley in his plastic boots; it took two weeks.

We did not order a helicopter as it would have taken a week to call one. Then before it came, several more days would have gone by. Who knows whether it would have been able to fly at all if the weather was bad?

On the way back from Kangchenjunga, I reproached myself bitterly for the way things had turned out. Worn out from the wind, cold and exertion I was

full of self-doubt. I could no longer see any kind of sense in such expeditions. I don't think it was so much tiredness and resignation that had dampened my enthusiasm for our enterprise, it was my illness. Above all, it was having to see how Friedl suffered. During the climb I had never enquired of myself whether it made sense or nonsense: during the period of effort, on this as other climbs, I was my own answer.

In the state of mind I was in, I wanted to abandon the rest of the expedition. What did it really mean to achieve such a hat-trick? Kangchenjunga had only been the start of a grand idea; setting out for Gasherbrum II and Broad Peak within the ensuing months would perhaps propel me into even worse hardships. Only the knowledge that we had come through by the skin of our teeth, enabled me to hold up my head. I was a man.

Death threat

My climb with Friedl Mutschlechner of Kangchenjunga's North Face was one of the most dangerous of my life. But the closest I ever came to death on a mountain still remains my experience on the Nanga Parbat crossing of 1970, my first ascent of an eight-thousander. Taking into account difficulties, effort, danger and hopelessness, no other adventure has superseded this one. I even believe that it would no longer be possible for anyone to traverse Nanga Parbat in the way Günther and I did in 1970. Perhaps if a thousand climbers tried, one might come through. I am sure that I could never survive those days a second time.

On Kangchenjunga it was the timing of the storm more than anything else that brought us close to the limit of our endurance – we were already suffering sickness and frost-bite. The storm hammered us just as we tired, coming down from the summit, when we had lost the curiosity that is the driving force on the way up. And it broke so violently it practically swept us from the mountain. It almost succeeded in extinguishing our spirit of life.

8   1956 Gasherbrum II   8,035m/26,360ft

The Easiest Eight-Thousander

Historical Highlights

Geographical Position: Karakoram, Baltoro Mustagh
Long. 35°46′, Lat. 76°39′

1909 An expedition led by the Duke of the Abruzzi and including the Italian photographer V. Sella explores the Gasherbrum Group from the north (Sella Pass) and from Chogolisa.

1934 An international expedition under the leadership of Swiss mountaineer G.O. Dyhrenfurth considers possibility of climbing Gasherbrum II from its south side; they reach an approximate height of 6,250m. This, with their other reconnaissance work, makes a solid foundation for future development.

1956 Austrian expedition under F. Moravec succeeds in making first ascent of Gasherbrum II by the Southwest Ridge. Having built up a small chain of camps and bivouacking once at 7,700m, S. Larch, H. Willenpart and F. Moravec complete the climb to the summit on 7 July by crossing to the East Ridge.

1975 By taking the South Rib to the east of the route of the first ascent, a French team under J.–P. Fresafond is second to reach the summit. One member is killed. The third ascent (and at the same time, practically a traverse) is made by a Polish group under the leadership of J. Onyszkiewicz. Three members climb from the saddle between Gasherbrums II and III (7,600m) up the 500-metre, rocky Northwest Face to the top by a new route. They descend the normal way. Shortly afterwards three more members reach the top by the Austrian route.

And three days later again, two Polish women climbers also climb Gasherbrum II. They are members of a separate expedition led by W. Rutkiewicz and primarily concerned with making the first ascent of Gasherbrum III, but the two teams co-operate well.

1979 A Chilean expedition claims to have reached the summit by the normal route. In July, German climber R. Karl makes Gasherbrum II his second eight-thousander. The two Austrians, H. Schell and K. Diemberger, collect their third and fifth eight-thousanders, respectively, with the ascent of Gasherbrum II.

1982 R. Messner, together with Pakistani mountaineers S. Khan and N. Sabir, climbs the Southwest Ridge to the summit of Gasherbrum II on 24 July. (8th ascent. Keeping exact records becomes increasingly hard. Because information reaching Europe is often incomplete, and several climbs have been made without permits – in other words are illicit or 'black ascents' – figures must of necessity be seen only as approximate. Ascents for which there is no corroboration are not included here.) In the same summer the French married couple, L. and M. Barrard, make it to the summit.

1983 The Swiss Three Eight-Thousanders Expedition under S. Wörner, makes the first ascent of Gasherbrum II by the Southwest Ridge. S. Wörner, F. Graf, A. Meyer, E. Loretan, M. Ruedi and J.–C. Sonnenwyl reach the summit. In the same summer Poles successfully climb the long East Ridge in three days. W. Kurtyka and J. Kukuczka open a new route from the saddle between Gasherbrum I, which they had already climbed, and Gasherbrum II.

1984 In the course of their traverse of Gasherbrum II and Gasherbrum I (Hidden Peak), R. Messner and H. Kammerlander open a new descent route, which leaves the summit where the Poles came up the previous year but takes new line down into the Gasherbrum Valley to the foot of the Northwest Face of Gasherbrum I. The same summer a Frenchman and a Swiss ski down from the summit of Gasherbrum II.

Reinhold Messner has climbed Gasherbrum II twice (by the 1956 normal route): in 1982 with Sher Khan and Nazir Sabir from a high camp in the Gasherbrum Valley with two bivouacs; and in 1984 from Base Camp with two bivouacs on the climb and one during the descent (B2), from where, with Hans Kammerlander in the course of their major Gasherbrum traverse, he came down by a new route.

There are five different routes on Gasherbrum II, all beginning in the Gasherbrum Valley. Further possibilities exist on the Pakistani and Chinese sides.

GASHERBRUM II 8035 m

B$_2$ 1982 / 1984

B$_1$ 1982

1 1984

Above left: View from Gasherbrum II down into the Gasherbrum Valley (1982). In 1984 Hans Kammerlander and Reinhold Messner climbed from Base Camp (on the dirty glacier at the bottom) up Gasherbrum II by the Southwest Ridge and back over the South Flank to the Gasherbrum Valley, then up the north side of Gasherbrum I (left in this picture). Coming down by the West Ridge and the glacier they were back in Base Camp after seven days.

Above: Gasherbrum III and Gasherbrum II from the southwest. The 1984 descent route follows the hanging glacier to the right of the French Ridge (1975), which runs diagonally from the summit of Gasherbrum II to the right of the picture. Further right is the big shoulder on the Southeast Ridge, over which the Poles Kurtyka and Kukuczka climbed to the summit (1983).

Previous double page: Balti porters in driving snow on the Baltoro Glacier. Each porter carried about twenty kilos of expedition gear, along with his own food, wood, blankets and sleeping mat. The march-in to base camp for the Gasherbrums today takes around ten days, with the porters marching between six and twelve hours a day.

Below left: The dead Austrian (left, 1982) was buried in the ice by Messner and Kammerlander during their Gasherbrum Traverse (right, 1984).

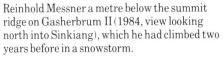

Reinhold Messner a metre below the summit ridge on Gasherbrum II (1984, view looking north into Sinkiang), which he had climbed two years before in a snowstorm.

Above: Hans Kammerlander on the summit of Gasherbrum II (1984). Behind, in the centre of the picture, Gasherbrum I, which the two climbed three days later as part of a single mammoth tour.

Right: Hans Kammerlander climbs down the first few metres from the summit of Gasherbrum II, looking north (25 June 1984). The little rock horn below him is a subsidiary summit, which must be about 8,000m high.

Gasherbrum II
Encounter with Death

I have never really worked in all my life. But I have done more than many people who take unquestioning pride in clocking up their eight hours a day. I have only ever done what I wanted to, what attracted me. That's the thing!
Max Frisch

Himalayan climbing could not exist without danger. Without risk there would be no adventure. That, I believe, is what gives it its worth.
Maurice Herzog

View from the West Ridge of Gasherbrum I to the summit of Chogolisa, touched by the first rays of morning sun. The moon still hangs in the sky. From the ridge on the left, lit by the sun, was where Hermann Buhl fell to his death. He was the first Western mountaineer to climb two eight-thousanders (1953 Nanga Parbat, 1957 Broad Peak).

After Friedl Mutschlechner and I had driven ourselves to our limits on Kangchenjunga – and at the same time also into a pit of despair – I wavered for a long time about the hat trick idea. Perhaps it was too much to try and climb Kangchenjunga, Gasherbrum II and Broad Peak in just one season. I certainly could not hope to accomplish the plan on my own, and Friedl had flown back to Europe to have his frost-bite treated. It would have been out of the question for him to go on in that condition. My first priority, too, had to be to get myself better.

I remained in Asia. After finding a doctor in Kathmandu, who diagnosed an amoebic abscess on the liver, for which he prescribed an excellent course of treatment, I proceeded to Ladakh. Within three weeks, I had recovered and had slowly begun to regain my strength.

Partly because I knew two old friends of mine, local climbers, would already be waiting for me in Pakistan, but really, too, because by then all my old ambition had come flooding back, in June I flew on to Pakistan. My equipment was already there. There were porters standing by. Everything was set; nothing need stop me going ahead as planned. Naturally, without Friedl, it would no longer be possible to traverse Gasherbrum II and Broad Peak the way we had hoped, let alone by new routes.

I had vaguely promised Nazir Sabir, who was without doubt the most successful climber in Pakistan, and Sher Khan, a young officer related to the Hunza royal family, that we could go on this expedition as a foursome. Now we were only three. All the same, I still wanted to try the climb with them.

They were full of enthusiasm at the prospect of doing the two eight-thousanders when I met them in Rawalpindi. We went on to Skardu, where our little expedition group assembled: 25 Balti porters, one cook, one runner and three climbers. We moved up to the foot of Gasherbrum II.

Gasherbrum II is generally considered to be the easiest of the eight-thousanders. Yet it was not as easy as we had expected in that year. There was quite a lot of snow on it in the summer of 1982.

Two Austrian climbers, a doctor and a scientist, had disappeared there some days before. When we arrived in Base Camp, an American expedition had already called off its attempt because one of its members had been killed in an avalanche. A German team was still functioning in the hopes of making it up the North Face of Gasherbrum I, but they too had spent weeks of fruitless effort, getting nowhere. The leader of that expedition was Gunther Sturm, whom I had known for many years. His team had opened the way into the Gasherbrum Valley, certainly, but there was no one on Gasherbrum II that could have been of any route-making assistance to us.

After a few days' acclimatisation, we went up the Gasherbrum Valley, to establish an advanced camp. When we came back down to base, we believed conditions were all right for us to attempt our climb. I was anxious to get started, especially while there was some slight chance that the two Austrians might still be alive. Perhaps we could help them?

In good weather Nazir Sabir, Sher Khan and I climbed with Rosi Ali and Little Karim, two famous high altitude porters, as far as Camp 1 at the foot of Gasherbrum II. From there, the next day we pressed higher. The porters came with us up the Southwest Face to a height of around 6,200 metres. There we pitched a tent and bivouacked. Next morning we packed everything up again and climbed on in the direction of the summit pyramid, beneath which we intended to make our last bivouac. It was a strange feeling to know that around here somewhere two climbers were missing.

I was way ahead of the two Pakistanis on this stretch, when I suddenly saw a tent in front of me. It was olive green and obviously the bivouac tent belonging to

Last bivouac of the two missing Austrians; the body of one of the men was later found by Reinhold Messner and Hans Kammerlander. Right foreground, Nazir Sabir; behind, Gasherbrum IV, which was climbed in 1958 by Walter Bonatti and Carlo Mauri. Gasherbrum IV is the highest seven-thousander.

Climbing over bodies

When I found a dead Austrian on Gasherbrum II in 1982 (who I later buried, in 1984), I was accused of 'climbing over bodies'. Even friends and relations of the dead man had some harsh words to say at first when they learned that I had found and inspected the remains of their dead friend/child/husband. On that first expedition I had done nothing more than photograph the man. It was necessary to have pictures in order to be certain who he was. I passed on to the relatives, unpublished, the diary and films I found in an abandoned tent lower down the mountain. Naturally, I tried to reconstruct what had happened.

The second time I was there – the body had by then been lying for two years out in the open – I buried the dead man in accordance with the family's wishes. It cost time and effort, and was certainly no pleasant task. Again other climbers condemned my behaviour. The very fact that I reported it was interpreted as sensation-seeking, profiteering. How happy I would have been to be able to go straight past as if nothing were there. At least a dozen expeditions had climbed on Gasherbrum II between 1982 and 1984, and none of them paid any heed to the dead man.

It is my view that the dead belong to these mountains every bit as much as the living. When we talk only of our successes, when we ignore the dead, young and inexperienced Alpinists don't appreciate just how dangerous this game is on the highest mountains of the world. Perhaps even we are gradually losing the feeling for reality up there. In recent years I have encountered 'the dead' on practically every eight-thousander, each one the subject of a macabre tale. The few times I have told their stories, and published one or two pictures, were not because people offered me money for them, but because they belong as part of the whole. Perhaps too, because they might save somebody else from a similar fate.

The fool is not the person who goes up there in full knowledge that this kind of climbing is hazardous, but the one who does not want to know about death, who shuts his eyes to the fact that even he could be killed.

Sher Khan and Nazir Sabir (behind) in mist on the summit ridge of Gasherbrum II. Messner's whole life has been one of balancing along such ridges with drops on either side. 'I have never regarded it as work.'

the Austrians. Nothing had been heard or seen of them now for several days.

There was no one inside the tent. I found only films and a diary, which indicated that this was the last place the two men had sheltered, and it was a week since they had set out from it to go for the summit. Under the circumstances, they would obviously only have bothered to take the barest bivouac essentials.

To read the diary was both moving and upsetting, but it gave no real clue as to what might have happened. When my two companions caught up with me, we kept going, but none of us could put the missing men out of our thoughts. Clinging to the tiny hope that they might still be alive somewhere up in the summit region, waiting for help, we quickened our pace. There were a few clues in the snow. A ski stick had been left behind at about 7,500 metres. In our 3-man tent we bivouacked just below the summit pyramid.

That night the weather broke. By morning a storm was howling around us. Dark clouds hung over the surrounding mountains. Although right above us, the summit of Gasherbrum was no longer visible.

Despite the stormy conditions and bad visibility, we set off. We wanted to look for the Austrians as we crossed under the summit pyramid. We did not expect to find much, but were anxious to do it all the same. There was no need to justify our actions, it was all perfectly natural.

We crossed the slope towards the right, in the direction of Gasherbrum's Northeast Ridge. Immediately below the Ridge, under a rock, we discovered a dead body. It was one of the missing men! He was in a half-sitting position as if waiting for someone. Clearly, he had bivouacked there and perished in his sleep. But where was his friend?

We did not disturb the dead man, simply photographed him and made a mental note of his equipment so that we could advise his relatives afterwards. Then we looked further. The other man must be higher up. We were able to follow his trail for quite a long way. In places it had been blown away by the wind, but in between we were able to pick it out again, until finally we lost it on the rock buttress under the summit.

The reason we were able to find our way to the top of Gasherbrum II that day despite the storm and cloud, was really only because the route went straight up and a knife-sharp summit ridge led to the highest point. The descent, though, turned out to be very dramatic. We followed the same route as we had come up, but the wind meanwhile had plastered long stretches of the trail with new snow. Trying to find somewhere to get ourselves off the ridge and back on to the Southwest Face suddenly made us unsure of ourselves. Where exactly was the place where we had to go down?

139

None of us could clearly remember any particular rocky pinnacle, any snow-drift, or any sort of landmark to show where the route turned off.

Frantically we began to search around One time we were too far down, another too far up. When we noticed that we were going wrong, it brought it home to us just how easily you can get yourself killed up here. It was a long time before we finally found ourselves safely on the right way to our last bivouac, the way back to life.

Every one of the fourteen eight-thousanders, even one like Gasherbrum II which is considered relatively easy, can be a serious undertaking if conditions are bad. When a storm blows up, if the climber has insufficient strength to get himself down quickly, he can soon find himself in a desperate position. Every eight-thousander can be fatal if you are not careful, or if you run out of luck. The next day we climbed down to Base Camp. There we handed over the note-books and films of the two dead Austrians to their friends. We still had no real idea what could have caused this tragedy.

Two years later, in 1984, when I came back to traverse the Gasherbrum summits with Hans Kammerlander, I again made the climb up Gasherbrum II. Originally we planned to do the traverse the other way round, climbing up Gasherbrum I, down the North Face, up the steep face between the Polish Ridge and the normal route, then back down the normal route. This would have meant keeping the easiest section of the route for the end. But in view of avalanche danger on the West Ridge of Gasherbrum I, we decided to reverse the expedition. It was Hans' idea. So, I climbed the normal route to the summit of Gasherbrum II for a second time. It was familiar territory.

Compared to before, conditions were easy. We had the best of weather, and the snow conditions were good. It was impor-tant not to let ourselves forget that reaching the summit of Gasherbrum II was only part of what we planned to do.

We must not give up once we had made the first traverse, and could only afford to expend part of our strength on this eight-thousander.

I was anxious to rediscover the body we found in 1982 and bury it properly. This young man had not been forgotten. We had come to know his relatives in the meantime, and they expressed the desire that he be left on the mountain – recover-ing a body from up there would not only have been exceptionally difficult, it would have been dangerous, and very expensive, too.

Several other expeditions, I knew, had passed close to the spot since I was last there, but none had interrupted their ascent long enough to commit the body to a crevasse – nor did Hans and I, right away. We were unsure whether we would have time to do so during the ascent, and in any case we were not keen

to confront a dead body so near the start of such a major undertaking. We needed to remain inwardly calm if we were to carry our plan through with undimin-ished enthusiasm.

On the way down, however, we did stop. The body had slid some distance downhill from where it had been in 1982. With our axes, we hacked the man clear of the restraining ice, then buried him a bit lower down in a crevasse. It cost us considerable time and effort, but was necessary, we felt. Everyone who climbed Gasherbrum II had to pass the body – in fine weather it would have been in full view. At this height, shelter-ed beneath rocks as it was, decades would have to pass before the remains dispersed.

Crossing Gasherbrum II only gave us one awkward moment – or rather an awkward few hours – on the following

Left: The first part of the Southwest Face climb on Gasherbrum II. Below, the Gasherbrum Valley; in the distance, the Abruzzi Glacier and above that Sia Kangri.

Right: Who among us is crazy? No one risks his life for a sponsor. But many people consciously accept risk in order to experience wilderness like this. Adventure without risk is not possible.

day when we were climbing down the face between the French and the Polish routes. This face would have been a real suicide route to come up. It is beset with seracs and concave in its lower section, so that the avalanches – all the serac debris – funnel into this one particular spot. Hans and I took it at the run in the very early morning.

The glacier was relatively quiet, yet we were naturally very aware of how much risk still remained. By choosing the best time of day, we were exposing ourselves to less danger and for a relatively short time, but there was still danger – immense danger.

The upper section below the bivouac camp was fairly easy. We traversed down to the left, where we had buried the body the previous day. Keeping upright and facing towards the valley, we crossed the snow flank obliquely and

then came down through a very steep passage between the seracs. We felt threatened from all sides. It did not need spelling out, we could sense the danger virtually throughout our whole bodies, especially in our backs, as we climbed down past these ice towers. They could have collapsed at any moment.

Only when we were right down to the bottom, when we had raced clear of the steep face out into the Gasherbrum Valley, did we allow ourselves to feel any sort of jubilation. We had escaped it! We could breathe freely.

A safe distance from the face, we sat down on our rucksacks to rest. Several times we looked up, retracing our descent route in our minds. We had climbed down this icefall! It was unbelievable, even to us.

When I think how tired I have been after every eight-thousander, I cannot

today imagine how we managed to do two together without stopping. In 1970 after Nanga Parbat I was close to death. In 1972 after Manaslu, I was sad and burnt out. In 1975 after Hidden Peak, my third eight-thousander, I was plagued by hallucinations. Now after the descent from Gasherbrum II, I still felt quite fresh. This certainly had something to do with the fact that we were committed to a double traverse from the start. We knew that the essential stamina would only come to us after the first eight-thousander.

It has, of course, been changes of attitude like this that have given the necessary impetus to climbing evolution. Grade 10 Climbs, consecutive big-wall ascents in the Alps (like climbing the North Faces of the Matterhorn, Eiger and Grandes Jorasses in a single day), and solo climbs of eight-thousand

Survived – the double-traverse

In my opinion, traversing the two Gasherbrum summits ranks as one of the hardest tours that have ever been done. At the same time, stylistically, it was one of the purest climbs made on an eight-thousander.

The most important factor was the length of time we spent at very high altitude. We were treading new ground not just in the mountaineering and geographical sense (though a major part of the four up and down routes was unknown territory), but also in an emotional sense. Other factors too, played their part. For instance, our medical, psychological and technological reactions to such a 'forced ride'.

Eight days in the 'Death Zone' without going back to Base Camp amount to rather more than that when you consider the critical circumstances: a week of hard physical effort with insufficient sleep, no fixed ropes, and little prior knowledge of the territory to be covered. Instructions such as 'You must ... it will need ... you ought not to ...' don't carry any weight there. I believe that every new frontier situation, whether on a mountain, in art or science, signifies a small revolution for existing standards and semantics.

Reinhold published a book some years ago, *Bergsteiger werden mit Reinhold Messner* (Become a climber with Reinhold Messner), which included the ten commandments for responsible mountaineering: boots with profile soles, spare underwear, personal identification, two prussik slings, toilet paper ... The Alpine catechism, you might say. The book outlines the approach that Reinhold teaches in his climbing school.

He has taken it to absurd lengths himself. We set off for the Gasherbrums with no climbing or sit har-

Hans Kammerlander

nesses, no compass, and no helmets. Candles and medical kit found a place in our equipment, but the 20 metres of 6mm line hardly constituted a rope.

A heretical father-superior with his apprentice? Two climbing outlaws who cannot obey the most elementary regulations? Certainly not! The Gasherbrum-Traverse Project was not realised by employing the ground rules of classical mountaineering. Only the rucksack – packed according to the commandment of theoretical safety – could not be dispensed with.

For this traverse, which took eight days of our lives, we played by the rules of the Messneric Koran (we were after all in Pakistan). We left all the book doctrine behind us in order to attempt what popular opinion deemed impossible. Our success proved us right, and if I now recall certain instances of the traverse, it is to point up where the textbooks need extending – not rewriting, just expanding.

It was our fourth climbing day when we began the descent of Gasherbrum II, down a steep, crevassed hanging glacier. Common sense

would most certainly have declared this forbidden territory. Yet we came safely down because we climbed in the very early morning on hard-frozen ice. The previous day we had given up the whole afternoon because we needed to come down this section at the most favourable time – first thing in the morning. We climbed unroped. There are not many other climbers who can crampon down as quickly and nimbly as Reinhold Messner.

Two days later, coming off the summit snowfield of Gasherbrum I, Reinhold took a bad fall. He peeled off backwards into space and was away. I have known people, trained sports climbers, who in such a situation, would not have come to rest till they hit the deck. But Reinhold was able to fling himself round in mid-air so that he was facing downwards, and then regain his footing several metres lower on steep, glazed rock slabs. It's not for me to eulogise here over this forty-year-old, beset at the time with all sorts of aches and pains; suffice it to say that quick reactions and balance like that aren't sold in any sports shop.

Further down, just before the glacier levelled out, we were nearly wiped out by a rock avalanche which came straight for us out of the mist. A huge rock pillar had collapsed on the ridge above. Why were we not killed? Sheer luck!

What people always take issue with us over is the 'signal' power of tours like this – according to your viewpoint they can be seen as setting good or bad examples. It is alleged that it encourages young people into this kind of adventure, to take such risks. Reinhold has always rejected such argument, believing in freedom of choice and the common sense of the individual.

Peak performances in any branch of life are not available on prescription, nor are they transferable one to another. The product of talent, intelligence, instinct and hard work is usually only sufficient for one activity, for one single exercise. Being able to evaluate it correctly, that is the main problem.

Anyone who has spent almost 20 years doing the most difficult routes in the Himalaya, practically without accident, is a phenomenon, however you want to look at it. You can't copy that. Even the luck that has held good for him cannot be duplicated. Anyone who has overcome all the hurdles is entitled to write a book about those hurdles – not in order to tear them down, but to emphasise their correctness.

Your instruction book, dear Reinhold, is born of long experience; that is its value. There is just one Commandment you have forgotten to put in. The eleventh: *'Quod licet Jovi, non licet bovi'*. Roughly translated it means, 'An ox cannot hope to do that which Jupiter can do'.

Hans Kammerlander
(Climber of seven eight-thousanders)

metre peaks would all have been unthinkable ten years ago, but now feature in the forward plans of several 'professional' climbers. Why should it not also be possible to climb two eight-thousanders in sequence?

To have reached what by today's standards we consider the 'ultimate' stage of development, has only been made possible thanks to improved equipment and an understanding of how to tailor diet to activity. However, I have never employed drugs here or anywhere else to get me to the top. I regard them in the same category as oxygen masks, expansion bolts, and all the false rhetoric so often spouted by would-be heroes.

Traversing the two Gasherbrum summits certainly counts as my boldest-ever adventure on an eight-thousand metre peak. I don't feel that, as a climb, it has ever been properly understood or recognised, either by specialists or laymen – perhaps because it is barely repeatable.

Looking back on it today, I see it was an undertaking ahead of its time. There

are any number of similar traverse possibilities, such as the traverse of Lhotse and Everest, for example, or of any two eight-thousanders close to each other.

There is also the traverse of the five Kangchenjunga summits, which has been tried but never accomplished. Four of the five are more than 8,000 metres high. It must also be possible to traverse Makalu, Lhotse and Everest one after the other, perhaps not today, but maybe in about ten years' time. It goes without saying, however, that the contender for such a traverse must bring not only skill, but the requisite experience, which can only be gained over a number of years.

Hopefully such a challenge will be realised by fair means, that is to say, without other expedition groups, or existing depots, or the route being prepared in advance. Otherwise it would not be the logical extension of what Hans Kammerlander and I did on Gasherbrums I and II.

Karakoram Breithorn

Historical Highlights

Geographical Position: Karakoram, Baltoro Mustagh
Lat. 35°48′ N, Long. 76°34′ E

1892 A British reconnaissance under W.M. Conway bestows the name Broad Peak to what was hitherto known as Falchen Kangri.

1909 The Italian V. Sella brings back photographs of the north, west and south sides of the mountain.

1954 A German–Austrian expedition under K.M. Herrligkoffer arrives at Broad Peak in the autumn. Dismissing the favourable West Rib, it attempts instead to climb the dangerous cracks and ice wall of the southwest side. This leads to several mishaps. Early in November the expedition has to be called off having reached around 6,900m.

1957 A small Austrian expedition under the leadership of M. Schmuck is the first to find success on Broad Peak. A strong 4-man team of H. Buhl, M. Schmuck, K. Diemberger and F. Wintersteller reach the summit. They do not use high-level porters nor bottled oxygen, and carry their own loads for the three high camps. On their first summit bid they are misled by a 'false summit' and retreat back to Base Camp to recover. Their second attempt is successful and they finally reach the summit on 9 June. 18 days later Hermann Buhl is lost on Chogolisa.

1975 Polish mountaineers under J. Ferenski follow the 1957 Austrian route as far as the saddle above the icy West Rib. From there they reach Central Summit (8,016m) via the rocky Southeast Ridge. Three of the 5-man summit team fall to their deaths on the way down. The second ascent of the Main Summit is made in the same year by two Japanese following the route of the first ascent.

1978 Y. Seigneur who had been forced to abandon an attempt of Broad Peak two years before, tries his luck again. This time he succeeds in reaching the long summit ridge at his second attempt (normal route), together with G. Bettembourg.

1982 On 2 August R. Messner climbs his third eight-thousander in one year. Accompanied by the two Pakistani climbers N. Sabir and S. Khan he makes it to the summit of Broad Peak with a variation on the normal route (6th ascent).

1983 The Italian R. Casarotto, having already made an attempt the previous year, now succeeds in making the first ascent of the North Summit (7,800m) by its difficult North Ridge. Polish women climbers set up a new record for womens' mountaineering at the end of June. In only two days K. Palmowska and A. Czerwinska climb the main summit without artificial oxygen and without porters. On the same day, Swiss mountaineer M. Ruedi and the Frenchman E. Loretan also reach the summit. Behind them come F. Graf and S. Wörner, and, later, P. Morand and J-C. Sonnenwyl, all members of the Swiss Three Eight-Thousanders Expedition.

1984 V. Kurtyka and J. Kukuczka successfully traverse Broad Peak from the West (North, Central and Main Summits). The 'low' eight-thousanders of the Karakoram again become the stage for extraordinary ideas, such as the Pole K. Wielicki's climb of Broad Peak in a single day. He leaves Base Camp (4,900m) at 02.00 hours, is on the summit at 16.00 hours, and at 22.30 is back in Base Camp. The major part of this climb of 3,150 vertical metres, is covered solo by this young sportsman. However, like the 'record ascents' of 1983 this does not rank as an 'independent tour'. The route is protected, trodden and supplied with food and camps. Incidentally, since 1957, much of the route has now become bare.

Broad Peak from the west. The route shown (with bivouac places indicated) is that which Reinhold Messner selected in 1982 for his climb with Nazir Sabir and Sher Khan. Apart from a variation at the start it follows the line of the first ascent (1957).

The full potential of Broad Peak has not yet been realised even though all three summits are often climbed. At least half a dozen logical routes still wait for first ascents.

BROAD PEAK 8047 m

B₂

B₁

BC △△△

Previous double page: View down-valley from the first bivouac on Broad Peak. Below, the wide sweep of the Godwin-Austen Glacier which flows from K2 (away to the right) towards Concordia. The two Pakistani mountaineers Sher Khan and Nazir Sabir are packing their rucksacks, the bivouac tent having already been dismantled.

Above: Broad Peak Base Camp with our cook, Rosi Ali. K2 is in the background. On all his expeditions Reinhold Messner sets up a team tent where everyone can eat together: members, cook, porters. Sleeping tents are then placed around, each housing just one or two people.

Right: Balti porters on the Baltoro Glacier. At the start of his 1982 expedition Reinhold Messner deposited a cache of stores at the foot of Broad Peak, to which he could return after climbing Gasherbrum II.

Below: Broad Peak from Concordia (southwest). Left is the broad-topped Middle Summit, right the Main Summit. The route follows the gap between the two summit masses.

View from the gap between Broad Peak's two highest summits, towards the fore-summit (which appears higher) and the main summit. Before making the first ascent in 1957, Schmuck, Wintersteller, Diemberger and Buhl retreated all the way back to Base Camp after reaching the fore-summit upon realising they had insufficient time to make it to the top. After a few days' rest, they tried again and succeeded in gaining the summit. Many Broad Peak aspirants content themselves these days with the fore-summit.

Above right: Nazir Sabir with the Pakistani flag on the summit of Broad Peak (2 August 1982). In the background, K2, which he climbed with Japanese mountaineers; they made the first ascent of the West Ridge (left skyline).

Below right: Nazir Sabir resting on the descent from Broad Peak summit. He is exhausted from the effects of strenuous exertion coupled with the heat and soft snow. There is a tendency to relax after attaining one's goal.

1982

Falchen Kangri
Only Height
is Measurable

*There is a gap between man's powers to
conceive and his ability to achieve that
can be bridged only by desire.*

Khalil Gibran

*It is a fantastic landscape, the Baltoro
Glacier; I call it the Champs Elysées of
the Himalaya. Imagine, if you can, an
ice boulevard of around 60 to 80
kilometres long, unbelievably long, and
the scenery does not change, even after
walking through it the live-long day.*

Marcel Ichac

Broad Peak, seen from K2 Base Camp (Middle
Summit on left, Main Summit right). The route
of the first ascent, which Reinhold Messner
followed with his two Pakistani companions,
runs from the right of the mountain (middle of
picture), diagonally left into the gap between
the two summits, then right along the ridge to
the highest point which is not visible here.

In the summer of 1982, a few days after
we had been to the top of Gasherbrum II,
Nazir Sabir, Sher Khan and I transferred our attentions to Broad Peak, or
Falchen Kangri as the local inhabitants
used to call it. With a few helpers we
moved our Base Camp. I was certain it
would only take us two or three days to
climb the mountain, and waited for good
weather.

My Pakistani companions, both now as
well acclimatised as I, proved themselves
ideal partners. Naturally, there was no
longer any question of doing the traverse I
had planned with Friedl Mutschlechner,
as they were insufficiently experienced.
It was not something anyone else had
attempted at that time.

We wanted instead to climb by the
Buhl route. It would be an opportunity,
exactly 25 years after Hermann Buhl's
death, to retrace his last summit climb.
It is was not sheer coincidence that I had
attempted Nanga Parbat, Everest, K2,
Dhaulagiri, and now Broad Peak, 25
years after their first ascents. At the
very least, it should serve to demonstrate
my respect for the pioneers.

Broad Peak was of special historical
interest. In 1958 Buhl, Schmuck, Diemberger and Wintersteller were the first
to set themselves to climb an eight-
thousander in Alpine style, and to a
great extent, they succeeded in this. By
dispensing with high-level porters, they
demonstrated how you could go one step
further and also do without fixed high-
level camps. But what really impressed
me more than anything was that on their
first attempt, they retreated all the way
back down from the fore-summit to Base
Camp when they realised that the Main
Summit was still too distant to be
attained that same day. They made it all
the way to the top on their next try.

If I succeeded in my ascent of Broad
Peak, it would mean that I had completed
the hat trick of three eight-thousanders
in one season, and this despite sickness and
the fact that Friedl had been forced to
give up.

Snow conditions were good when we
started. Climbing in a leftwards arc
from Base Camp, we were able to leap-
frog the Camp I that Buhl and his
companions had needed. We found remnants of fixed ropes from previous
expeditions scattered over the face.
Halfway up this steep flank, which was a
good 3,000 metres high, we installed
ourselves in our first bivouac.

When, fully rested, we were about to
set off again next morning, we were

Voytek Kurtyka is one of the most
independent-minded of Polish mountaineers.
Reinhold Messner invited him to join his
winter expedition to Cho Oyu.

surprised to see two climbers coming
down towards us. I was curious because I
knew we were the only ones with permission to be on Broad Peak at that
time. As the pair drew closer, we recognised them as Jerzy Kukuczka and
Voytek Kurtyka. The two Polish climbers, among the best in the world, had
made a side trip to Broad Peak from K2
and had climbed it in Alpine style. K2
they would try later. We chatted briefly,
then they continued down, and we
resumed our climb.

Had we gone all out for it, we could
have reached the summit that second
day, even though we were carrying

about 20 kilos in our rucksacks, but instead we bivouacked once more. At more or less the spot where the first ascent party had placed its last camp we put up our tent, the same one we had dismantled in the morning after our first bivouac.

The next day, 2 August, the weather was fantastic. The route up between the Middle and Main Summits looked long, but we did not doubt for a moment we would make it. We kept to the ridge all the way. It took quite a while to reach the fore-summit, but then, towards the top, the angle eased, the rocky crest became more broken and we had no difficulty in reaching the highest point.

For me, Broad Peak presented no particular problems. It was, perhaps, the easiest of all my 8,000 metre climbs, no more strenuous and technically easier than any one of the great classic Alpine tours. Objectively, it certainly does not rate as the easiest eight-thousander, but, being subjective, for me it was, if I take difficulty, conditions and weather into account.

A light, high cloud hung in the sky, but the weather held. We did not feel any pressure to hurry down, either on account of weather or from any diminution in our own strength. Besides, the view from the summit was stupendous, like something from another planet. K2 stood to the north, immediately in front of our Central Summit, which although it is nearly 8,000 metres high is clearly recognisable as being only a subsidiary summit.

These many subsidiary summits of the fourteen eight-thousanders, mostly now climbed, have insufficient geographical importance in themselves to hold much appeal for climbers. But, as intermediate summits, on traverses, taken in conjunction with their main summit, they offer an added attraction.

It surprises me how many people attribute special worth to the eight-thousanders merely because they are 8,000–and–more metres high. The 'Quota-8,000' has become a kind of trade mark, as if this alone were enough to guarantee quality. How superficial such a standpoint is! The value of a climbing tour cannot be measured. 8,000 is only a number, after all – it is the mountain, and the experience behind it that counts.

When we got back to Base Camp, we still were not completely exhausted. We could have climbed a fourth, perhaps even a fifth eight-thousander if we had been prepared for it. That was when I took the decision to personally climb all the eight-thousanders.

I wanted to be the first to do this, but I did not see it as any kind of competitive struggle between me and Jerzy Kukuczka or Kurt Diemberger, who in any case were too far from completion at that time to be able to overtake me. For a while, I kept the idea to myself. Later I took one or two people into my confidence and with that, a whole avalanche began to roll, which was finally to sweep me along with it. As the media seized upon the story, the 'race' for the eight-thousanders got blown up into a bloody hand-to-hand duel. In truth, however, this imagined contest never existed.

Realising this new ambition of climbing all the eight-thousanders was not to be my exclusive aim in the next few years, however; nor was it the most important. It would come, when and if it did, more by way of a bonus, an extended possibility, out of the final aggregate of my climbs.

On Broad Peak, as earlier on Gasherbrum II, my experiences with local climbers had only been good ones. It is well known that in Pakistan, Tibet and China there are now some very fine mountaineers. I was convinced that in a few years they would at least be able to match us on their own mountains, if not outstrip us. For one thing, they certainly acclimatise better than we do. At very high altitude, they are almost always stronger than European climbers. Technique they can acquire, in the same way as we acquired it.

Alpinism originated in Europe. We have often behaved to the peoples of Asia like colonial masters. Until recently, local people were employed mainly as porters or assistants. In future, they must work towards becoming independent climbers, or even guides. Himalayan people will play a much bigger role than formerly in the climbing of their own mountains.

It is true that today the Sherpas in Nepal, or the Baltis in the Karakoram, do the bulk of the hard work on many expeditions. On Everest it sometimes happens that Sherpas prepare the entire route for the sahibs; the latter can then perform their 'heroics' up a well-fashioned trail, like a footpath.

Sherpas and Baltis are underpaid, especially the ones who work above Base Camp and actually bear the responsibility. I would be glad to see indigenous high-level porters developing organisational talents in future, alongside their willingness to serve. They need to organise themselves socially and politically, to realise that collectively they have an important voice, and can influence what happens to them. They should aspire to the stage where they achieve adequate payment for all their hard work.

In the long term I hope that the Baltis, the Sherpas and the Tibetan high-porters can become a kind of guide-corps. If Himalayan climbing finally splits into two disciplines, as I think it must, they will always have work. In future I believe on one hand there will be many normal-route expeditions, virtually package tours, organised by European agencies. The less experienced and not especially well-trained 'adventurers' among them could be led to the summit by local climbers. The other development I foresee is expeditions with ever more eccentric objectives. Strong, exceedingly powerful climbers from all over the world will want to do new things on these mountains without the help of high-level porters. They won't just be looking for new routes, attempting traverses, and linking

The Eight-Thousanders and Their Subsidiary Summits (over 8,000m) – First Ascents

(From *Pyrenaica*)

No.	Name: Main/ Subsidiary Summit	Other Names	Height	Date	Expedition	First Ascensionists
1	Everest	Chomolungma, Sagarmatha	8848 m	29 May 1953	British	E. Hillary, Tensing Norgay
a	South Summit	—	8760 m	26 May 1953	British	C. Evans, T. Bourdillon
b	Northeast Shoulder	—	8393 m	Unclimbed	—	—
2	K2	Chogori	8611 m	31 July 1954	Italian	A. Compagnoni, L. Lacedelli
a	West Summit	—	8230 m	Summer 1982	Japanese	N. Sabir and a Japanese
b	South Summit	—	8132 m	Unclimbed (?)	—	
3	Kangchenjunga	Kangchanfanga	8586 m	25 May 1955	British	G. Band, J. Brown
a	Central Summit		8482 m	22 May 1978	Polish	W. Branski, Z. Heinrich, K. Olech
b	South Summit	—	8476 m	19 May 1978	Polish	E. Chobrak, W. Wroz
c	Yalung Kang	West Summit	8433 m	14 May 1973	Japanese	T. Matusuda, Y. Ageta
4	Lhotse	—	8516 m	18 May 1956	Swiss	F. Luchsinger, E. Reiß
a	West Int. Summit	—	8426 m	Unclimbed	—	—
b	East Int. Summit	—	8376 m	Unclimbed	—	
c	Lhotse Shar	East Summit	8400 m	12 May 1970	Austrian	S. Mayerl, R. Walter
5	Makalu	Makalufeng	8463 m	15 May 1955	French	J. Couzy, L. Terray
a	Southeast Summit	—	8010 m	22 May 1970	Japanese	H. Tanaka, Y. Ozaki
6	Cho Oyu	—	8201 m	19 October 1954	Austrian	H Tichy, S. Jöchler, Pasang Dawa Lama
7	Dhaulagiri	—	8167 m	13 May 1960	Swiss	K. Diemberger, A Schelbert, Nawang Dorje
8	Manaslu	Kutang	8163 m	9 May 1956	Japanese	T. Imanishi, Gyaltsen Norbu
9	Nanga Parbat	Diamir	8125 m	3 July 1953	German/Austrian	H. Buhl
a	South Summit	—	8042 m	17 August 1982	Swiss	U. Bühler
10	Annapurna	Morshiadi	8091 m	3 June 1950	French	M. Herzog, L Lachenal
a	Central Summit	—	8064 m	3 October 1980	W. German	U. Böning, L. Greissl, H. Oberrauch
b	East Summit	—	8029 m	29 April 1974	Spanish	J. Anglada, E. Civis, J. Pons
11	Hidden Peak	Gasherbrum I, K5	8068 m	5 July 1958	American	P. Schoening, A. Kauffman
12	Broad Peak	Falchen Kangri	8047 m	9 June 1957	Austrian	M. Schmuck, F. Wintersteller, K. Diemberger, H. Buhl
a	Central Summit	—	8016 m	28 July 1975	Polish	K. Glazek, M. Kesicki, J. Kuliś, B. Nowaczyk, A. Sikorski
13	Shisha Pangma	Xixabangma, Goisainthan	8046 m	2 May 1964	Chinese	6 Chinese and 4 Tibetans
14	Gasherbrum II	K4	8035 m	7 July 1956	Austrian	F. Moravec, H. Willenpart, S. Larch

ridges, rather they will impose on themselves so many limitations that new styles will be brought into being. What is not possible today, will become tomorrow's impulse. An innovator is someone who tries to go one step further than anyone in the Himalaya has been before, not someone who only lops time off something others have already done.

With my successful completion of this first hat trick of eight-thousanders in mountaineering history, my publicity ratings went up. That brought certain financial benefit, but at the same time, more malicious criticism. I was now 'public' property and under close scrutiny. It became much more difficult to organise my practical life without continual disturbance, more difficult, too, to dedicate the necessary time to developing new ideas or preparing new expedition projects.

The subsidiary summits of the eight-thousanders, even though more than 8,000 metres high and often difficult to climb, cannot be considered as independent mountains. At the Himalayan Conference in 1983 (organised by the German Alpine Club) this was re-emphasised. The subsidiary summits listed here are the most important ones, but on Gasherbrum II, Gasherbrum I, Shisha Pangma, Nanga Parbat and Lhotse, there are other lesser ones. Climbers who have been to them are the only ones capable of assessing the importance of subsidiary summits. At the moment there are 'officially' only fourteen eight-thousanders.

So I learned to reduce the time I spent on something which hitherto had demanded my full attention: my 'work'. Whereas I used to spend three months a year on expeditions and nine raising the money to live and to go on these expeditions, I wanted gradually to reverse the relationship. In future I would have nine months 'free' and 'work' for only three. Work for me was also tied up with strange conditions: deadlines, compromises, publicity. Unfortunately, creative work is not very different from that.

Three times now, I have climbed an eight-thousander with local climbers: Kangchenjunga in 1982 with Ang Dorje, the strongest Sherpa I have ever known; and, also in 1982, Gasherbrum II and Broad Peak, with the two Hunza climbers, Sher Khan and Nazir Sabir. On both these expeditions responsibility weighed more heavily on me than if I had been with European climbers. The reason for that, of course, was that their climbing competence was no match for ours. However, because I appreciated their attitude towards mountains, and knew they lacked nothing in tenacity and purpose, their presence was no handicap – in fact it was quite the reverse. I have learned a lot from local climbers in the Himalaya and Karakoram. They see their surroundings rather differently from us, and are superior to us in instinct. Doug Scott has a few things to say on this (*see* page 75).

Reinhold Messner, who was born in 1944, was 20 years old in 1964 when the last eight-thousander was climbed. He arrived on the scene, therefore, too late to make a first ascent of any of the fourteen. However, his climb of Hidden Peak in 1975 was only the second time the summit had been reached. He climbed two other eight-thousanders as third ascents, two as fourth, one as fifth, etc. All his climbs of 8,000m peaks fall into the first 20 successful ascents. No one else will ever be able to match such a low count. The South Tyrolean artist Luis Stecher has dedicated this etching of the fourteen eight-thousanders to his achievement. It was in 1982 that Reinhold Messner consciously resolved to climb all of the eight-thousanders. A strong desire for extreme experience was the motivating force.

MOUNT EVEREST 8848M

K2 8611M

CHO OYU 8202M

DHAULAGIRI 8157M

GASHERBRUM I 8068M

BROAD PEAK 8048M

156

KANGCHENDZÖNGA 8598M   LHOTSE 8511M   MAKALU 8481M

MANASLU 8156M   NANGA PARBAT 8125M   ANNAPURNA I 8091M

SHISHA PANGMA 8046M   GASHERBRUM II 8085 M

Ang Dorje, Sher Khan and Nazir Sabir were all determined to get to the top, yet I had not initially invited them on a summit climb. At the same time, they saw in these mighty mountains something holy, deserving of respect. Between this respect and wanting to climb to the highest point, they were less sure than European mountaineers, but less intense, too. We think rationally and can focus unequivocally upon the summit. Over 200 years, we in Europe have amassed a lot of experience and are schooled technical climbers. They live in the mountains.

I could not have undertaken an extremely difficult route with Ang Dorje, nor with Nazir Sabir or Sher Khan. We prepared the route on Kangchenjunga for Ang Dorje, in as much as we fixed ropes – without them he would not have been able to manage it. Only the last bit of the route we accomplished in Alpine style, where he could climb without danger.

Ang Dorje climbed Everest twice and also Kangchenjunga without artificial oxygen. He was among the first Nepalese climbers, and the only Sherpa, to have climbed both of the highest mountains in his country without using oxygen apparatus. The third time he tried to climb Everest, however, Ang Dorje was killed.

Sher Khan and Nazir Sabir are still climbing. Nazir Sabir has not only climbed K2, Gasherbrum II and Broad Peak, but also many of the smaller six-thousanders in his Pakistani homeland. Sher Khan has been three times to the summit of Gasherbrum II.

Sherpa Ang Dorje on the summit of Kangchenjunga. He was later killed on Mount Everest.

Nazir Sabir (left), Reinhold Messner and Sher Khan in Dassu before setting off for Gasherbrum II and Broad Peak.

Survived – on big mountains

When Hermann Buhl fell to his death in 1957 and I was left to find my own way back down through the mist to the valley, across the snowfields and icefalls of Chogolisa, it certainly cost me one of my seven lives. In the summer of 1986, when I was making a summit attempt on K2 with Julie Tullis, and not only my companion but four others in our group of seven lost their lives, those long days of storm and the never-ending descent just as certainly robbed me of another. How do you explain survival? Left on your own, where does the 'Never give up!' come from? It is something that has often puzzled me.

Even if my style of climbing is different from that of Reinhold Messner – and really the two are not at all comparable – I know that we both owe our survival largely to the strict adherence to rules we hold to be right, whatever others might think; and that can also extend well into the region of instinct. When I think how often people going to the summit on big mountains – or more particularly, coming back – find themselves in borderline situations, I can only marvel that someone who has climbed all fourteen eight-thousanders, some by their most difficult routes, has survived to tell the tale.

'An eight-thousander is only yours if you get down safely – until then, you belong to it.' That is something I once wrote in my diary. For me, big mountains are like people, each has its own character, with moods and humour that can change from day to day. The mountain will tolerate me or it will not. If I can build a relationship with it, then I may bind my life to it in the sense that I am able to climb to its summit. I call that the 'inner voice rule' – that is, what says yea or nay, and recognises the right moment to

Kurt Diemberger

make a move. Without being able to pinpoint occasions exactly, I know I have often had it to thank for saving my life.

Something else that is terribly important is a meditative ability, or rather a sort of trance which, once achieved, enables you to endure days of storm in a tent, or even withstand an open bivouac at great altitude. I'm certain that is what kept me alive on K2 during the bitter tragedy of 1986.

Last but not least is the 'ratio'. Before every climb, you have to make a countdown of the necessary equipment, and be quite precise about it, to the point I would say of being pedantic. More than that, you have to make an assessment of all the possibilities. My companion, Julie Tullis, and I had reached a rare harmony in the way we approached mountains. (Julie had accompanied me on almost all my trips to eight-thousanders in recent years, filming and climbing; we were known as 'the highest film team in the world' and had filmed on K2, our

dream-mountain, from both north and south-east in the course of three expeditions.) We used to take into account the requirements of 'creative climbing', and at the same time those of safety. With us, speed was not a prime factor, as it has become in recent sport-mountaineering developments on eight-thousanders. Above everything else, we needed the capacity to be able, if necessary, to hold out at great heights, coupled with the ability to make a fast descent in emergency. On K2 we twice carried our own Camp 4 to around 8,000 metres, and had we been able to make our summit bid on 3 August, as planned, Julie would still be alive.

I consider it of the utmost importance that anyone who climbs to such heights should be constantly aware that above 8,000 metres no rescue is possible, and that you should not spend a single unnecessary day up there. The many expeditions you find these days on eight-thousand metre routes can certainly lead to greater international co-operation, on the one hand, but equally can increase the overall danger.

I believe what is important for survival is that the people who climb high must not just aim for the top single-mindedly, but also be very critical of the way they carry out their undertaking. Reinhold Messner has described me as the 'only mountaineer to have survived throughout the whole history of eight-thousand metre climbing and remained active'. I have to say, I have seen a lot of changes.

Kurt Diemberger
(Climber of six eight-thousanders)

159

10 1954 Cho Oyu 8,201m/26,906ft

The Turquoise Goddess

Historical Highlights

Geographical Position: Nepal
Himalaya, Mahalungur Himal
Lat. 28°06′ N, Long. 86°40′ E

1952 A British team explores the northwest approaches of Cho Oyu. E. Shipton, E. Hillary and W. (G.) Lowe climb as far as the great ice barrier at 6,800m.

1954 Small Austrian expedition under H. Tichy makes first ascent of Cho Oyu. H. Tichy (despite frost-bite), S. Jöchler and the Sherpa Sirdar Pasang Dawa Lama reach the summit on 19 October without artificial oxygen. Their route follows West Ridge and West Face to the summit.

At the same time Frenchwoman C. Kogan and Swiss R. Lambert make an unsanctioned attempt on the peak – they try for the summit after the withdrawal of Tichy's team. A storm turns them back at around 7,600m.

1958 In the course of an Indian expedition under K. Bunshah, Sherpa Pasang Dawa Lana, together with S. Gyatso (Sikkim), climb the Austrian route to the summit (2nd ascent). An expedition member dies of pulmonary oedema.

1959 C. Kogan returns to Cho Oyu with an international womens' expedition. She is killed, together with a Belgian woman and two Sherpas, when avalanches destroy Camp 4.

1964 An alleged 3rd ascent by the German F. Stammberger, member of a ski expedition led by R. Rott, remains unratified on account of controversial photographic 'evidence'. On descent Stammberger has to leave two exhausted team members, A. Thurmayr and G. Huber, behind at Camp 4, in the 'Death Zone'. It is nine days before a rescue party reaches them, by which time it is too late. Both die.

1978 On an unsanctioned summit climb, Austrians E. Koblmüller and A. Furtner make the first ascent of the difficult Southeast Face. Travelling as trekkers, they have no permit to go to the top, and their 'raid' causes much ill-feeling in Nepal, resulting in a ban of several years for the climbers.

1982 German, Austrian and Swiss mountaineers, hoping to climb the Southeast Face in the spring are dogged by bad luck. R. Karl is killed in his tent by an ice avalanche and W. Nairz badly injured. O. Oelz has to be flown home to Zurich with cerebral oedema, and toothache forces R. Meier into the Hillary Hospital in Kunde.

1983 Having been driven back by bad snow conditions in the winter, R. Messner sets off for Cho Oyu again in the spring. With F. Kammerlander and M. Dacher he climbs to the summit on 5 May by a partly new route on the southwest side (4th ascent).

1984 During a Czech–American–Nepalese expedition under V. Komarkova, two women and two Sherpas reach the summit in the spring. In the autumn, Yugoslavs reach about 7,600m on the South Pillar.

1985 Polish climbers (among them J. Kukuczka) make a successful winter ascent of the Yugoslav 1984 route (12 and 13 February). In the spring, Chinese and Spanish expeditions complete the ordinary route. A Polish–American expedition fails on the East Ridge but manages to climb the normal route, as does a Canadian–American–Czech team in winter.

1986 Poles reach the summit in the spring by the Southwest Ridge; so too does an international expedition with ascents on three separate days. A Swiss expedition under E. Loretan fails in the autumn on the Southwest Face when a member falls to his death (P.A. Steiner).

Reinhold Messner went to Cho Oyu in two consecutive seasons. In December 1982 on the Southeast Face, which had first been climbed by the Austrians Koblmüller and Furtner (1978), and in spring 1983. On the first expedition Messner's South Tyrolean expedition failed only 700m below the summit. Five months later he reached the top by the Southwest Face with Michl Dacher and Hans Kammerlander. Using only two bivouacs the three made the climb in Alpine style after having installed an advance base camp immediately below the Nangpa-La. Today there are four separate routes on Cho Oyu as well as a few variations to the normal route. The Tibetan north side in particular has several worthy first ascent possibilities.

CHO OYU 8201 m

B₂ 1983

△ C₃ 1982

△ C₂ 1982

△ C₁ 1982

Sherpa woman in the Solu Khumbu. For her Cho Oyu is a holy mountain.

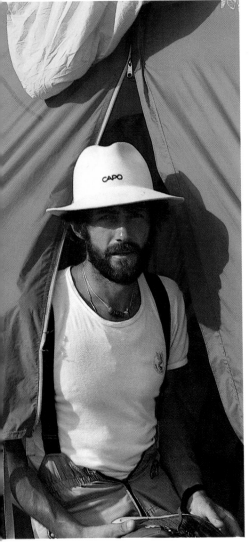

Hans Kammerlander, who climbed Cho Oyu in 1983 with Reinhold Messner. This was his first eight-thousander; the Cho Oyu attempt of the previous year was the first time he accompanied Reinhold Messner on an expedition.

Elderly yak in new snow on the way to Base Camp under Nangpa-La (1983).

Masked dancers in the monastery at
Thame (Solo Khumbu) at the foot of
Cho Oyu. Once a year, usually in
May, the Mani-Rimdu festival is held
in Thame.

Snow in Namche Bazar. The Sherpa
capital is a tourist centre.

Above: Hans Kammerlander and Reinhold Messner on the Southwest Face of Cho Oyu.

Left: Hans Kammerlander on Cho Oyu Southeast Face in winter. Blank ice on the lower part of the climb hampered ascent; higher, unstable avalanche snow rendered further progress almost impossible.

Right: Michl Dacher and Reinhold Messner on the summit of Cho Oyu, a huge snow-dome (5 May 1983). Looking north towards Tibet.

Previous double page: Hans Kammerlander and Michl Dacher below the col which leads over the border ridge, giving access to the Southwest Face of Cho Oyu south of Nangpa-La.

Cho Oyu
Astride Two Worlds

What is within, the intuitive state of mind, is so much more important that it is what I have always to win over first.

Peter Handke

Is it too late to stop mountaineering becoming a commercialised rat-race, where individual spontaneity and creativity are overwhelmed by mechanistic ego-tripping rituals, sponsored by manufacturers, approved by social do-good institutions and propagated by the mass-conditioning of the press media?

Rob Wood in *Mountain*

Cho Oyu from the south. The Southeast Face route (1978) runs diagonally from lower right to the summit. Reinhold Messner attempted it with a South Tyrolean expedition in the winter of 1982, reaching a point just above the last seracs. The southwest side of the mountain (left) is not visible in this picture.

On 17 February 1980, Polish mountaineers became the first to climb Mount Everest in winter. Officially, however, the climb was never recognised as a winter ascent. To be so, according to Nepalese 'rules', it would need to have been climbed during the period 1 December – 15 February. All the same, as far as I am concerned, this was the first ascent of an eight-thousander in winter.

When the Nepalese authorities started issuing permits to climb their highest mountains during the winter months, they encouraged a completely new ball game. Even though at first I was sceptical that eight-thousanders would be climbed 'by fair means' in winter, certainly without masks, I decided to try it for myself in the winter of 1982–3. That was still before any eight-thousander had been climbed during the 'official' winter months.

At the beginning of December, however, while we were making an attempt on the southeast flank of Cho Oyu, a Japanese expedition reached the summit of Dhaulagiri. Knowing just how extreme conditions can be in winter, they had planned their expedition to run over from post-monsoon into winter, laying their preparations in November. Their lower camps were established, therefore, before the onset of winter, so that in the first days of December they could climb through to the summit. Such a tactic – a trick, really – we were not prepared to employ on Cho Oyu.

I invited five mountaineers on this expedition, but also two artists from South Tyrol – the painter, Luis Stecher, and the author, Bruno Laner. These two, each in their own way, were to capture impressions of big mountains from the standpoint of men versus nature. Our *baroque* winter expedition to Cho Oyu was thus something of a new departure; and for me, a most rewarding experience.

We climbers were able to relax better whenever we came down to Base Camp. I found it possible to completely forget the mountain as we sat together in our big communal tent, talking deep into the night. And the talk was not just about climbing and eight-thousanders, but of God, and the world, too.

Acclimatising first down in the Gokyo Valley, we then climbed Island Peak under the South Face of Lhotse. The climb proper we began on 1 December. All the climbers left Base Camp, making swift progress as conditions were good. Lower down on the mountain wind and cold were no great handicap. It was only when we reached 7,500 metres, from where we hoped to launch our summit bid, that we got bogged down in new snow.

Preparing for this expedition, I had made an error in my reasoning. Observations led me to conclude that on the Southeast Face in winter we would be protected from the dreadful storms that roll in from the northwest. On all other flanks, jet stream winds, which blow from Tibet at this time of year over the high mountains, are the greatest handicap. This wind can be fatal at high altitude, but in the wind shadow, on the opposite side, I hoped to be able to make good headway.

This indeed proved to be the case when we were climbing steep passages which did not hold the new snow. We were only aware of the wind by the streaming banners of spindrift way above our heads. But once we had put Cho Oyu's main climbing difficulties behind us and reached the point where the angle eases off, we were confronted with masses of waist-deep snow. It was simply impossible to wade up through it. Bearing in mind what might happen if this slope was to give way, Hans Kammerlander and I, who were in the lead, decided not to go for the summit even though it was so close. It was too risky and too effort-consuming to force the climb further. Anxiety turned us back.

In the final analysis, every expedition to an eight-thousander, Cho Oyu included, resolves down to a struggle with oneself, any inner insight gained being infinitely more valuable than the view from the summit. I am the last person to suppress my ambition, yet climbing for me is first and foremost a quest. It is not a struggle, not a battle against 'naked rock', not a competition with other climbers, but an attempt to put something I have carefully planned into action.

On this Cho Oyu expedition in the winter of 1982–3, we frequently passed the place where Reinhard Karl had been killed six months earlier. He was attempting the Southeast Face in the pre-monsoon period as part of an expedition led by Wolfgang Nairz. At the foot of the actual summit wall, at around 6,500 metres, the two were overwhelmed by an avalanche at dawn one morning. Wolfgang crawled free, but Reinhard lost his life.

They were not far from the summit when the accident occurred, full of confidence, full of life. Afterwards,

Wolfgang Nairz called off the expedition. It remains a mystery why such a successful and wary climber as Reinhard Karl could have camped in an exposed spot like that. There is nothing to be gained from brooding over the tragedy. Anyone who is first and last a climber knows that he lives dangerously; even when he is not looking for danger, it can find him. We reached a good 1,000 metres higher than Karl and Nairz. But that did not alter the fact that we also failed.

This winter expedition was the first time Hans Kammerlander partnered me at altitude. Within a few days I had complete trust in this young South Tyrolean climber, such as I have rarely felt for other mountaineers. He was not only strong, he accepted everything as a matter of course. Like *Bulle* Oelz, Friedl Mutschlechner, or before that, my brother Günther, he soon became more than just a climbing partner, and I invited him to come back to Cho Oyu in

Memorial cairn *(chorten)* to Reinhard Karl in the Gokyo valley. Cho Oyu behind to the left.

the spring of 1983. Michl Dacher came too – by now he had grown into West Germany's most successful high altitude climber.

For the 1983 expedition we had a permit for the southwest side of Cho Oyu. This was an easier side of the mountain, but not easily accessible. The Nepalese Government had made it a condition that I did not cross over the Nangpa-La into Tibet. This is the Himalayan pass over which the Sherpas migrated from Tibet to Nepal in the seventeenth century. From Namche Bazar, in the Solo Khumbu, therefore, we set off towards Thame and beyond that, to the valley under the Nangpa-La.

Not far below the pass, at a height of 5,000 metres, we set up our Base Camp and sent back our yaks; they had struggled breast-deep in snow practically as far as the Nangpa Glacier. Above, on the Nangpa-La itself, we set up our first high camp, a kind of advanced base camp.

From there, we tried to traverse on to the southwest flank of our mountain across the Nangpai Gosum. This is just a small pass, a gap, which is relatively easy to cross, and if you descend on the other side it brings you into Tibet without having to go over the forbidden Nangpa-La. That way we detoured round to Cho Oyu. We were indeed in a forbidden world, but had attained it by legal means. I had kept to the instructions given to me by the Ministry of Tourism, yet had still reached my sanctioned route. Since no Sherpas accompanied us, we were heavily loaded.

The climb to the summit lasted three days and passed without special incident. There were no serious difficulties. On our last day, Michl, Hans and I gained more than 1,000 metres of altitude. Up on the great summit plateau, more than anywhere, the mountain seemed set to go on for ever. Coming through the wind-sculpted snow-fields, we kept thinking every last hill was the summit, only to find another, still

Advanced Base Camp under the Nangpa-La, 1983. The smaller tent was home to two Sherpas whenever they brought supplies of food up from our main camp. We occupied the larger one. In the background, Nangpai Gosum.

Stonefall

The hardest part on the Cho Oyu Southeast Face was an ice slope between 7,000 and 7,400 metres. We dared not make use of the crack by which Koblmüller and Furtner climbed to the summit in 1978, as it ran underneath a huge, dangerous piece of serac. Climbing there would be lethal. We therefore kept to the right. Even so the face was almost vertical. Ice ribs appeared to be glued to the face, with drifted snow between them! The whole thing was like a gigantic gâteau, generously loaded with snow instead of cream. The climbing required absolute concentration.

Hans Kammerlander, Hans Peter Eisendle, Voytek Kurtyka and I had spent ten days preparing the route. Now Hans and I found ourselves on the stage of the face where it gently begins to lean backwards. I was anchored to a stance 40 metres below Hans, belaying him. Hans, climbing deliberately as always, followed a crack across to the left under vertical rocks. Suddenly, high above us, a rock as big as a dinner table broke loose. I watched it fall down the face. First it slid, then jumped through the air in several bounds, past Hans and directly towards me. I stared as if hypnotised, all the while hanging trapped in the rope, unable to free myself. Even with a knife I did not have sufficient time to cut the rope free, so quickly was the rock coming for me.

Like a condemned man, I waited till the very last moment when the stone was right above my head, before tearing myself to one side. The boulder whizzed a few centimetres away from me and into space, disappearing minutes later in the great glacier basin at the foot of the face. Paul Hanny, who was climbing below, bringing up gear, had also been staring at it, spellbound, as if he would divert it from me with sheer will-power. When the danger was over, he breathed a sigh of relief, but was white with fright, as was I.

It only came home to me later just how dangerous this moment on Cho Oyu had been. When I think about it today, the piece of rock takes shape again in my mind's eye. I see how it breaks away and aims straight for me. As then, I know that my only chance of survival is to wait till the last minute to be able to dodge it accurately. The trajectory of a falling stone can only be exactly gauged in those final moments. Only the correct movement at the correct time decides between life and death.

Paul Hanny on the steep ice flank of Cho Oyu (about 7,300m), shortly after Reinhold Messner was nearly hit by a falling rock. Later that day the attempt on the Southeast Face was abandoned. Right, in the background, Mount Everest and Lhotse.

Cho Oyu from the southwest with the route taken by Michl Dacher, Hans Kammerlander and Reinhold Messner on the left. Thanks in no small part to Michl Dacher's many successes, Germany was the first mountaineering nation to be able to claim ascents of all the eight-thousanders. In the 'conquest' period (1950–1964), however, they were not successful in making a single first ascent among the fourteen. Later – and it still applies today – they were content to repeat ascents of the normal routes and other popular lines. The most innovative climbers today are the Poles, Americans, French and Spanish.

higher, behind – and then another, and then another. Was there no end to it?

We made it: on 5 May we stood on the highest point. We photographed each other, then climbed down. The next day we were back at our advanced base camp on the south side of the Nangpa-La.

On this expedition, unlike the first one, we did not have the time nor leisure to study the mountain, to write or to read. The climb was quickly accomplished. It was all too short. I do not believe any expedition before has gone to a summit so quickly without first acclimatising. Being constantly on the go like this is not so enjoyable. The contemplative side of climbing has become as important to me now as the necessity every so often to 'push the limits'.

On this spring expedition in 1983, I did not just cross the boundary between China and Nepal, I transcended the boundary into a new life. The hazards encountered on a mountain, living as one with nature, had become essential to me, unquestionable. You could say I was addicted to them. If I had to stay too long in Europe, I became bad-tempered. To stay alive, I needed the week-long, month-long solitude of Himalayan mountains, either alone or with a few chosen friends.

This was a half of my existence. Then, back in Europe, I was similarly happy to be among a throng of people, giving a lecture somewhere. On the one hand I needed solitude, on the other I was always glad to go back to civilization, to 'work', and to everyday stress. I am one of those people driven by ideas, who has to be active in order to stay physically and mentally healthy; but for the generation of new ideas, pauses are necessary. I now played my life half and half: one half in the total isolation of the Himalaya, the other in the hectic rhythm of a mid-European town. I was

searching for heights and depths, and needed the contrast, not just to be in mountains.

The change from one extreme to another during the course of a year became so natural to me that I could go from living one day in a hotel to the next in a tent, without upset and without any sense of loss for what I had left behind.

I never experienced any contradiction in this 'double life', as others seem to imagine there must be. Just when I began to tire of schedules, questions, and all the bustle, I would be setting off on my travels once more. In many respects, the pace of life in Asia completely reversed the way I felt about things. My 'gods' were once more the mountains, the streams, the clouds.

People there regarded me with the same curiosity as I them. In as much as I kept coming, it was obvious to them that I loved their land and their mountains. I adopted several of their customs: since 1981 I have worn a Xi-stone around my neck and have learned to barter with the same enthusiasm as the Khampas or Kashmiris. I am quite at home in the Himalaya.

Reinhold Messner has formed close relationships with the Sherpas and Tibetans through his many visits to their countries. He wears a Xi-stone, between two coral beads, around his neck (middle picture), which he obtained in Tingri at the northern foot of Cho Oyu. Such stones are said to have magic properties, being barometers of the soul. Sherpas and Tibetans (who still take their yaks across the Himalaya over the Nangpa-La, almost 6,000m high) are surprised to see him wearing it, as are the Hunzas in Pakistan. People keep coming up and touching it; they often treat Messner as one of themselves.

Survived – with new insight

More than 30 years have passed since we – Tyroleans Sepp Jöchler and Helmet Heuberger, Sherpa Pasang Dawa Lama and I – reached the summit of Cho Oyu for the first time. The struggle for the eight-thousanders had then only just begun. Our success lay somewhere around half-way – Cho Oyu was the fifth mountain above the magic 8,000-metre level to be climbed. Incidentally, it has 'grown' since then: when we climbed it, its official height was 8,153 metres, today it is given as 8,201 metres. Is this because the Himalaya are rising, or does it reflect more accurate measuring, or is it some combination of both?

I have often been away in the years since then, and with the growing number of expeditions, have lost touch with what is happening in Himalayan mountaineering. Maybe I have too little interest in such Alpine undertakings – I am no climber in the extreme sense of the word. Away in Nepal, where I have lived for a long time, it was difficult to learn particulars about successful or ill-fated expeditions.

We did once sit up all night, though, talking of 'our' Cho Oyu and reliving the past. That was in Bhaktapur near Kathmandu, when I met our Sirdar Pasang decades later. From his faraway gaze you could see he was not long for this world, and indeed he died a couple of months later in Darjeeling. Remembering old times and shared experiences kept him wide awake as night gave way to morning. We had spent many months travelling together in a Himalaya that was then completely cut off from the world, very remote.

This long conversation between Pasang and I took place in 1982 when Reinhold Messner was making his

Herbert Tichy

first attempt on Cho Oyu. We knew hardly anything about that at the time. Even now, as I write these lines, I am not familiar with the details of Reinhold's triumph. But I don't need them to understand the magnitude of his achievement.

Take the so-called Death Zone, in which everyone who wants to climb an eight-thousander has to spend more or less time. Life there becomes a thrilling and happy experience – or so at least I found on our summit climb. True, thoughts become confused, but vision – and I don't just mean what you see, I mean inner vision, too – becomes more acute. It allows you to forget everyday worries. That may sound contrary, but most people who have been above 8,000 metres – and there are now many of them – will vouch for this experience.

When we went to the summit we endured one very bad night in Camp 4. It was only at 7,000 metres, but in a most exposed position. The tent poles broke in the storm, and the tent fabric wrapped around us like a net around fish. We thought then, we poor fish, that we had no hope of surviving as the force of the hurricane was so great.

Since then equipment has improved significantly and experience has taught new strategies for survival. Many mountaineers before and since have survived critical situations. Viewed from today's standpoint, perhaps we only found ourselves in an 'awkward' predicament. But I remember the actual thoughts that went through my mind at the time. My life would have been measurably poorer had I not experienced Camp 4 on Cho Oyu.

Thinking now about Reinhold Messner brings back to me those hours in Camp 4. For him, Cho Oyu was only one of more than a dozen of the world's highest mountains. Doubtless he has withstood critical hours as we did in our camp. The views – external and internal – that he has gained from such situations, seem to me to be every bit as valuable as the 'Record of all the Eight-thousanders'.

Herbert Tichy
(First ascensionist, Cho Oyu)

The First Eight-Thousander

Historical Highlights

Geographical Position: Nepal Himalaya, between Kali Gandaki and Marsiandi
Lat. 28°36′ N, Long. 83°49′ E

1950 Up to this time Annapurna is as good as unexplored. The French expedition under M. Herzog, originally heading for Dhaulagiri, has first to reconnoitre its own way in. Approaching from the west, it succeeds in getting into the glacier basin to the north of Annapurna, from where a possible route is revealed via the sickle-shaped glacier. As the start of the monsoon is fast approaching, no time can be lost. Despite inadequate footwear M. Herzog and L. Lachenal launch an attempt and on 3 June 1950 stand on the summit. This is the first ascent of an eight-thousander. Retreat from the mountain, however, is anything but triumphal. Crevasse falls, avalanches and bivouacking in the open all badly affect Herzog, Lachenal, and their rescuers; the drugs they take only make matters worse, and the expedition doctor, Oudot, is forced to amputate fingers and toes while still on the return march.

1970 The second ascent of the main summit of Annapurna is made by a British expedition following the same route as the first. Shortly afterwards the third ascent goes to D. Whillans and D. Haston. They are members of a very strong team of Alpinists, who have come to Annapurna with C. Bonington to climb the extremely difficult South Face for the first time. 4,500 metres of fixed ropes are employed; the new Himalayan style is established. I. Clough is killed.

1974 Spanish expedition under J. Anglada makes the first ascent of Annapurna East Summit, 8,026m.

1977 Dutch open a new route on the north side of Annapurna, to the left of the Sickle Glacier. Three men reach the summit.

1978 An American womens' expedition follows the Dutch route; two members and two Sherpas reach the summit. An English and an American climber fall to their deaths.

1979 On the French ski expedition two members climb to the summit by the route of the first ascent. Y. Morin dies in an accident skiing down.

1981 A Polish expedition under the leadership of R. Szafirskis climbs the right-hand pillar on the South Face. Two members make the first ascent of the Middle Summit, 8,051m, by a new route. A Japanese expedition under H. Yoshino places two members on the summit via the British South Face route.

1982 British group discovers a new line on the South Face, to the right of the Bonington route. The expedition is called off when A. McIntyre is killed by a stonefall. (Two Spanish climbers complete this extremely difficult route a couple of years later, in Alpine style.)

1984 Swiss team attempts the traverse of the East Ridge, which had been tried a number of times before. After only a 3-day climb E. Loretan and N. Joos stand on the East Summit, then continue over the Central and Main Summits, from where they descend by the Dutch Route. They thereby traverse the three Annapurna summits in Alpine style.

1985 R. Messner, with the South Tyrolean H. Kammerlander, completes a route on the previously unclimbed Northwest Face, reaching the summit of Annapurna on 24 April (12th ascent).

The Northwest Face of Annapurna is difficult and dangerous in places, especially under new snow. The icefall below Camp C1 is not particularly crevassed and for the most part can be avoided by rocks on the left. The summit ridge is long and exposed. Left of the route, which was first climbed by Reinhold Messner and Hans Kammerlander in 1985, is the line which twice defeated Troillet and Steiner. It remains a fascinating possibility. Also unclimbed is the spur on the upper part of the face.

All the routes on Annapurna are steep and difficult apart from the route of the first ascent (1950), which is, however, extremely dangerous. The mountain has been well explored from all sides.

ANNAPURNA 8091 m

Left: Swami Prem Darshano (originally Luggi Rieser), a member of the 1985 Annapurna expedition, talking with an Indian guru in Nepal.

Right: Camp 1 at the foot of Annapurna Northwest Face. Reinhard Patscheider, Hans Kammerlander, Prem Darshano and Reinhard Schiestl stand around the tent. The route runs up the mixed wall to the big serac, over this to the right and up slabs to the ridge. From the shoulder it goes from right to left to the summit.

Below left: Porters and Swami Prem Darshano cross the Kali Gandaki by a suspension bridge. The approach to Annapurna from the north.

Below right: Porters below the Thulo Begin, which has to be crossed on the approach march.

Left: Reinhard Schiestl, unroped, negotiating a crevasse below the bergschrund.

Previous double page: Annapurna (extreme left), Shoulder and Fang (the rock tower in the background) after a new fall of snow. Storm winds blow snow from the sides of the Northwest Gully. A huge avalanche pours down the start of the route attempted by French and Canadian climbers under Henri Sigayret in 1983. It was the first expedition on this side of the mountain. Reinhold Messner and Hans Kammerlander made the first ascent of this face (24 April 1985).

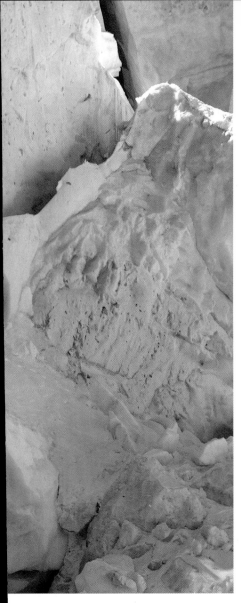

Above: Reinhard Schiestl in the icefall below Camp 1 on Annapurna.

Right: Blank ice at the top of the combined wall below the ice 'balcony' at around 6,000m above sea level.

1985

Annapurna
The Biggest Hurdles
are in the Mind

It is a desperate thing to eliminate despair, for it is despair that makes our life what it is.

Erich Fried

There is a third less oxygen in the air at 8,000 metres than normally. That means it takes all your willpower just to draw another breath. The whole body concentrates itself on this single task: inhale one more breath. And it takes some time to achieve a slow and steady breathing pattern, before you can begin to live again.

Maurice Herzog

View of Annapurna from the north. One of the major achievements of modern Himalayan mountaineering was the traverse of the East Ridge made in Autumn 1984 by the two Swiss climbers Norbert Joos and Erhard Loretan (from left to right of picture, taking in East, Middle and Main Summits, the obvious rocky upthrusts), followed by a descent down the Dutch Spur. The first ascent route (Herzog/Lachenal, 1950) runs to the left of the sharp edge (North Spur, unclimbed), which separates the Northwest Face from the North Flank.

It has never been my object in the mountains merely to repeat something others have done ten years before me, only faster. Whatever I did, I wanted to push one step ahead of all my predecessors. That way I could be assured of the quality of what I was doing.

With the ascent of the Rupal Face on Nanga Parbat in 1970, I was in at the beginning of a second phase of Himalayan climbing, the struggle for the difficult faces on the highest mountains. By 1985 most of these faces had been climbed; a few were still untried. Only a very few had been tried without success. One of these was the Annapurna Northwest Face.

Annapurna, whether by chance or providence, was the first eight-thousander to be climbed, in the year 1950, and its South Face later became the first big wall on an eight-thousand metre peak to receive an ascent. In 1977, from Dhaulagiri, I was able to get a good look at its northwest side, one of the most difficult of all Himalayan faces, and was immediately struck by the hazardous nature of this vast concave wall. I planned a visit there for the spring of 1985, and put together a team with which, it seemed to me, I had a slight chance of being able to climb the face.

It included the Tyrolean climbers Reinhard Schiestl and Swami Prem Darshano as well as the South Tyroleans, Hans Kammerlander and Reinhard Patscheider, who had climbed the Eiger's North Face in around five hours. Thomas Bubendorfer had done it even faster and also wanted to come to Annapurna, but unfortunately I had to refuse him because he did not fit readily into my team. It is important on a project like this that all the members not only get on well together, but work at equal speed.

In choosing members I noticed that the younger climbers viewed this sort of expedition quite differently than we did fifteen years ago. They were not just going to the face, they were also going to the 'market-place'. This was understandable – with a successful expedition, it was possible to increase the value of your name, and with it, your income. So I felt that they had a legitimate interest.

So many professional climbers have sprung up recently that the competition has become harder. That is a good thing. What I don't like is a new kind of charlatanry, which peddles half-truths. There are a few people who sell their tours with dubious information, comparing their deeds to those of earlier epochs in order to appear superior to the majority of other climbers around, when in fact they cannot hold a candle to them. Others feign solo ascents which are only done with outside help or a very long preparation. There were some people recently who got their expedition into the papers by proclaiming that they wanted to take their three-year-old child to the summit of Makalu. I do not intend to go further into this here, naming concrete examples, but just to remark that a lot of incorrect information is floating around in mountaineering circles and that it has become difficult to distinguish real pioneering performances from blown-up sensationalism. There have been mountebanks in every age, but previously these were usually recognised and exposed as such.

In the spring of 1985 we left Kathmandu for Pokhara. From there we went over the Gore-Pani-Pass in the Kali Gandaki valley, then climbed over the Thulo Begin, a ridge of more than 4,000 metres, to bring us to the foot of Annapurna. This was a difficult approach: it snowed and the porters threatened several times to strike. As some of them did not want to go any further, I dismissed them, equipped the others with boots and jackets and organised rotating duties. We lost much time.

At long last, we approached the foot of the face at the beginning of April, and Reinhard Patscheider went on ahead to find us a suitable spot for Base Camp. When I got a close look at our

In the photograph:

Sept. 24. 83
† YANGKEUN JUNG
TIKARAM MANGAR
MAILA HARKA

24 SETT.
1973

LEO CERRUTI
MILLER RAVA

SADATOSHI TAKAHASHI
MASANORI HAMA
TADASHI USHIOE
KAZUMI KATAGIRI
RINJI SHERPA
18 MAY 1973

---

proposed route, I have to confess my hopes sank almost to rock bottom. Had Reinhard not pressed to stay and at least try, I might have backed off there and then, in favour of the French 1950 route.

The real 'hurdles' on these very big mountains are often not to be found in the face itself, but come from within ourselves: feelings of isolation and apprehension, and frequent waves of dizziness, all of which I experienced with particular acuteness here at the foot of Annapurna. These are what so often rob me of my enthusiasm for a climb, my courage and with it, my strength. Once on the face, climbing, I calm down. If I make progress, however slow, if I see I am rising to meet the difficulties, then the doubts fade away – they have no place any more. Only sometimes, when I have to wait about, and in the tent, do they come back.

The knowledge that I can endure cold, and thrive on climbing into the wind doesn't help at all. But once I am out of my sleeping bag in the morning, all these worries and doubts disappear. It's in the grey light of dawn, or at the foot of a big wall, and sometimes, too, during the organisation and preparation for a tour, that they present such an inhibiting barrier. They hardly ever make an appearance when I am actually climbing, even when things are not going well and there is no knowing how they will end.

Our tactics for Annapurna were that Hans Kammerlander and I, after we had reconnoitred the way right to the foot of the face and set up our first high camp there, should take a look at the French route. At 6,000 metres we wanted to install a small gear dump, so that we could use this route as an emergency escape route if we had to. If

we did manage to get up, we did not know whether we would be able to climb down the difficult Annapurna Northwest Face again.

Having made up my mind to adopt a line straight up the concave centre of the face, Sheistl, Patscheider and Swami Prem Darshano got busy fixing ropes on the lower sections. They demonstrated great skill and what is more, for 'novices' to Himalayan climbing, the two Reinhards were uncommonly fast.

During this preparation work, Hans and I twice went off to take a look at the mountain from a bit further away. Once we climbed up the normal route, once the slope opposite. What we saw was both worrying and exciting. When the three others came back to Base Camp for a rest, Hans and I went up to establish Camp 2. At the same time, we wanted to find out whether we would be able to continue from there in Alpine style or whether we would have to fix the second half of the face with ropes as well.

Two days later we erected the camp, with just a single tent first of all, placed under a vertical ice wall on the edge of a crevasse. This was not an ideal spot for a tent, but safer at least than anywhere else around. Above us loomed the summit wall, steep and dangerous.

Since we were carrying sufficient food and equipment in our rucksacks, we pushed on further the next day. It went much faster than we expected; we kept to the right as far as the second big serac. Hans managed to bypass this by a series of difficult little traverses around a compact rockband, which from below had looked impassable.

On a snow ramp far above this balcony of ice, we made our first bivouac, having been forced to stop by a storm. From there, the next day, we climbed another 300 vertical metres and again had to bivouac because of storm conditions. Having got this far, we decided to go for the summit on 24 April, despite the bad weather.

Without having properly surveyed the face beforehand, we climbed the summit ridge. What exposure! Going round the two big seracs on the upper third of the face had been difficult, but the summit ridge, though not particularly sharp, was very broken and the crux of the whole climb. There were frequent steep and exposed upswings. Sometimes we climbed to the left, sometimes the right of the ridge. Here, between the Northwest Face and the South Face, level ground was a rarity. Added to this, we had the hurricane.

Its full fury met us only when we reached the summit area: an even stronger storm was blowing in from the Northwest, threatening to brush us off the ridge altogether. It had been steadily rising in strength since morning. For hours we were battling at the very limits of our powers – and we still had the descent to face afterwards. Then, at last, there was the summit!

Reinhold Messner, photographed by Hans Kammerlander, on the upper third of the Northwest Face: 'When I look at this picture, I only remember the good moments. I blank out all memory of the uncertainty, the cold, the storm, even though that's what life is all about up there.'

Reinhold Messner on the summit ridge of
Annapurna. Cold and storm made these last
200 vertical metres a walk on the extreme side.

The partner as a mirror-image

On the summit ridge of Annapurna
Hans Kammerlander was climbing
ahead of me. The wind swept in from
our left, from the northwest. To our
right, in the wind-shadow, masses of
snow clung almost vertically to the
face, snow which I feared to touch lest
it break off and take us with it. The
storm battered us with all its might,
and it was barely possible to keep on
the ridge. Hans climbed steadily on. I
kept shouting for him to stop, but
he could not hear me, the wind
smothered the words as they left my
mouth. So he pressed ahead, and I
followed.

He was aware of the danger as was I.
He could hear it in the noise of the
storm; smell it in the broken rock;
feel the whiplash of the gusting wind
in his face. In these situations it was
of great help to have Hans with me, to
be able to see him. I could see he was
not being blown away by the wind –
that was comforting. To know that he
still had strength enough to keep
going gave me similar strength. I saw
him as if I was looking at myself in a
mirror. Through him, I appreciated
my own position, moving as he moved.
Although danger increased as we went
higher, climbing unquestioningly like
this, anxiety did not keep pace. Had I
not been embedded in the idea of
being one of a team, and thereby, if
only to a slight degree, embedded in
the strength of my partner, I would
have plunged from that ridge.

We climbed down right away, taking
the tent with us, calling to the others for
help. That was the only thing that kept
us alive.

The situation grew more critical the
further we went. There was now a lot of
snow lying on the face. Luckily, Patscheider and Schiestl came up towards
us from below. They piloted us down
through the relatively flat couloir in the
middle of the face, nursed us into the
camp, and helped us pull through the
long night. Avalanches poured over the
tents all night long, and had Reinhard
Patscheider not gone out, hour after
hour, to shovel them free, perhaps in my
exhausted state, I would have just let
myself suffocate inside the tent under a
huge mass of snow.

This climb seemed to uphold the law
that risks increase in proportion with
height. During the descent, however,
we made decisions for which there were
no rational explanations, but which
afterwards proved to be right.

After the snowfall we all went
together back to Base Camp, where we
recovered quickly. Hans and I waited so
that another rope could have a chance of
going for the summit. Patscheider and
Schiestl were in superb condition. They
had everything it takes for reaching the
summit of this mountain. Swami Prem
Darshano wanted to accompany them.
Although they were three, they initially
made good progress.

At around 7,200 metres, where the
face rises steeply, they saw that there
was still too much snow, and turned
back. Then, in those first few steps down,
Reinhard Patscheider made a 'mistake'.
He sank into a snow hole, tripped and
lost his balance. He tumbled backwards
off the mountain, and fell 400 metres
down the ice face. Luckily he was able to
cast off his rucksack, and at the last
minute managed to brake his fall before
going over a 100-metre icefall. He escaped
death by the skin of his teeth.

I did not see the fall from below, as the
face was enshrouded with mist. We only
learned about it when the three arrived

back in the second camp. Patscheider, a self-taught mountaineer, has withstood many dangers in his time – falls, freezing bivouac-nights without protection, the loss of crampons on steep ice faces. He has mastered the art of survival better than many other summit-climbers.

The three decided not to make another attempt and came back down to base. They had recognised that in the Himalaya other principles come into play than in the Alps, that with these

Reinhard Patscheider

distances, this accumulation of danger, ability and endurance is not enough on its own; you need luck as well. To reach the summit, all the prerequisites have to be right.

In general, you can say that around half of today's expeditions to the eight-thousanders are successful, the other half not. With small expeditions attempting difficult objectives like we were on Annapurna, less than half are successful. With Annapurna Northwest Face, I had now made ten first ascents on eight-thousanders, ranging over a period of fifteen years in the Himalaya. But, also, I had often given up – during the same period I had failed ten times on eight-thousanders.

The middle third of the concave wall, just below the summit rock bands, was where Reinhard Patscheider lost his footing. He fell 400m down the hanging glacier, and stopped just above the serac girdle a third of the way up the face.

189

Whenever I felt I was lacking in strength or stamina, I intensified my training. My will, too, was schooled by this same long training, and by the climbing itself. Failure gave me the incentive to go on, to better earlier achievements with each new step; but in this, I could only hope to succeed if my powers of concentration, my commitment and my knowledge kept expanding.

My activities no longer aroused the same interest as they did in 1978 – they had become too frequent, perhaps too successful. That worried me less than the knowledge that I could not live for any length of time without the stimulus of extreme experience. My motivations were no longer the same as they had been on Nanga Parbat in 1970; without doubt they were stronger. There was no question of giving up.

To climb eight-thousanders is less a matter of skill and know-how, which is what rock climbing demands; far more, it requires an optimum combination of endurance, will-power, and instinct, and an ability to tolerate suffering. The right thing to do at any given moment is only learnt over decades. You can compare an expedition like this with a kind of *Tour de France* or *Giro d'Italia*. These long competitions last for weeks and exact the utmost from professional cyclists every day of that time.

On eight-thousanders it is not important whether you are a professional in the commercial sense of the word, as I am, or an amateur. It is like art. A pro has no more time to train than an amateur, than someone who works in any other field of life. Whether you climb in your free time and are able to go on expeditions in your annual holidays, or whether you divide your time between mountain activities, lecture halls and management is unimportant. The only thing that matters is how seriously you take what you do, and how creative you can be at it.

I finance not only my expeditions but also my life indirectly from climbing

Survived – the most difficult route

Annapurna occupies a special place in the history of Himalayan expeditioning. The story really begins in the year 1950. British mountaineers had tried their luck several times on Mount Everest and had climbed to heights of more than 8,500 metres. But before 1950 no one had been to a summit of more than 8,000 metres; none of the eight-thousanders had been climbed. This was the year of the great breakthrough, when French mountaineers climbed Annapurna. It was a fantastic episode: and their first task had been to discover some way of reaching the mountain.

Having found a route, they built high camps; and one morning two men set out from Camp 5 – Maurice Herzog and Louis Lachenal. The weather was fine, but very cold. After many hours the pair gained the summit. The first summit of more than 8,000 metres had been surmounted. But the descent became an epic with avalanches, bivouacs, and frost-bite. Toes and fingers had to be amputated.

The route of the first ascent runs

Henri Sigayret

up the north side of the mountain. It winds between rock ribs and fissured glaciers. Blocks of ice, thrown into imbalance by the advance of the glacier, frequently break off and crash down with a fearful roar. After periods of bad weather there are enormous snow avalanches, which destroy everything on the slopes, and even on neighbouring ridges and buttresses as well. Facts speak for themselves: in ten years there have been more than 25 people killed on this route alone!

The south side, too, was 'conquered'. British climbers, led by Chris Bonington, climbed this steep face in 1970. They succeeded in accomplishing what till then had been considered impossible – the climbing of extremely hard passages above 7,000 metres. On the way down one member of the group was killed by a falling serac. Again, the hand of tragedy.

Today, in the Western World at least, we no longer have national expeditions. Equipment has become lighter, oxygen flasks have been 'outlawed'.

In 1984 when my companions and I attempted a new route on the north side of Annapurna – right of the Main Summit, over a shoulder which we called 'Peak of No Name' – a tent in which two of my friends were sleeping was swept away by an avalanche. We were never able to find them.

and directly from marketing the 'waste products' of climbing. But I have to spend the greater part of the time that I am in Europe at the writing desk, or standing on a platform, or consulting with business partners, or designing improved items of equipment. It requires considerable professionalism to manage such a job successfully; and professionalism takes application, skill and time, which is then lost to training.

Only if a climber keeps forcing himself to train, if he lets himself be driven by his own fanaticism to the outposts of his potential, can these limits be moved – his personal limits, that is, as well as the limits of Alpinism. To be fully stretched means being in perpetual momentum, being dragged along. Only thus is the climber capable of dismantling the inner barriers when he finds himself, after months of work and preparation, at the foot of a big wall. Only thus can he cope with the isolation, the apprehension and the spells of faintness that are much harder to overcome than all the rocks in the world. Good fortune and benign providence are presents from the gods, as the Tibetans say; they are an extra. But the prerequisites for success the climber has to acquire for himself – they are never given freely, anywhere.

Since 1950 many expeditions have attempted Annapurna. A dozen variations and new routes have been opened up. Only the Northwest Flank remained unclimbed, and this promised to be a formidable proposition, even for the dauntless. It is a receptacle for avalanches, and very steep, with barriers of crumbling rock and overhanging balustrades of ice. A multi-crevassed glacier guards the foot of the mountain, making passage on to the face a problem in itself. It is as if climbing were being resisted there.

In an article that appeared in 1983, I wrote: 'The face is both steep and high (Base Camp would have to be established at 4,000 metres, a height gain of more than 4,000 metres would therefore be involved). By present-day standards of expedition Alpinism it would be a very bold and serious undertaking; stonefalls and avalanches render it exceedingly dangerous.'

In 1985 Reinhold Messner wanted to climb Annapurna. He could have climbed the normal route on the North Face in his usual fast manner and easily 'bagged' his eleventh eight-thousander. But he refused the sure and simple option of climbing the mountain in two or three days, turning his attention instead to the Northwest Face. There, with resolution and in exemplary expedition style, he selected a direct and complex route. Two camps were established; and after two further bivouacs, he reached the top.

At that time, there were very few Alpinists who could stand head and shoulders above the rest. They were all men who, confronted with natural problems, were able to come up with more or less interesting solutions. Rarer, were those climbers who, forswearing the obvious, engineered original and elegant solutions to their problems. These were the innovators, the forerunners of later trends. Often criticised by the mediocre or jealous, they accomplished what others have considered impossible and did so with a certain brilliance and facility. Reinhold Messner is such a one.

Rarer still, are those Alpinists who stand out from their contemporaries in such divergent disciplines as free-climbing, ice-climbing and Himalayan mountaineering. Reinhold Messner is such a one.

And how seldom do you find Alpinists whose passion, which is the driving force for pioneering feats of vision, has not waned over such a long period of activity. Reinhold Messner is such a one.

Finally, singular phenomena indeed are those Alpinists who have understood how to preserve their experiences faithfully in word and picture, and thus enable others to share them. Such a one, too, is Reinhold Messner.

Reinhold Messner is truly *the* most extraordinary mountaineer. That is a fact. But it is an inadequate definition. Above all, he is a man of stature, an extraordinary human being.

Henri Sigayret
(Climber of Annapurna, Expedition Leader)

The White Mountain

Historical Highlights

Geographical Position: Nepal Himalaya, Dhaulagiri Himal
Lat. 28°42′ N, Long. 83°30′ E

1950–1959 The first aerial pictures are taken in 1949, and French, Swiss, Argentines and Austrians make successive expeditions to Dhaulagiri. All attempts on the north side fail around the 8,000m mark. A particularly difficult feature is 'The Pear'. Altogether, three climbers die.

1960 An expedition organised by the Swiss Max Eiselin is first to reach the summit; it follows the Northeast Ridge. On 13 and 23 May Swiss climbers E. Forrer, A. Schelbert, M. Vaucher, H. Weber, Austrian K. Diemberger, German P. Diener and Sherpas Nyima Dorje and Nawang Dorji reach the summit 'without oxygen'. Members and equipment are flown to the North Col by a light aircraft (the 'Yeti').

1969 On a repeated attempt of the dangerous Southeast Ridge by an American Expedition under B. Everett, five team members and two Sherpas are lost under an avalanche on this 'suicidal' route.

1970 Following the route of the first ascent, Japanese climbers under the leadership of T. Otah succeed in the autumn in making the second ascent.

1973 An American team under J. Morrissey makes the third ascent by the Northeast Ridge.

1975 A Japanese expedition led by T. Amemiya loses two members and

three Sherpas in an avalanche accident on the South Pillar.

1978 A Japanese expedition succeeds in the spring in making the first ascent of Southwest Pillar. One member dies. After reaching the summit by the South Face and the Southeast Ridge, another Japanese post-monsoon expedition suffers loss of four mountaineers.

1979 Spanish under J. Pons are the next to make an ascent by the normal route.

1980 A Polish expedition under the leadership of V. Kurtyka, in which British and French also take part, climbs the East Face for the first time during the spring – not, however, right to the summit, which is reached a few days later by the Northeast Ridge.

1980 20 years after his first successful expedition Max Eiselin runs a commercial expedition to Dhaulagiri, on which out of 17 participants, 14 climb the Northeast Ridge to the summit. Among them F. Luchsinger, at 59, is the oldest man to have climbed an eight-thousander. The Sherpa Ang Rita has now climbed to the summit of Dhaulagiri three times.

1981 In the course of a Japanese expedition, 3 climbers operate Alpine style on the East Face. H. Kamuro goes alone to the summit. In the autumn, Yugoslavs, attempting the South Face to the Southeast Ridge, fail at about 8,000m.

1982 Japanese mountaineer A. Koizumi succeeds with the Sherpa Wanchu in making the first official

winter ascent of Dhaulagiri (according to Nepalese rules) and with it, the first ascent of any eight-thousander in winter. They climb with oxygen, but it runs out before the summit so that the descent is only achieved with much hardship.

1984 In the autumn a French team succeeds on the Southwest Pillar. A Czech group makes the first ascent of West Face. One member falls to his death on the descent. Polish mountaineers climb the Northeast Ridge in winter.

1985 On 15 May R. Messner and H. Kammerlander (S.Tyrol) climb the Northeast Ridge to the summit in a bad storm (20th ascent). In the winter a Swiss group climbs the East Face and Northeast Ridge to the summit.

1986 A German–Austrian travel group reach the summit of Dhaulagiri by the normal route in a season when most other expeditions fail.

From a mountaineering point of view, Dhaulagiri is one of the most interesting eight-thousanders, even today. In 1977, Reinhold Messner failed to climb the South Face; he failed again in 1984 on the Northeast Ridge (route of the first ascent, 1960), but finally climbed the mountain by this route in 1985 with Hans Kammerlander.

Half a dozen different routes have now been climbed, and as many variations. At least as many other possibilities still wait for first ascents. Because this mountain is so often beset by bad weather, it is especially dangerous.

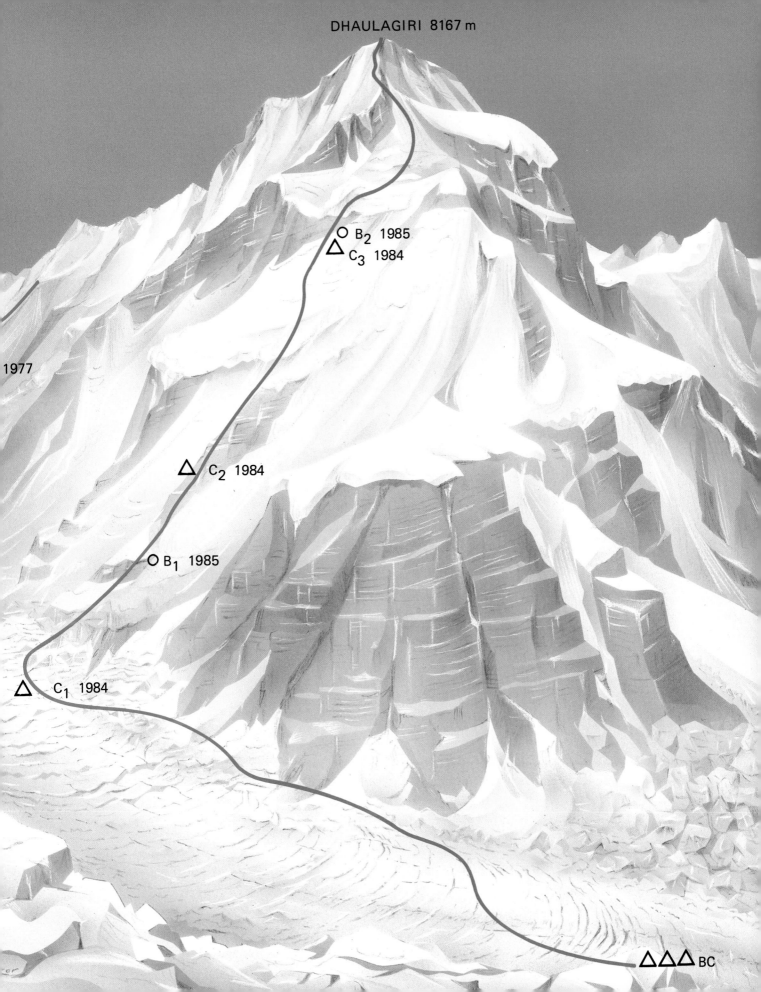

DHAULAGIRI 8167 m

1977

○ B₂ 1985
△ C₃ 1984

△ C₂ 1984

○ B₁ 1985

△ C₁ 1984

△△△ BC

Above left: Base Camp at the northern foot of Dhaulagiri.

Below left: Hans Kammerlander and Reinhold Messner enjoying breakfast at Base Camp. They only spent two nights in this tent (1985): one before the climb to the summit, one afterwards.

Previous double page: Dhaulagiri from the south from the GhoRapani pass. On the right is Tukche Peak. The left pillar (Southwest Pillar) was first climbed in 1978 by Japanese. Far right is the long Southeast Ridge, a difficult route which was also climbed by Japanese mountaineers (1978). Yugoslavs reached the same ridge further left via the South Face (climbing the blunt pillar right of centre of the face), but were unable to reach the summit. The true South Face is unclimbed. Reinhold Messner attempted it unsuccessfully in 1977 with a small international team.

Above: Dhaulagiri, seen from Annapurna. On the right is Nilgiri Peak (not all in picture).

Above: Reinhold Messner abandoned his 1984 attempt on Dhaulagiri's Northeast Spur (route of the first ascent, 1960) with a North/South Tyrol expedition. But in 1985 he climbed to the top this way with Hans Kammerlander in only three days.

Hans Kammerlander a few steps from the top of Dhaulagiri (15 May 1985). What the picture does not show is the electricity in the air, a tension which manifested itself in crackling and buzzing.

Left: First bivouac on the Northeast Spur, Messner/Kammerlander 1985.

Dhaulagiri
The Records Game

There are times in life, you can count them in minutes, when you experience an awareness far greater than you usually find in a whole year.

F.M. Dostoevsky

The human body is absolutely remarkable. It is very perfectable, very resistant, and I believe it is still capable of greatly increasing its capacity for achievement in all areas.

Nicolas Jaeger

Dhaulagiri from the South. The Japanese route (1978) follows the prominent pillar on the left, and long sections of fixed rope are still hanging there. The face to the right of that, attempted unsuccessfully by Reinhold Messner in 1977, remains unclimbed and is one of the finest problems left on the eight-thousanders. The face, however, is extremely dangerous.

From a surfeit of enthusiasm, or obsession perhaps, call it what you will, I wanted to go straight to Dhaulagiri immediately after our Annapurna climb in 1985. On Annapurna I had felt that Hans Kammerlander and I were still capable of more, that we could still progress one step further.

Critics will now ask how there can be a 'step further' on the normal route of Dhaulagiri. There can be none if you are only taking the difficulty of the mountain into consideration. But our plan was to climb from the Kali Gandaki valley to the summit in a single push, without any rest days. No one had attempted anything quite like it before. What we didn't know was whether it was physically possible to climb non-stop from a height of 2,000 metres to the top of Dhaulagiri. Equipment at least was no problem; we could use what we had brought for the Annapurna expedition.

During my climbing career, I have developed many new items of equipment for this sort of expedition: tents, boots, crampons. They have to be as light as possible, yet at the same time robust. When I've drawn up the designs, I frequently take them somewhere to be made up, going into partnership with whoever undertakes the production and marketing.

Naturally, such equipment is not suitable for every climber. A high altitude tent, for example, is no use for an Alpine bivouac. It is windproof, but not watertight; all right for snow, but not for rain. Atmospheric dampness is no problem in the Himalaya.

The plastic boots I wore on Everest in 1978 were one of my own developments. At the time they were a great source of amusement, but everyone now climbs in plastic boots. They dry so much faster than leather at altitude, and the inner-boots are not so compressed as in most traditional boots, which helps resist frost-bite. Ideally the liners should be made out of Aveolite, a material that guarantees better insulation than either felt or leather.

It is important that the customer knows exactly what he wants. He cannot blame the supplier if he finds himself sitting in a high altitude tent in the pouring rain, getting soaked to the skin. If he goes to Patagonia with a tent designed for the eight-thousanders, that's his stupidity, not the fault of the manufacturer.

I was well aware of the risk involved in turning our attentions to Dhaulagiri immediately after coming off Annapurna. Trying to climb two eight-thousanders in such quick succession would not only be very draining, it would place a great strain on luck. Everyone has luck, but only up to a point. Once it is spent, a climb becomes dangerous and it may no longer be possible to mobilise those reserves that are so vital in emergency. Perhaps we would find ourselves too tired to carry through such a climb. *Kaputt.*

Hans Kammerlander was not very enamoured with my idea to start with – he would have preferred to go home. The weather was poor and it could not be long before the monsoon hit us. For my part, however, I had failed on Dhaulagiri twice before and hoped with this attempt to spare myself the long approach a third time. We were at the very foot of the mountain.

On my first attempt at the South Face in 1977 with Otto Wiedemann, Peter Habeler and Michael Covington, we got no higher than 6,000 metres. It proved an uncommonly dangerous and difficult proposition. With the experience we then possessed, we had really taken on far too much in this massive, concave face. It was swept by avalanches almost daily. We were not prepared at the beginning to consider climbing either the left or right-hand edges of the wall, preferring to go straight up the middle. Later on, it was too late to alter the route. We failed, and to this day, no one else has succeeded on this face.

Between the foot of the mountain and the summit lie around 3,000 metres of steep mountainside, the rock looser and more dangerous than the notorious North Face of the Eiger, and nearly twice as high. Experts had called it impossible, but that was exactly why I found the South Face of Dhaulagiri so fascinating. *Almost* impossible, I told myself before setting out to attempt it in the spring of 1977. From the first moment I saw it, I could not wait to get to grips with the problem: to find a line and lead a team to it.

The summit was not important – nor has it been on any of my eight-thousander climbs – it is the attempt that counts. This face is one of the world's highest unclimbed sweeps of rock and ice, elegantly proportioned. Like a citadel in the glass-clear, oxygen-starved air of the 'Death Zone', it soars above the shimmering, dark Nepalese jungle.

Not that the air is always clear up there, nor the mountain always still. Dhaulagiri attracts more than its share of bad weather. Storms rage in from Tibet, with winds of often more than 200 kilometres an hour, stringing snow banners kilometres long to the summit ridges. In the evening, it often seems as if the mountain is on fire. It glows then like a volcano about to erupt.

It's true, Dhaulagiri is like a volcano. It came home to me forcibly after I spent four long weeks getting to grips with the South Face – observing, then tackling it. Its summit wall discharged so many avalanches that fear was something we had to learn to live with. All four of us, usually so assured, were stretched to the limit in the face of one of the last great mountain adventures.

We knew how the damp mist from the Nepalese highlands gets trapped in the hollow of this great frozen face, how it collects up there and can turn the face to a hell on earth within minutes. What we didn't know was that out of four weeks, we would be granted only two usable climbing days – that we would never have believed.

And so we kept up our attempts. The decision finally to call it a day came

when an avalanche swept down too close for comfort. The air blast alone was strong enough to blow us away, and the avalanche, had it been a fraction closer, would have buried us for good.

It had not taken us long to register that the route we originally planned up the central section of the face was far too dangerous. It seemed to us that to climb the South Pillar would be safer, even if at the same time it was steeper. But climbing across, between the pillar and the face, we abandoned the attempt.

That we should have found this face impossible was something that many of our fans, the sponsors and even the cameramen who were making a film of the Dhaulagiri South Face attempt refused to accept. That gave the critics something to get their teeth into. People

who themselves had never climbed on an eight-thousander, knew exactly how it should have been done. Others claimed equally to have 'known' that it had been madness from the start. Down on the flat, talk is easy.

It's always like that with us. Not only outsiders, but observing cameramen and even expedition members think differently in the security of Base Camp than they do on the face. Back home, we can often not understand how we could have 'run away' in the face of danger. Towards the end of the expedition, Otto Wiedemann, then a German military climbing instructor and the youngest man in our team, was scared to death of the face and its terrifying avalanches – not without reason. But no sooner had he flown home, than it seemed to him he had been too weak, and he was asking

Left: Base Camp at the foot of Dhaulagiri South Face. Reinhold Messner has spent the equivalent of several years in base camps like this and managed to gain from the experience, instead of letting frustration and hatred build up in the face of such inactivity, as so many climbers do.

The left-hand section of Dhaulagiri South Face after a fresh fall of snow.

himself if he had pushed 'the attack' hard enough.

There was no question that he had not put enough into the climb; yet at the same time, he had not risked too much. In big mountaineering, striking the exact balance between the commitment required to bring about a successful outcome and needless self-sacrifice is a fine art. If I am still alive today, it is not because I am a bolder climber, but rather that basically I am a fearful one.

For me, climbing – the conquest of the useless – represents a kind of sport with possibilities for creative expression, not an *ersatz* religion, and still less some kind of war game. For that reason I do not plan and lead my expeditions in a military way, nor do I control the input of my companions. Each of us four climbers had an equal say on Dhaulagiri, and

each was as responsible as I for the outcome of the expedition.

I had not made my companions sign any form of contract before we started, binding them to absolute obedience or forbidding them to write anything about the expedition. My job, as I saw it, was to raise the bulk of the money for the expedition, provide the team with the best possible food and equipment, lead them to the mountain and to be prepared on the most dangerous passages to climb out in front.

Financing was only possible with press and television contracts, support from the trade and help from private patrons. Naturally all that raises expectations, but I never raised false hopes. The chances of success were always narrow, and just because we were prepared to push it to the 'limits of the impossible',

it should not be inferred that we were some kind of suicide squad. 'Death or Glory' was no motto of ours.

On Dhaulagiri, we were not climbing for the public, not for a TV channel or any other institution. We were certainly not climbing for our country nor any Alpine organisation, but just for ourselves. When, via the Press and television, we accepted a transient and widely scattered audience, it did not mean that we agreed to play the heroes. We were not prepared to heroically sacrifice ourselves.

I was not, and never have been, willing to feed the mass media with the usual clichés about climbing – calling it a contempt of death, recklessness, or playing with lives. I think perhaps some time I will go back to the South Face of Dhaulagiri, but not out of any heroic or glorious gesture, rather out of curiosity. Should I go again, however, it will be with the same principles as regards risk discipline as on the first occasion. If I had any wish to kill myself, I know simpler methods and less beautiful places.

In 1984 I came back to Dhaulagiri with Wolfgang Nairz. He was leading an expedition of climbers from both North and South Tyrol, to which I had attached myself. In the back of my mind when I set off was the idea that a traverse of Dhaulagiri might be possible. At least I ought to have no difficulty getting to the summit by the normal route.

But, again we were unsuccessful. To start with, we took the ascent too lightly; then it snowed almost without ceasing. Several times we had to turn back because of avalanche danger. Once our tents were completely snowed in. Finally, when we had climbed to our top camp and were preparing to leave for the summit, bad weather forced us back down yet again.

Only on my third attempt did my ambitious project succeed. Early in May 1985, Hans Kammerlander and I left the Kali Gandaki Valley, crossed the Dhampus and French Pass to reach Base Camp on the north side of the mountain. There we stayed one night. On 13, 14 and 15 May we climbed the Northeast Ridge to the summit in Alpine style.

It was not easy finding a way around the fractured icefall which blocked the way on to the ridge. We kept to the right, between the ice and rock. Often we were forced to climb vertical rock slabs, and twice we left rope 'handrails' to keep our return route open. On the Northeast Ridge we chose a route much further to the right than in the previous year and reached over 6,000 metres on the first day. On our second climbing day we pushed steadily higher. By afternoon we reached the place where we had bivouacked almost exactly a year before. This time we had less trouble setting up our tent. It was a smaller one and fitted comfortably on to the platform after we had re-levelled it.

The last part of the climb was epic. There was so much electrical activity around the summit region that we literally gave off sparks. Our axes and crampons buzzed. Our hair stood on end. A sort of fizzing was coming from the rocks, and there was arcing everywhere, between the ridge and sky, between sleeve and glove, between rocks and crampons.

It was a wonder we were not struck by lightning, as we moved up the sharp and exposed ridge. The nature of the climbing was such that we had to stand erect most of the time. It was not always possible to duck out of the way. Even on the summit, passing between the two horns of rock, we remained unscathed. We could hardly believe it. At any moment we could have been killed. As the hours went by and still the lightning missed us, it gave us a sense of invulnerability. Up against the wall, like this, I ceased to care what else happened.

At least twice in my life I have been given up for dead. This time no one besides our Sherpas in Base Camp knew that we were on the summit of Dhaulagiri during this storm.

Camp 1 on Dhaulagiri (1984). It was these continuous falls of new snow that put a full stop to progress and caused Reinhold Messner and Hans Kammerlander to give up their attempt.

View from the summit of Dhaulagiri, looking west. 'Summit experiences like this are what changes a person. They help you to grow and you always need them.'

Mountains are not fair or unfair – they are dangerous

The fact that we were not struck by lightning on the summit of Dhaulagiri surprised even us. A few months afterwards when I was travelling in Tibet and learned that my brother Siegfried had been killed by lightning, the fact of my survival seemed even more inexplicable, shocking even. It seemed so unfair that I should still be alive and he was dead.

Siegfried was head of the climbing school I set up in South Tyrol. He was with some clients on the Vajolet Towers when a bolt of lightning pitched him off his stance. He fell down the face and into a gully where he lay unconscious. He was recovered alive, but died in hospital a few days later.

Siegfried was a good climber. He had made a few first ascents, but never sought out the extreme, whereas, for 25 years, I had been doing something 'crazy' at least once a year. Relentlessly, I drove my climbing to the limits of possibility,

over and again. I pushed myself further all the time. In the beginning it had been on to increasingly difficult routes, and later, up ever higher mountains. I needed constant danger. Siegfried, on the other hand, would deliberately steer clear of danger. He was quite the opposite to me.

In the mountains, he radiated confidence and a zest for life. Never for a moment did I think he could have an accident. As a mountain guide he was responsible not only for himself, but at all times also for the safety of those who climbed with him. Yet, it was *he* the lightning struck, and not me. Even though I was perhaps more exposed to it in those few hours near the summit of Dhaulagiri than he had been in his whole life, I came safely back.

Presumably, if I had been standing where Siegfried was on the Vajolet Towers, I too would have been killed. But at the fateful moment, I was not there; when Siegfried died, I was in

Tibet, on Kailas, the holiest mountain in the world.

I am not trying to say that the mountains like one person and not another. The mountains are neither wicked, nor kind to us. They are nothing more than an organic mass. For us men, they appear unpredictable, and they are not fully understood scientifically. They have no will of their own, no emotions. They do not draw us to them, but equally they do not shake us off. They represent for us a marvellous opportunity for experience. And because they are infinitely bigger than we are, they remain a dangerous medium at all levels.

By comparison, we are tiny. Our instincts are ill-developed, our endurance quickly runs out and our strength is limited. Big mountains, therefore, will always remain a useful medium for us.

Reinhold Messner on the North Ridge of
Dhaulagiri (1985). Below left is the French Col
and behind it the Hidden Valley. Still further
left lies the village of Dolpo, a Tibetan refuge.

The professional mountaineer

A new guild of top mountaineers
have successfully begun to market
their climbing achievements in one
form or another. In other forms this
tendency has been around for half a
century. In those days climbers
earned reputations with first ascents
and participation on expeditions, and
this brought them profitable opportunities. Many climbers wrote books,
took pictures, made movies, gave
lectures and so earned themselves a
little income, perhaps even a salary,
or at least a contribution towards
incidental expenses and extravagant
projects in the mountains.

The appearance of pictures of
Reinhold Messner on this or that
summit has transformed climbing
into an accepted profession, and in
commercial terms has knocked all
earlier efforts in this field well into
the shade. A marketing concept has
been developed that is comparable
with that found in other professional
sports.

One offshoot of the process has
been the appearance of such uncom-
fortable ventures as a 'contest' to
become the first person to climb all
the world's eight-thousanders, and
this clearly conflicts with certain
ethical ground rules for climbing.
Without doubt it also leads to greater
exposure to danger. But at the same
time, behind this record-chasing,
amazing qualities of a technical
and physical nature can be seen; it
may be possible to pave the way to
the mountains for these 'star-
performers', but in the final analysis
they are alone, and have to endure
prodigious pressures.

Karl Erb
in *Sport-Information*

I am certain that lightning in the Himalaya is less dangerous than in Europe. I would never have left the hut in the Alps with such tension in the atmosphere. On Dhaulagiri it was quite different. We heard the thunder and the concussion of impact, and further to the south we saw flashes of fire, but there were obviously no lightning strikes around us on the mountain.

We climbed back to our top bivouac the same day, slept there and went all the way down to Base Camp the next day. I am often asked whether climbs like this become a matter of routine. My answer is that there is no such thing as routine when it comes to eight-thousanders. For every new objective I embark upon, I have to prepare a suitable and individual new plan. Even then the tactics have to be adapted hour by hour to suit changed circumstances – if the weather turns or my strength starts giving out.

As for the experiences and sensations on the summit – these too are different every time. They are so diverse! If the sense of being on top was always the same, I would only have had to climb up once. They grate on my nerves, those climbers who rather pompously claim to be nearer to God on the summit, or feel they are special to have been on top.

I have experienced perfect peace on a summit, but also total despair. Nothing has so strongly unsettled me as being overwhelmed by its negative blackness. But usually the dominant, most disturbing preoccupation is one of getting down again in good time. Hope and anxiety react together to tell you that you must not linger too long in such an exposed situation.

Max Eiselin

Survived – Dhaulagiri, too

That Reinhold Messner has survived on Dhaulagiri, too, I put down to his great expedition experience, which has seen him through on his other eight-thousanders. Naturally a hefty chunk of luck comes into it, as well; I remember particularly the first time he attempted this mountain, when, having taken on the exceedingly dangerous South Face, he made a dramatic yet unscathed retreat from it. Messner's ability to turn back on a mountain was put to the test again on his second Dhaulagiri attempt seven years later, when, in the face of extreme bad weather, he favoured a timely withdrawal to struggling on at all costs. This was no easy decision with all that lost time and expense of preparation, the bureaucratic formalities and the long march-in.

Yet Reinhold Messner is such a shrewd tactician and husbandman, he acts as if he did not find it unrewarding to struggle for weeks on end against the superior might of the unbridled elements, 'burning himself out' from the effects of the storm and the altitude in so doing. He possesses a maturity which enables him to wait patiently, and then at a precise moment to 'strike' with elegant speed.

He owes his eventual summit success on the third attempt to this multi-faceted ability. Clearly, he is not exaggerating when he remarks that it was 'a wonder' they were not struck by lightning on the exposed summit ridge. Yet, to this 'wonder' his own survival instincts made a contribution, as did the mountaineer's luck – without which, in Alpinism, simply nothing 'goes' – and his speed of movement, born of his extraordinary condition.

Reinhold Messner has always had the inner calm and assuredness to know exactly when the time was right to return to the scene of a retreat – even after years. He is not only a brilliant climber, but a splendid organiser. He applies the same diligence and rigid discipline that have made his hardest mountaineering deeds possible, to equally hard commercial and publicity work, and has managed to create the necessary foundations for his expedition activity, which so many people envy.

Reinhold Messner need feel no shame in attaining his economic goals. It has brought him nothing; hard work and iron discipline alone have led to his well-earned success.

Max Eiselin
(Leader of the Dhaulagiri Expedition, 1960)

The Great Black One

Historical Highlights

Geographical Position: Nepal
Himalaya, Mahalungur Himal
Lat. 27°53′ N, Long. 87°05′ E

1954 Although already observed and photographed by other expeditions, this is the first to go specifically to Makalu. Americans under the leadership of W. Siri attempt Southeast Summit, but only reach 7,056m. New Zealanders under E. Hillary have to give up their summit hopes because Siri's group hold permit for it, but 25 other peaks are climbed, all above 6,000m, and the north side of Makalu explored. Hillary and McFarlane sustain considerable injury in a crevasse fall. Post-monsoon a French expedition under J. Franco visits northwest side and reaches a height of 7,880m on the North Ridge.

1955 Building on his experience of the previous year, J. Franco returns in the spring. This time the venture is a complete success: all nine members and their Sirdar reach top in three groups on 15, 16 and 17 May. The expedition runs without incident.

1961 A British–American expedition under E. Hillary attempts to repeat the French route. As part of a high altitude physiological experiment they climb without oxygen which almost costs the lives of some members. Two come to within 120m of the summit.

1970 A strong Japanese team attempts Southeast Ridge and makes the first ascent of Southeast Summit, 8,010m. Two members with only limited oxygen reserves go on to within 180m of Main Summit and from there without masks to the top.

1971 Bad weather conditions prevail when in the spring a French expedition under R. Paragot attempts the mountain. In snowstorm and extreme cold the very difficult West Ridge is climbed, making the third Makalu ascent a 'direttissima'. Summiteers are B. Mellet and Y. Seigneur.

1974 W. Nairz's Austrian expedition fails on South Face.

1975 In the autumn A. Kunaver returns to Makalu for a second time with a Yugoslav expedition. The summit is reached on four occasions by the South Face Route. Four climbers are injured.

1976 In the course of the Czech expedition under J. Cervinka, the Pillar under the Southeast Summit receives its first ascent. Two Czechs and a Spaniard reach the Main Summit. On the descent one of the Czechs dies and the other suffers severe frost-bite injury.

1978 An international expedition under the leadership of the German H. Warth, with three Sherpas as official members, has to give up its planned traverse, though it reaches the Main Summit by the French route in three groups.

1982 In the course of a Polish–Brazilian expedition, A. Czok climbs the West Face solo and continues over the Northwest Ridge to the summit.

1984 After Makalu has already defeated Canadian, American and British mountaineers, a Spanish expedition under M. Abregos climbs to the summit from the northwest.

1986 At the beginning of the year R. Messner fails on his attempt of a winter ascent of Makalu. In the autumn he goes again to the mountain. Together with H. Kammerlander and F. Mutschlechner he attains the summit on 26 September by the French Route (17th ascent).

Reinhold Messner has been four times to Makalu. In 1974 he unsuccessfully attempted the South Face, which was first climbed a year later by Yugoslavs. In 1981 he visited the Southeast Ridge, but made no attempt on the mountain. The Normal Route (1955) defeated him during the winter of 85–86, but was the way by which he eventually made it to the top – in 1986 with Friedl Mutschlechner and Hans Kammerlander.

With five routes as well as four variations, Makalu still has other fascinating opportunities in store like the West Face in particular, but also the Northeast and North Flanks (Tibet). Along with Lhotse, it is an 'eight-thousander with a future.'

MAKALU 8463 m

1986 C₃

1986 C₂

1974 C₃

1985 C₁

C₁ 1986

ABC 1985

BC

Above left: Makalu from the south. The dome on the left is Makalu II. Immediately to the right of the main summit is the Southwest Ridge (French Route, 1971), bearing left further down. It separates the West Face (only the left side of which has been climbed, by Polish Route 1982) from the South Face, which was first climbed by Yugoslav climbers in 1975). To the right, above the rounded pillar, leads the Czech Route (CSSR Pillar, 1976) which joins the Southeast Ridge (first climbed by Japanese in 1970).

Above right: From the highest settlement it is a day's march to Base Camp under the West Flank of Makalu following the edge of the dead glacier. In the background are Baruntse (left, in cloud), Nuptse, Lhotse and Lhotse Shar, with Mount Everest extreme right before the rocks.

Left: Porters on the way to Makalu Base Camp.

Right: Porters around the camp-fire after delivering their loads.

Previous double page: 1974. Reinhold Messner calls his first halt on the way to Makalu. With Austrian mountaineers he hoped to make the first ascent of the South Face. The expedition failed. Two more trips followed, but it was not until 1986 that he was able to reach the summit.

Left: Looking down from the summit ridge to the Makalu-La. Friedl Mutschlechner and Reinhold Messner in the steep gully to the right (going up) of the summit.

Above right: Reinhold Messner and Hans Kammerlander on Makalu summit (26 September 1986). The top of Everest can be seen far right.

Below right: Reinhold Messner on the final ridge of Makalu, just below the summit.

Below left: View from Mount Everest towards Chomolonzo, Makalu II, Makalu-La and Makalu I (1980).

Makalu
Happy Feet!

*What shouldn't be any of my business?
Only my own business should never be
my business – phooey! to those egoists
who think only of themselves!*

Max Stirner

*Makalu is without doubt one of the
hardest propositions of all.*

Edmund Hillary

*The race for the eight-thousanders will
only end when Messner has finally
climbed them all.*

Erhard Loretan

Makalu from the south with Base Camp, 1974.
Reinhold Messner has camped here on three
separate occasions: 1974, 1981 with Doug Scott
in the hope of making an East-West traverse,
and 1986 in winter. None of these expeditions
were rewarded with success. In the autumn of
1986, Messner's expedition moved Base Camp a
day's march higher up.

When I fail on an expedition, I usually return home with the intention of going back and trying the mountain again. I failed three times on Makalu.

In 1974 with Wolfgang Nairz and some other Austrian mountaineers, I made an attempt on the South Face. We got to about 7,500 metres before being forced to give up. We were not strong enough and were employing the wrong tactics. We took too long over the initial preparation work on the wall, and then failed to switch to an easier alternative route in good time.

I still regret that I was not able to make the first ascent of the Makalu South Face. Such a beautiful wall! So elegant! A year later a Yugoslav team successfully climbed it. It was a fascinating route; they discovered an ideal line. All the same I was not too put out by our failure. The South Face was only one possibility.

In 1981 I went back to Makalu. With Doug Scott I wanted to traverse the mountain from southeast to northwest. This would have been a completely new experience in exposure: two people climbing one of the highest eight-thousanders in Alpine style all the way from the Base Camp, and then coming down the opposite side.

But that, too, was not to be. After climbing Chamlang Middle Summit as an acclimatisation exercise before the traverse, I learned that my daughter Layla had been born in Kathmandu. She was in an incubator. Without hesitation, I abandoned the Makalu climb and raced back to the capital. In two days I was in Kathmandu. It upset me to leave Doug Scott like that without a partner, but I was far too agitated to climb. My child at that moment was more important than all the eight-thousanders put together.

My third encounter with Makalu was in the winter of 1985-86, a few months after the death of my brother Siegfried: Hans Kammerlander and I wanted to make the first winter ascent of the mountain. At that time none of the five biggest eight-thousanders had been climbed in winter without artificial oxygen. We hoped to climb the north-west side of the mountain, just the two of us, by the French 1955 route, up to the summit and back.

We failed, however, just above the Makalu-La, the pass that separates Makalu I from Makalu II, the next summit to the north. We only got as high as 7,500 metres.

I had learned of my brother Siegfried's death in Tibet a few months before the expedition. The news did not hit me quite as hard as the loss of my brother Günther on Nanga Parbat fifteen years earlier. I had still been very young then, and life seemed endless. Death had no place in it, had not remotely entered into my thoughts. When it struck, it was such an enormous shock it took me years to accept the reality of it.

In Tibet in 1985, this land where death belongs to life, when I learned that Siegfried was dead, I took the news quietly, accepting the irrationality of it as somehow inevitable, although it still grieved me deeply. My mother, who had now lost two sons in the mountains, did not try and persuade me to give up expeditioning. She only asked me to promise to give up the eight-thousanders if I were to climb all fourteen of them, and not to do any more after that. So, in the knowledge that my mother understood, I kept on going.

In the autumn of 1986 I came to Makalu for the fourth time, this time with Hans Kammerlander and Friedl Mutschlechner. My plan was to climb Makalu and Lhotse one after the other, as a single enterprise. During the two previous years and particularly just before I set off, the mass media really played up the 'battle for the eight-thousanders', and above all the 'fierce competition' that raged between Jerzy Kukuczka and myself, so that many observers really believed my sole ambition in life was to be the first to climb all fourteen eight-thousanders.

Even the Swiss climber Marcel Ruedi was drawn, wittingly or unwittingly as a rival contender, into this supposed final sprint to the finishing line. It was constantly reported that the two were climbing the big mountains in my shadow.

For me at least, this bitter struggle, as the newspaper columns and headlines would have it, and as for that reason many lay people saw it, certainly did not exist. Granted, I had the ambition to be the first person to climb all fourteen eight-thousanders, but without any thought of it being a competition. I was looking for excellence. I saw it as the realisation of an idea, never for a moment as a competition with other people, as that was something I didn't care for. In any case, the idea to do it came to me well before the others were any 'competition' to me at all.

When it is asserted that other mountaineers were 'standing in my shadow', that is fundamentally untrue; and I would like just once to turn round and say, perhaps *they* are standing in *my* light. As a result of media interest in the eight-thousanders – and equally, of the active publicity surrounding me – climbing has become of far greater interest to a wide section of people. Other well-known climbers are also now able to finance their exploits on the open market – perhaps thanks to years of publicity work on my part. And who doesn't compare his deeds to mine simply in order to gain more attention from the mass media? This happens not only in Italy, Germany or Japan, but also in Poland, the USSR, Spain and France. This both amuses and saddens me – not on account of pleasant or unpleasant publicity here, but much more because what we do today has become regarded in a more superficial and often too biased way.

I was always a dreamer, and am still a dreamer. Whenever an idea took hold of me, it would bring with it a spontaneous burst of strength, and this is a reaction that has become stronger over the years. It was a feeling of relief that permeated to the very tips of my toes; it was like a great weight being lifted from my chest, even in the knowledge that I was committing myself into danger. With a new idea in my head I became single-minded, guided by this idea, carried along, driven. There could be no more freedom then.

People who say I planned my adventures for mercenary reasons have no conception of this inner explosion of the soul. Calculating people are usually faint-hearted, seldom capable of going to the limits. Gamblers who have lost their nerve interest me more. Man is not born as Ulysses; he allows himself to be tempted out of his everyday tracks by curiosity, even by ambition, but never by money, and still less by envy.

No one had climbed two high eight-thousanders in a single season before 1986 but we were not the first to try it. What caused the others to fail? We wanted to do it! We wanted to climb two of the five highest mountains in the world in the space of two months, without using artificial oxygen. What we needed above all for this was energy, the sort of energy that only springs from enthusiasm. No tail-end Charlie can shake the Pillars of Hercules!

During that summer of 1986, a few weeks before our success on Makalu, Erhard Loretan and Jean Troillet climbed the North Face of Everest in 43 hours, including the descent. They slid down from the summit on the seats of their pants. This audacious achievement, which was barely noticed by the media, was as far as I was concerned worth far more than a dozen eight-thousanders.

In the autumn of 1986 when we arrived on Makalu we had Base Camp to ourselves. Our accompanying film team and the organisers from Trekking International necessary to it worked with us as a single expedition. It was a harmonious gathering. But ten days later a dozen expeditions moved in on

Friedl Mutschlechner and Reinhold Messner on the summit of Makalu. 'It's a good feeling, going to the top with a friend. Mutual trust brings so much peace.'

us. They all had permits for different routes, or for Makalu II, but, without exception, all made use of the route to Makalu-La which we had prepared with fixed ropes.

The fact that expeditions have been allowed to overlap has dramatically changed big mountain climbing in the last few years. In Nepal, Pakistan and China permits for the eight-thousanders are given out almost indiscriminately, and most involve a sharing of route. This has brought a great reduction in the quality of such climbing.

It took Hans Kammerlander, Friedl Mutschlechner and I three tries to finally reach Makalu summit. On the first attempt, we got as far as the Makalu-La, where we had already been the winter before, but we decided there was still too much snow higher up for us to reach the summit. The conditions were prohibitive. We were not yet fully acclimatised, though we would have been capable of making it to the top had we found firm snow and ice on the summit plateau, as in the winter. So we came back down to Base Camp.

On the next attempt, Hans and I climbed to about 8,000 metres. Friedl was not feeling well and had turned back from a little beyond our third camp. We got bogged down in new snow at the start of the big plateau under the summit buttress.

Only on our third attempt were we successful in planting our happy feet on the summit. 'Kallipe' say the Tibetans, meaning happy feet; and I have also learned this from them: up there, only he who travels thoughtfully will not stumble.

Friedl, Hans and I had gone up to our last bivouac in two days, using a pre-placed camp at 7,800 metres. From there, on 26 September, we climbed the last stretch to the summit in good weather. We got there in the morning, out of breath but with happy feet.

We had plenty of time to look around and take photographs. We enjoyed standing up there, with no feeling of fatigue and without being under any pressure to hurry down. We knew we had enough reserves of strength to get back. There was such a spectacle, as the mist below us seemed to boil; and such peace when we stopped clicking cameras! Hans had himself photographed on top with a Coke can, something that was later to infuriate several 'moral guardians'. The fact that it was empty was a joke only comprehended by a few.

Once back at our top camp, Hans continued down on skis the same day. He walked the last bit into Base Camp, arriving in the evening. Friedl and I meanwhile packed up the top camp and cleared the route down to Makalu-La. Together with our Sherpas we climbed down to Base Camp the next day, the day after our summit attempt. We then left.

The other expeditions remained on

Reinhold Messner first met Wanda Rutkiewicz on Noshaq in the Hindu Kush in 1972. Since then they have frequently found themselves attempting the same mountain, including Makalu in the autumn of 1986.

Makalu. A Polish group, Italians, and French, were all now attempting to climb the normal route even though they had no permit for it. Wanda Rutkiewicz was among the Poles. With Nanga Parbat, K2 and Everest, she was the only woman to have climbed three eight-thousanders, and it was a great shame that she later failed on Makalu. Wanda is living proof that women are capable of achievements at altitude that many men only dream of. It cannot be more than a decade hence before a woman, too, has attained the magic goal of standing on top of all fourteen eight-thousanders in the world.

I did not personally experience any critical moments on Makalu in 1986, but two other expedition members were very lucky to survive their summit bid which was made just before ours. Our camera-man Denis Ducroz and the doctor

Guigliano de Marchi had promised themselves they would go to the top. I did not want to stop them. They had responsibilities within the expedition, but wanted to take advantage of our rest days to climb the prepared route to the summit. I could appreciate such a desire and gave them my support.

Guigliano had to go straight home after the Makalu expedition, and was therefore in a hurry. He and Denis set out from the last camp relatively late. They followed our tracks to about 8,000 metres, but above that, had to break their own trail, which was a hell of a job. They kept approximately to the line of the French 1955 route, but were stopped by nightfall just below the summit. The snow on the ridge was soft and in danger of giving way. Neither of them knew exactly which direction the route took, and so they turned back. In the moonlight they retreated to their top camp.

We were already in Camp 1 on our climb when they came down. I was appalled by their appearance, not only because Guigliano was frost-bitten, but more because I could read in their faces the strain of what they had been through. Only someone who has experienced it can know what it's like to break trail in very deep snow at 8,400 metres, to be forced to turn back just below the summit of an eight-thousander, or to stand at night on a heavily-corniced snow ridge. Only someone who has done it can know what it means to climb down snow-covered rock slabs by moonlight.

How they managed to get back down those steep cliffs to their camp, through avalanche runnels and across interminable snow slopes, even I find it hard to imagine. Luckily, they both stayed calm, and demonstrated great fortitude. Had they stopped in that snow, they would almost certainly have died. The most we could have done for them would have been to go looking, nothing more.

But a few days later we were called upon to face something worse. When

Right: The permit for Makalu (Autumn 1986). Reinhold Messner had two permits for Makalu and Lhotse, the normal routes and the south sides.

Hans Kammerlander on the traverse above the third camp on Makalu. In the background are Lhotse and Everest from the East. Marcel Ruedi had already negotiated these snowed-up rock slabs safely on his fatal descent.

Hans, Friedl and I were on our way to the summit, we learned that Marcel Ruedi was in trouble on his way down. He had just climbed Makalu as his tenth eight-thousander.

From the Makalu-La we had been able to see Ruedi, Switzerland's most famous high Alpine climber, making his way down. The Polish climber Wielicki, who had been to the summit a few hours before him, was able to get back before dark to his top bivouac, which was a little way below our own tents. There he waited anxiously all night for Marcel Ruedi, who obviously could only have reached the summit in the late evening. Wielicki waited in vain. Why didn't he come? Had he slipped?

Worried that Ruedi must have fallen somewhere near the summit, Wielicki left his tent in the morning and wandered despondently over towards our camp on the Makalu-La. He was obviously desperate. When he was about ten metres away, we shouted to him that we could see Ruedi coming down. He was descending just below the summit. Wielicki threw himself into the snow, tore off his rucksack and

bellowed for joy. A great weight had been lifted from his mind.

We could make out Ruedi picking his way down between 8,200 and 8,000 metres – slowly, continually stopping, but seemingly all right. Then the tiny figure disappeared behind a snow slope. We waited and waited, with tea and food ready for him. But he didn't come. When we climbed up, we saw Ruedi sitting in the snow just below his camp. He was dead. Tracks showed that he had slid down the last bit from the camp. We couldn't tell what had killed him. Obviously he'd met with some sort of accident. Whether he had fallen or died of exhaustion, what does it matter now? Death had overtaken him, that's all we know – a possibility he would not have cared to acknowledge even to himself, when he set out to climb all fourteen eight-thousanders in one massive spurt of activity.

Marcel Ruedi was one of a number of eminent victims of high altitude climbing. He was not the first and will not be the last. Sadly it is so often the most able and successful who do not come back. In a mere two years, between 1982 and 1984, eight of the world's most

experienced mountaineers died on big mountains. Reinhard Karl was lost in May 1982 on Cho Oyu. He was the best all-round mountaineer in Germany. Peter Boardman and Joe Tasker died a little later on Mount Everest. They represented the most successful partnership in modern high altitude climbing. Alex McIntyre was killed by a falling stone on the South Face of Annapurna in autumn of the same year; he was the most consistent performer on steep Himalayan faces in modern style. Then on Mount Everest in December 1982, Yasuo Kato disappeared, the man who had climbed the highest mountain in the world three times – in spring, autumn and winter. It was from this last winter mission that Japan's most truly innovative climber failed to return.

In Spring 1983, Nejc Zaplotnik, an exceptionally fine Yugoslav climber was killed by an avalanche at the foot of Manaslu South Face. With his first ascent of the South Face of Makalu, the West Ridge of Hidden Peak and the West Ridge Integral of Everest, he had earned world-wide admiration. In the autumn of that year Hironobu Kamuro,

HIS MAJESTY'S GOVERNMENT
MINISTRY OF TOURISM
MOUNTAINEERING SECTION

EXPEDITION-PERMIT

NEPAL

2037

No. Exp 3-1-.....Makalu (1986 Autumn) S. No. 3   Date:—1986/8/15

It is hereby notified that His Majesty's Government of Nepal has granted permission to the undermentioned expedition party to carry out the expedition on the peak mentioned below during pre/post monsoon/winter Season of the year 19 86.............

1. Name of the expedition party __Messner Makalu Expedition_____

2. Country of origin __Italy_____

3. Name and height of the peak permitted to scale __Makalu I (8463m)__

4. Caravan route __Kathmandu-Tumlingtar-Khadbari-Seduwa-Arun Khola-__
   __Barun Valley- Base Camp.__

5. Climbing route __South West Side__

Subarna Jung Rana

Joint Secretary

a man who had climbed Dhaulagiri on his own, died on Everest. Naomi Uemura disappeared in February 1984 on Mount McKinley. This Japanese climber had climbed hundreds of big mountains alone and made a solo trek with dogsled to the North Pole. He vanished without trace during a winter ascent of the highest mountain in North America.

All these men belonged to the dozen climbers who encompassed more success and experience than any others of their generation. If not among the all-time top ten of big mountaineering, they are certainly in the top twenty. Their deaths, therefore, are felt as a great shock – or a grim warning. Had these great, classical climbers pushed so far that the risks they incurred were no longer calculable? Had the margin between getting up and getting killed become so narrow that for those who go seeking new dimensions, it is only luck that separates the two? Is it only every second or third who survives to tell the tale? If that were true, then what we are doing is surely madness. It would no longer be tenable.

No one of us sets out to be the best. There's no such thing as the best mountaineer in the world, nor the fastest, nor the most outstanding. These are attitudes invented only by journalists or publishers. Perhaps an adolescent rock climber may have occasionally promoted himself with superlatives like these, because he knew that in big mountaineering there were no gold medals or world titles.

Personality alone is what counts, along with the capacity for survival in increasingly more demanding situations. Mountaineering is not measurable in points and seconds, its only calculable absolutes are metric heights and grades of difficulty. It is capable of expression through the management of risk. The bigger the risk, the more difficult it is to do what is right, and what is right is that which permits us to survive. Coming home safely is all that matters. So here again, the question is have the possibilities – the products of mountain, experience, equipment, know-how – become so great, that we are running blindly into a trap? Are we human beings too human with our longings and our ambition?

Climbing, which arises out of ideas and big mountains, develops an individual dynamic. It is only justifiable when we stop where the control of risk runs out. Someone who exposes himself to dangers which cannot be avoided is either a fool or afflicted with a death wish – he is certainly not a climber aware of his responsibilities. That is something I have always striven to be – striven harder than on all the summits of this world.

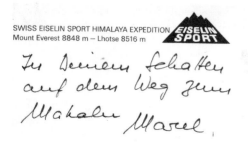

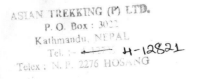

Greetings card from Marcel Ruedi to Reinhold Messner.

Survived – fourteen times

A lot of people, including myself, believed that Messner would eventually climb all fourteen eight-thousanders, that his success hung in the air. All the same, as an Alpinist who has been much influenced by Reinhold Messner, I was delighted when he pulled it off.

As I try and follow his example, the scale of Messner's human achievement is clear. Climbing a summit of over 8,000 metres in a small group or alone, without oxygen equipment, in Alpine style, by difficult routes – these 'Messnerish conditions' form the basis of top climbing activity today. His attempt to push out mental and physical limits in increasingly adventurous 'games', without at the same time being dependent on artificial aid in the way of apparatus or equipment, has become a new mountaineering philosophy.

When Messner appeared in the world of Himalayan Alpinists, such thoughts were rare. He only felt challenged on the summits of the world, and not by mountains. His methods, full of romanticism and new ideas, were unthinkable before then. He discovered and demonstrated them. His record is therefore exceedingly impressive and fascinating. It is as if he alone constituted the whole history of modern mountaineering.

Messner was the first to practise a systematic training for his activity in the Himalaya: exercises to rob you of breath in preparation for climbing under extreme conditions and on high summits. He has achieved a mental and physical toughness and an endurance that is unique.

Climbing all fourteen eight-thousanders is an unbelievable feat. It must have been a hard road for Messner. His twenty-nine expeditions to eight-thousanders in sixteen

Takashi Ozaki with his son Makoto.

years tell little of the immeasurable energy necessary to keep a firm grip on the resolution and the *Kampfgeist*, of the overcoming of self-doubt and of his many set-backs. Above everything they demonstrate his total harmony of body and mind, the bedrock upon which his philosophy is founded.

Climbing at top level, in the demanding conditions of extreme altitude, certain death can be expected from even the slightest error. Whether an Alpinist can come through such demands unscathed or not depends upon his self-regulating facility. That means, whether he has or has not the instinctive, practical and intellectual capability to distil life from death. Messner 'climbed over the dangers' that came at him thick and fast. That was, and is, his art – an art nourished by judgement sharp enough to be able to evaluate dangerous situations precisely, and a relish in decision-making. He has earned the skill to do this from his numerous high altitude experiences. Real adventure (which does not exist without extreme danger) and survival are two opposing problems. Messner has established that you can come back alive. Even out of hell.

On those expeditions where Messner has met with no climbing success, I have been amazed by his clear and humble attitude. If the danger is incalculable, he turns his back on it, time and again. Messner faces the unknown with the strength of an innocent and childlike heart. He has tried to discover this within himself, and in so doing has furthered his own potential.

That way Messner has uncovered many wonderful 'play opportunities'; with his own hands, feet and his heart, he has furnished proof of a whole new secret world within ourselves. The fourteen eight-thousanders, the 'record' itself, which he has gained, is important. But what he has done that is more important is that he has awakened dreams and hopes and the spirit of adventure in people throughout the world.

Takashi Ozaki
(Climber of six eight-thousanders)

14 Lhotse 8,516m/27,940ft

Satellite of Everest

Historical Highlights

Geographical Position: Nepal
Himalaya, Mahalangur Himal
Lat. 27°58′ N, Long. 86°56′ E

1955 Initially reconnoitred in conjunction with earlier Everest expeditions. Lhotse lies only 3km south of Mount Everest, from which it is separated by the South Col, and is thereby considered an independent mountain. The first climbing attempt is made by an international expedition under the leadership of N. Dyhrenfurth. Surveys are carried out in the pre-monsoon period of the south side of the mountain. E. Schneider works on a topographical map. After the monsoon the Lhotse Flank is visited from the Khumbu Glacier and in September the complete icefall descended on short skis. A summit attempt from the Western Cwm (E. Senn) fails at around 8,100m. Autumn storms at the end of October force the expedition home.

1956 Swiss Everest expedition in the spring, under the leadership of A. Eggler, also makes the first ascent of Lhotse on 18 May. F. Luchsinger and E. Reiss reach the summit by way of the West Face.

1970 An Austrian team under S. Aeberli climbs Lhotse Shar (East Summit, 8,400m) for the first time by its South/Southeast Ridge. S. Mayerl and R. Walter reach the top. Because the permit was for Lhotse, the expedition is officially regarded as having failed. (Lhotse Shar had already been attempted in 1960 by the New Zealander

N. Hardie, who reached 6,700m. In 1965 Japanese had to give up on the same route at around 8,150m.)

1973 Japanese make first attempt on Lhotse South Face but are unsuccessful.

1975 In the spring a strong Italian team under the leadership of R. Cassin and including R. Messner comes to Lhotse. They are hoping to find a route up the South Face. About 1,000m below and well to the left of the summit, the attempt has to be called off.

1977 German climbers under G. Schmatz and Sirdar Urkien climb Lhotse from the Western Cwm. One member dies.

1979 In the spring Austrians under E. Vanis climb the route of the first ascent to the main summit. The same route is taken by Polish climbers in the autumn when they reach the top in two groups of four.

1980 The French climber N. Jaeger has great plans. He wants to traverse Lhotse and then Everest. He fails at around 6,000m on the South Face. Attempting to reach the summit by way of Lhotse Shar, Jaeger is then lost on the mountain.

1981 Yugoslav climbers under A. Künaver succeed in climbing the Lhotse South Face to a height of about 8,000m – a great achievement! Shortly before, Bulgarian climbers reach the summit by the normal route.

1983 In the autumn a Japanese expedition puts three teams – seven members, including T. Ozaki and Sherpa Dawa Norbu – on the summit.

1984 A Czech expedition under I. Galfy makes first complete climb of the South Face of Lhotse Shar.

1985 Poles abandon their attempt on Lhotse South Face at about 8,100m after one of their members falls to his death. Similarly the attempt of a French South Face group is unsuccessful.

1986 In the spring Japanese climb the normal route to the Main Summit. In the autumn R. Messner climbs Lhotse with the South Tyrolean H. Kammerlander. On 16 October he stands at the summit of his fourteenth eight-thousander (8th ascent overall).

On Lhotse in 1986 Hans Kammerlander and Reinhold Messner climbed to the summit by a route prepared by the Everest expedition. (Lower section the same as for Everest, *see* Chapter 4.) The Eiselin group's Camp 3 served as their second camp (C2), from where they went for the top. An attempt on the South Face (right) with an Italian expedition in 1975 was abandoned just above the third camp (C3). Lhotse has been little developed and offers fascinating opportunities for the future.

LHOTSE 8516 m

C$_3$ 1975 △

△ C$_2$ 1980/1986

Above: In 1975 two avalanches at the foot of Lhotse South Face devastated Base Camp of the Italian Expedition of which Reinhold Messner was a member. Fausto Lorenzi and Mario Cunis are digging out their tent in the foreground, while Riccardo Cassin (Expedition leader, centre) is relaying news of the disaster by radio to the higher camps.

Right: After the catastrophe: crushed tent near the edge of the avalanche track, and (below) half-buried store tent and oxygen apparatus. It was the experience of this large-scale expedition that convinced Messner of the advantages of lightweight expeditioning, and he resolved never to resort to oxygen apparatus.

Above right: Injured Sherpa on the morning after the avalanche.

Below right: For his second and third attempts on Lhotse, Reinhold Messner set out from this West Base Camp: in 1980 to make a solo attempt via the Western Cwm in parallel with an Italian Everest expedition, and in 1986 with Friedl Mutschlechner and Hans Kammerlander in the wake of an international commercial expedition on the same route.

Left: The Khumbu Icefall is the most
dangerous section of the whole Lhotse
climb. Reinhold Messner helped
reconnoitre and prepare a route through
the ever-changing tumbled ice in 1978
when climbing in conjunction with an
Austrian expedition. In 1980 expedition
leader Santon let him share the same
route with his team despite protests from
other members. After their Makalu climb
in 1986, Messner contracted an agreement

with Max Eiselin for his group to make use of the fixed ropes and ladders installed for Eiselin's commercial expedition, led by Fredy Graf.

Above: A few weeks after his Makalu climb, Reinhold Messner was already on Lhotse. Because of the route-preparation done by the Eiselin expedition which had already been there for two months, it was possible for Messner and Kammerlander to reach the summit in three days (seen here under cloud in the background, 16 October 1986). For the first time a team had successfully climbed two large eight-thousanders in one season.

Next double page: Reinhold Messner and Hans Kammerlander return to Base Camp. Kammerlander has climbed seven eight-thousanders, Messner all fourteen, four of them twice. Another half an hour will see the danger behind them; they will be back through the icefall and have done it. More importantly, they will have survived.

Lhotse
Climbed to be Free

Lhotse from the South, in evening light. This face, which has already been attempted half a dozen times, is one of the most exciting problems remaining in the Himalaya. The logical route starts left and joins the gully running down the centre of the face from the summit (attempted by Yugoslavs, 1981). The Polish Route (attempted 1985) gains the same gully by coming in from the right. So far there is only one route to the main summit of Lhotse, which has made it necessary for all Lhotse climbers to operate 'on the backs' of concurrent Everest expeditions, as Reinhold Messner did with his climb in 1986.

With success on Makalu in the autumn of 1986, and a permit in my pocket to attempt Lhotse immediately afterwards, I knew that at long last I stood a chance of realising my goal – one of my goals, that is. I would probably have to forgo climbing one of the eight-thousanders in winter. If I really did manage to climb Lhotse, and thereby complete ascents of all fourteen of the world's highest mountains, I wanted to keep the promise I had made to my mother, not to embark on any more expeditions to the eight-thousanders. At least, not with the intention of going to the top myself.

I have done almost everything there is to do on the eight-thousanders. I have been on big expeditions, small expeditions, made solo ascents; I have climbed in spring, summer and autumn; I have climbed them by easy ways and by their most difficult routes; I have traversed them; I have climbed them with various partners, but I have never got to the top of one in winter. I have had to turn back often enough to have learned how to 'lose' without giving up. This has saved my life.

My one regret, after promising myself I would go to the top of an eight-thousander in every season of the year, is not to have climbed one in winter. After my Nanga Parbat solo climb, I did also entertain the vague ambition of climbing an eight-thousander as one of a couple – one man, one woman. It does not bother me now that in this I was anticipated by the French pair, Maurice and Liliane Barrard. They climbed Gasherbrum II and Nanga Parbat before I got around to finding my ideal partner; and they died together after climbing K2 in the summer of 1986.

Today I often ask myself where I found the strength and motivation to keep setting out afresh, after success and after failure. It was purely discipline – mental, physical and spiritual – that made such an extended achievement possible. In the final analysis, it wasn't ambition. Having the potential to raise money before and after an expedition was also a great help, but that was not the incentive.

When we arrived on Lhotse from Makalu, we had a long detour behind us. Originally, I had planned to cross two 6,000m passes – the Sherpani and West Col – to bring us from Makalu to Everest Base Camp (which also serves as base camp for the normal route up Lhotse). But having lost so much time on Makalu, and the weather being relatively bad, I decided instead to come right down into the valley, where we could declimatise. Camping lower down, our blood would have a chance to thin out, and we could take the opportunity of 'fattening up' a bit. We had lost a considerable amount of muscle-mass during our Makalu climb. We flew by helicopter from Sedoa, a village on the Arun, to Lukla, and from there climbed on foot up to Lhotse.

Active on Lhotse and Everest that autumn, 1986, were Swiss and French climbers, an Argentinian, a Belgian, and a Canadian. They were members of a commercial expedition – 25 men and one woman – organised by Max Eiselin, from Lucerne. Fredy Graf was the leader. They had been joined by Eric Escoffier, one of the fastest European Alpine climbers, with his own small party. Escoffier had plans to climb six eight-thousanders that year, and wanted in particular to set a new record time for climbing Everest. He was not to be successful in this, however.

When Friedl, Hans and I met up with the expedition in October, it was already apparent that there were tensions within the international team. The equable Fredy was working flat out to keep everybody happy. Not only had he personally prepared a large part of the route, his presence offered a haven of calm within the disparate group. It was thirty years since a Swiss expedition climbed Everest and made the first ascent of Lhotse; Fredy Graf wanted to celebrate the anniversary by climbing the two peaks in conjunction once more.

His team included some good Alpinists,

who had 'sold' the expedition to press and industry in order to finance their share of the cost. But there were also some 'Sunday mountaineers' among them, who from the outset, never had a hope of getting to the summit of either mountain. After two months of hard effort, with Fredy himself mostly out in the lead, the attempt bogged down in deep snow on the South Summit of Everest. Even with the summit so close, he was forced to turn back on grounds of safety.

What impressed me most was how, at his age, he still climbed superbly. He was an inspiration, and convinced me that I must not give up climbing, not yet – at 42. He is living proof that it is possible to continue climbing at a high level for very much longer.

For a few days Friedl, Hans and I waited down in Base Camp, because a strong wind was blowing and also because we wanted to accustom ourselves to being on the mountain. When we did set off, we knew we had little more than a 50–50 chance of getting to the top. There was too much wind. A northwest storm was already raging around the upper slopes of Everest and Lhotse. It was whipping up the snow and had already stopped the Swiss. Even Escoffier had to admit defeat. Lower on the mountain, the icefall became 'alive' and new crevasses gaped daily.

The three of us, still accompanied by the camera team which had filmed our Makalu expedition, climbed into the Western Cwm, following the route prepared by the Swiss. At least the Swiss camp was still standing and we could make use of it. We had reached an agreement with Max Eiselin back in the summer, allowing us, for a fee, to make use of some of his expedition's equipment in the icefall. That way we could climb over the Lhotse Face to the north side of the mountain without restraint.

All those who think that to some degree, we reached the summit of Lhotse on the shoulders of the Swiss, are right, but it does not bother me at all. I had allowed my permit for Lhotse South Face to lapse when I failed on Makalu the previous winter. To try and do Makalu and the South Face of Lhotse in a single season would have been presumptuous; more than that, it would have been crazy. And, really, I wanted to be finished with the eight-thousanders that autumn, and be free to do other things.

All Lhotse expeditions from this side have been built on parallel Everest expeditions. I had already been on two expeditions to Lhotse before this last successful one. In the spring of 1975 I attempted the South Face as a member of an Italian expedition. It was the only 'national' expedition in which I have ever participated. Sponsored by the CAI, the Italian Alpine Club, and under the leadership of Riccardo Cassin, one of the most prolific climbers of the 1930s, we were generously equipped. Even so, we failed.

There were a few nasty moments. When an ice avalanche carried off our Base Camp, I believed we would all die. Higher on the face, when climbing a huge avalanche-prone ramp, the snow surface could have peeled off at any moment with us on it, but it held. We climbed up towards the summit ridge, under enormous threat, and knowing

Survived – the avalanche catastrophe

Around midnight, I heard a great rumbling and a crash, followed by a terrific wind. Someone was shouting. I switched on a torch to see my whole tent had been flattened. I shook it and could feel the snow heavy upon it. I went outside and saw Messner, half-dressed and covered in snow dust. His tent had been quite demolished by the rush of air and the snow from an avalanche down the Lhotse Face, and those of the Sherpas were damaged.

Messner was invited in with Mariolino Conti and I crawled back into the wreck of my own tent, vowing to fix it in the morning. At around 6 a.m. I got up to inspect the damage in the daylight. Looking around, I saw Messner's tent on the ground and the rest of the damage. Then I scrutinised the face to see where the avalanche had come from, but was unable to pinpoint the exact spot as it was snowing lightly.

I went back into my tent to rest, and don't know how much time passed before, half asleep, I heard another great rumble. It was followed by a tremendous roar and a crash, then a fierce wind that drowned out everything. I felt a huge weight pass quickly over me, and instinctively tried to raise my arms over my head to protect myself. I struggled to get up but was immediately sucked back down.

At last, after a while, the inferno calmed down, and with some difficulty I struggled out of the tent again on all fours. It was a terrible sight: there was nothing left of our precious village of tents. Everything had vanished as if a monstrous bulldozer had flattened the lot, leaving only a thick blanket of snow.

The first people I saw were Messner and Conti, both completely white from

Riccardo Cassin

head to foot. With them, I went over to where the Sherpa tents had been and where we could hear moans. With ice axes and knives, we dug the trapped men free. One Sherpa was having trouble breathing, others were hurt, but fortunately none seriously. We managed to dry them off a bit with towels for they were soaking wet and covered with snow and might easily have died of hypothermia, it was so cold. We bundled them into sleeping bags as quickly as we could to give them at least some protection.

Our equipment boxes and the 30-kilo gas cylinders were scattered over a radius of more than a kilometre around where our base camp had been. I tried to contact our colleagues at Camps 1 and 2, but was not able to make myself heard until 7.30, the time of our normal morning link-up. When I finally did get through, their total astonishment was easy to

understand. They were completely unaware that anything had happened. Even from Camp 1, where you can usually see Base Camp with the naked eye, they could not tell anything was amiss because of the light snowfall. It was merely white like everywhere else. I asked them to come down quickly and help us.

In the meantime the sun came up and the temperature grew milder. Everyone tried to round up his belongings. We spent three days searching for all our clothes and things, which were strewn all over the glacier. It was fortunate there had only been five of us at Base Camp with fifteen Sherpas, cooks and assistants, otherwise the consequences would surely have been much more serious.

Our friends from Camp 1 reached us around 9.30. We were worried whether the Sherpas would be prepared to continue with the expedition or not. They seemed to want to go on, however, so we called a meeting to decide whether to continue ourselves or go back to Italy. We were still missing the four from Camp 2, who were not down yet . . .

Riccardo Cassin in his book *Fifty Years of Alpinism*
(Leader of 1975 expedition to Lhotse)

Prayers – for survival

Below Mount Everest on the south side, the Khumbu Icefall blocks the way up into the Western Cwm, or the Valley of Silence as it is sometimes called. The plan was that Dati – Dawa Tensing Sherpa – should accompany me through the Icefall. But before we were able to set off through the shambles of moving snow and ice, Dati's wife arrived in Base Camp to beg him not to go. She threatened to leave him if he went up against her will.

Dati's mother, too, had sent a letter to Base Camp a few days before, entreating him not to climb. In the letter, it said that she had visited the head lama, who had advised her that the signs did not augur well for Dati. The lama felt that a great danger was steadily approaching her son. He would be wise to remain in Lhotse Base Camp. It would be a safer place for him. Were he to decide to climb higher, something was going to happen to him – bad frost-bite, or perhaps even death.

The lama promised to procure a *shouga* for the worried mother, a bundle of prayers bound round with yarn, worn by Sherpas and Tibetan

Dati (right) with our liaison officer on Lhotse.

buddhists around the neck. Dati's wife was to bring these prayers to her husband to protect him. They took a long time to make, and even with them, Dati was warned not to climb any higher.

In 1981 Dati was 26 years old. According to Tibetan belief, the ages 26 and 32 are bad for men, 25 and 31 for women. At these ages, they have to withdraw for a period of two or three days to pray. They have to go with a few lamas to the top of a hill or ridge and build a little *chorten*, or memorial cairn, there.

When Dati became 26 he was in Europe, and after he returned to Nepal, he immediately began preparations for this expedition. He did not have the time to carry out the prayer ritual, which he had to do before he set off into any dangerous situations.

already that it was hopeless. (We would not have fared much better on the other side, the North Face, without making a great detour.)

I have also failed once on the normal route of Lhotse. That was in 1980 when I tried to go to the summit alone after my only Sherpa, Dati, had refused to climb with me. He was not in a position to accompany me for religious reasons, he explained, and remained in Base Camp. I understood, and did not press the point.

This time, my third attempt, I was hoping for a more positive outcome. Hans, Friedl and I spent a night in the Swiss Camp 2, but the next morning,

Friedl, who had been suffering from toothache for some time, turned back to Base Camp. An air pocket under some dental work was giving him a lot of pain in the thin atmosphere up here, and it was getting worse by the hour. He was forced to give up this eight-thousander, which otherwise he would certainly have been able to climb.

Hans and I did not leave camp until late morning. The wind grew even stronger the higher we went, and it was already getting dark when we reached Camp 3, in the middle of the Lhotse Face, at 7,500 metres. We stretched out in the half-wrecked Swiss tent, but did not get a wink of sleep that night. Next

day we were still keen to go on, but worried in case the climb would not be possible in such a storm.

All the same, we crawled out of the tent on the morning of 16 October. We were dressed as warmly as possible and, wearing crampons, started to climb into the storm. The ropes which the Swiss had fixed on the Yellow Band and above had blown loose, or been carried away by the wind. So we climbed without, trusting just to our ice axes and our sense of balance.

Snow conditions were so good that initially we made swift progress, despite everything. The only bad moment came just below the narrowing

Hans Kammerlander, Wolfgang Thomaseth and Friedl Mutschlechner near the top of the Khumbu Icefall.

Lhotse Groove which runs from bottom left to top right towards the summit, where with the snow knee-deep in places, we were only able to advance with great difficulty. In consequence we slowed right down. At one point, in the upper part of the groove, in the gap between two steep rock walls, we were practically hurled upwards. With uncanny strength the wind caught us from behind. It shoved and thrust us up the gully.

How often on expeditions have I wished for a lift that could transport me up the last bit. The force of this wind was so strong, that in places for 20 or 30 steps together, we had only to move our feet one in front of the other. Naturally we had to take short rests in between, because even maintaining balance costs energy. Sometimes we were actually hoisted off our feet and carried up. Never before have the last 200 metres to the summit gone so quickly as on that day on Lhotse.

I had thought I might stop for a moment just a few metres below the summit of this, my last eight-thousander, as a kind of gesture of respect. Now, harried and hustled by the storm, it was no longer possible. My helplessness alone was obeisance enough. With no desire to be a hero, or even an anti-hero, I followed Hans.

At the end of the couloir, in a little gap, we stopped. Taking a firm grip on our axes, which we had rammed into the snow, we endeavoured to recover our breath. We knew we dare not make the slightest mistake when climbing this last rock and ice pinnacle, the left of the two summit pyramids. It would require the utmost concentration to manage it safely. We would have to wait for the lulls in the storm if we were not keen to learn to 'fly'.

To be blown off your feet in the groove was not too serious, but beyond its protection, we faced wind on steep, open slopes. We had to cling to our axes for dear life, so as not to be blasted away. Neither of us had a free hand to take photographs. In any case both cameras were frozen up – we had noticed that down in the gully half an hour before. As we reached the summit, one behind the other, we turned immediately and set off back down again.

You have reached the summit when there's no more up, not when you're tired, or frightened, or don't want to go any further. And you stand up there, wanting nothing more than to be safely back down on flat ground, where it's warm; back down where it is possible to rest; down where your friends are waiting. In this almost airless void, no one lasts long. It is not just that there is insufficient oxygen; there is also too little human warmth, too little sense, too little love.

Stooped over like a chronic invalid, I stood on top, unable to do more. The snow under my feet was hard and a long way away from me; only my crampons linked me to it. I shut my eyes as the storm gusted, shut my eyes and doubled up even more tightly. Only my mouth remained wide open. When the din let up, I saw a bit of sky, like frosted glass. Behind, it was the black of eternity. Spindrift shot vertically into the air. The air not only had substance, but strength. With an animal instinct I knew this nameless place. I was there. All around me was hell intensified: storm, cold, the void.

You very quickly become worn down up there, unlike anything at lower levels. Those few minutes spent really high were only sustainable, because I now knew that the sort of luck I had been seeking up here, for weeks on end

The eight-thousanders, the Yeti and the Press

'It has to be admitted that climbing all fourteen eight-thousanders is a fine record. We applaud it. But it could have been even finer and more significant, and impressed us even more, if Messner had not surrounded himself with the by-now familiar band of big businessmen, sponsors and the Press.'

This and the citation below came from Walter Bonatti, the leading European climber in the years between 1950 and 1965, and was published in the Italian newspaper *La Repubblica*. I don't want to reflect the mirror back on him here, only to reiterate what I have already said in the final chapter of my last book, *Wettlauf zum Gipfel*, (Race for the Summit) about all the false rubbish like this that gets bandied around. I was not surprised that my book was torn apart – I have come to expect a certain narrow-mindedness.

I would willingly talk to Walter Bonatti. He would find me open, self-critical, aggressive, as I am with all who challenge me. I am used to saying what I think. Yes, I am subjective. There is more than enough balanced 'gossip'. Even though I know it makes people unpopular to speak their truth, I speak mine – always. I have never ingratiated myself with any journalist; all my adult life I have defended my egoism. But I have never set out to be a hero, that sort of heroism disgusts me.

The slogans have been invented by other people, I go my own way – even when it does not please Walter Bonatti. *Noblesse oblige*, it was once called. Today, however, we seem to live only in the time of personalised slogans.

'Thanks to Messner, we live longer, according to one press notice. For years we have been accustomed to seeing the image of our hero promoting some product or another. When people speak of him, they even run the risk of their own words being put to use as testimonies and appearing in some advertisement.'

I have great respect for Walter Bonatti, because of his achievements – not because I need him. Nor did I need the Yeti. The stories about my seeing it were invented by reporters; I wanted the right to reply, as always.

Some friends of mine organised a celebration in Sulden on the Ortler to mark the successful completion of the fourteen eight-thousanders. At my request, all the people still living who had climbed with me on these summits were invited, including Michl Dacher and Peter Habeler. I was sorry that Walter Bonatti was not able to be there too.

But my generosity took something from the pride that I always get in the mountains. In future I must think more of myself.

and time and again over 16 long years, only exists lower down.

On Lhotse we ventured our summit climb in a storm, the like of which I had only previously endured coming off a mountain. On none of my earlier expeditions to eight-thousanders would I have considered setting out in that sort of weather.

I don't know why we risked more this time than before. I can only say that Hans and I felt safe making the climb. Only when we stood between the two summit horns of Lhotse did we hesitate a moment. We could smell the danger, but the proximity of the summit strengthened our confidence. To go on meant the whole business could be concluded.

On the summit this time there was no time for joy, only an anxiety to get back down. The descent, too, needed our fullest concentration. Only the next day, when we had safely recrossed the icefall and were nearing Base Camp, did a sort of elemental joy wash into me. Not so much, 'Hooray! We've done it!', but rather a joy of being alive at all, coupled with the feeling that I was now free for other things.

There was no sense of heroism or conquest after finishing the fourteen eight-thousanders, merely the satisfaction of having realised a complex idea, a target I had set myself. The obligation to climb all the eight-thousanders without bottled oxygen and in as 'fair' a style as possible, was something I had assumed voluntarily. No one had set out rules or conditions for me in advance, apart from Nature. Because, to a certain extent, I had fulfilled the obligation, I was pleased with myself, at least in this respect. All the same I know it is not only a tragedy *not* to achieve one's goal, it is perhaps an even greater tragedy to do so.

For the time being I have no worries about my future. There are plenty of new ideas, new goals. The eight-thousanders are ingrained deeply in the mind of the public, but they don't interest me that much. Not just Alpinists, but millions of ordinary people are beginning to take the eight-thousanders seriously, at a time when they should no longer be taken so seriously. Now, because I have survived ascents of all fourteen, this realisation has outlived its importance – at least, it has for me. This kind of adventure has become outmoded. It is now an institution, and by assuming a mundaneness has become, therefore, antiquated.

I will have to begin from the beginning if I want to go on from here. I have to learn it all again. In any different field I have to master what has already been done before, in order to be able to take a step forward, in the same way as everyone who has gone before me. My life takes a new direction. So long as I am criticised by the older as well as the younger climbers, I am reassured, I know I am on the right lines.

It has become easy for me today to finance my expeditions. I am as proud of that as of my other achievements. I have not yet found a true sponsor, in the sense of someone who gives me money for my enterprises without hope of return, but I have made so many contacts, and scoop in so many royalties from my books, that I can 'indulge' my wildest schemes.

The practical side of my life has been shaped to an extent by my predecessors, in as much as I have lifted and developed many mountaineering ideas from history. I knew that the only way I could do something 'new' was to know what everyone had done before.

I have modelled myself on Walter Bonatti, Hermann Buhl, and Paul Preuss – even when it came to developing new techniques for negotiating lecture fees or clinching advertising contracts. All three not only achieved exemplary 'work' with their climbing deeds, they stood also as examples of how to organise a life as an independent adventurer. Apart from the few friends that I have, it is they who have given me most practical help. I could not have done it alone.

The others, who have assisted me, the readers of my books, the people who come to my lectures, the fans, were like the wind on Lhotse. Without their recognition I would have starved emotionally, would have given up somewhere along the line. Without the trust of my business partners I would never have been in a position to get so far, and certainly not 'to the top'.

If I have not given enough answers, don't come looking to me for more, go to the mountains! We humans give too many answers – each day there is a different one. The mountains have an answer for everyone.

Reinhold Messner 1986 after climbing Lhotse: 'Freer than ever before.'

Appendix

List of all Climbers with four or more Eight-Thousanders

(Arranged in order of first four, as on 16 October 1986)

1. **Reinhold Messner** (b. 1944) Italy

Nanga Parbat 27.6.70; 9.8.78 solo
Manaslu 25.4.72
Hidden Peak 10.8.75; 28.6.84
Mount Everest 8.5.78; 20.8.80 solo
K2 12.7.79
Shisha Pangma 28.5.81
Kangchenjunga 6.5.82
Gasherbrum II 24.7.82; 25.6.84
Broad Peak 2.8.82
Cho Oyu 5.5.83
Annapurna 24.4.85
Dhaulagiri 15.5.85
Makalu 26.9.86
Lhotse 16.10.86

2. **Kurt Diemberger** (b. 1932) Austria

Broad Peak 9.6.57; 18.7.84
Dhaulagiri 13.5.60
Makalu 21.5.78
Mount Everest 15.10.78
Gasherbrum II 4.8.79
K2 4.8.86

3. **Hans v. Kaenel** (b. 1940) Switzerland

Lhotse 8.5.77
Makalu 10.5.78
Mount Everest 1.10.79
Dhaulagiri 13.5.80
Manaslu 7.5.81

4. **Robert Schauer** (b. 1953) Austria

Hidden Peak 11.5.75
Nanga Parbat 11.8.76
Mount Everest 3.5.78
Makalu 25.4.81
Broad Peak 8.8.84

5. **Michl Dacher** (b. 1933) West Germany

Lhotse 11.5.77
K2 12.7.79
Shisha Pangma 7.5.80
Hidden Peak 22.7.82
Cho Oyu 5.5.83
Manaslu 4.5.84
Nanga Parbat 12.7.85
Broad Peak 16.8.86

6. **Siegfried Hupfauer** (b. 1941) West Germany

Manaslu 22.4.73
Mount Everest 16.10.78
Shisha Pangma 11.5.80
Hidden Peak 22.7.82
Broad Peak 16.8.86

7. **Jerzy Kukuczka** (b. 1948) Poland

Lhotse 4.10.79
Mount Everest 19.5.80
Makalu 15.10.81 solo
Broad Peak 30.7.82; 17.7.84
Gasherbrum II 1.7.83
Hidden Peak 23.7.83
Dhaulagiri 21.1.85
Cho Oyu 15.2.85
Nanga Parbat 13.7.85
Kangchenjunga 11.1.86
K2 8.7.86

Jerzy Kukuczka

8. **Doug Scott** (b. 1941) Great Britain

Mount Everest 24.9.75
Kangchenjunga 16.5.79
Shisha Pangma 28.5.82
Broad Peak 27.6.83

9. **Fredy Graf** (b. 1936) Switzerland

Dhaulagiri 17.5.80
Manaslu 9.5.81
Gasherbrum II 15.6.83
Broad Peak 30.6.83

Erhard Loretan

10. **Erhard Loretan** (b. 1959) Switzerland

Nanga Parbat 10.6.82
Gasherbrum II 15.6.83
Hidden Peak 23.6.83
Broad Peak 30.6.83
Manaslu 30.4.84
Annapurna 24.10.84
K2 6.7.85
Dhaulagiri 8.12.85
Mount Everest 30.8.86

11. **Marcel Ruedi** (1938–1986) Switzerland

Dhaulagiri 17.5.80
Gasherbrum II 15.6.83
Hidden Peak 23.6.83
Broad Peak 30.6.83
Manaslu 30.4.84
Nanga Parbat 3.6.84
K2 19.6.85
Shisha Pangma 14.9.85
Cho Oyu 5.5.86
Makalu 24.9.86

12. **Voytek Kurtyka** (b. 1947) Poland

Dhaulagiri 18.5.80
Broad Peak 30.7.82; 17.7.84
Gasherbrum II 1.7.83
Hidden Peak 23.7.83

13. Takashi Ozaki (b. 1952) Japan

Broad Peak 8.8.77
Mount Everest 10.5.80; 16.12.83
Manaslu 12.10.81
Lhotse 9.10.83
Kangchenjunga 19.5.84
Shisha Pangma 10.9.86

14. Ang Dorje, Sherpa (1949–1984) Nepal

Mount Everest 16.10.78; 23.5.84
Annapurna 6.5.80
Kangchenjunga 1.5.82
Manaslu 22.10.83

15. Noboru Yamada (b. 1950) Japan

Dhaulagiri 21.10.78; 18.10.82
Kangchenjunga 9.5.81
Lhotse 9.10.83
Mount Everest 16.12.83; 30.10.85
K2 24.7.85
Manaslu 14.12.85

16. Günter Sturm (b. 1940) West Germany

Lhotse 9.5.77
Shisha Pangma 7.5.80
Hidden Peak 22.7.82
Manaslu 11.5.84

17. Andrzej Czok (1948–1986) Poland

Lhotse 4.10.79
Mount Everest 19.5.80
Makalu 10.10.82
Dhaulagiri 21.1.85

18. Hans Kammerlander (b. 1956) Italy

Cho Oyu 5.5.83
Gasherbrum II 25.6.84
Hidden Peak 28.6.84
Annapurna 24.4.85
Dhaulagiri 15.5.85
Makalu 26.9.86
Lhotse 16.10.86

19. Norbert Joos (b. 1960) Switzerland

Nanga Parbat 10.6.82
Manaslu 11.5.84
Annapurna 24.10.84
K2 19.6.85

20. Krzysztof Wielicki (b. 1950) Poland

Mount Everest 17.2.80
Broad Peak 14.7.84
Manaslu 20.10.84
Kangchenjunga 11.1.86
Makalu 24.9.86

21. Hanns Schell (b. 1938) Austria

Hidden Peak 11.8.75
Nanga Parbat 11.8.76
Gasherbrum II 4.8.79
Shisha Pangma 19.5.85

22. Peter Habeler (b. 1942) Austria

Hidden Peak 10.8.75
Mount Everest 8.5.78
Nanga Parbat 12.7.85
Cho Oyu 5.5.86

23. Maurice Barrard (1942–1986) France

Hidden Peak 15.7.80
Gasherbrum II 12.6.82
Nanga Parbat 27.6.84
K2 23.6.86

24. Eric Escoffier (b. 1960) France

Gasherbrum II 15.6.85
Hidden Peak 22.6.85
K2 6.7.85
Shisha Pangma 10.9.86

25. Peter Wörgötter (b. 1941) Austria

Lhotse 11.5.77
Manaslu 19.5.81
Shisha Pangma 10.5.85
Broad Peak 21.6.86

26. Viktor Groselj (b. 1952) Yugoslavia

Makalu 10.10.75
Manaslu 4.5.84
Broad Peak 28.7.86
Gasherbrum II 4.8.86

27. Andrej Stremfelj (b. 1956) Yugoslavia

Hidden Peak 8.7.77
Mount Everest 13.5.79
Broad Peak 29.7.86
Gasherbrum II 4.8.86

28. Fausto Destefani (b. 1952) Italy

K2 4.8.83
Makalu 1.10.85
Nanga Parbat 15.8.86
Annapurna 21.9.86

29. Sergio Martini (b. 1949) Italy

K2 4.8.83
Makalu 1.10.85
Nanga Parbat 15.8.86
Annapurna 21.9.86

30. Gianni Calcagno Italy

Broad Peak 27.6.84; 13.7.86
Gasherbrum II 6.6.85
Hidden Peak 19.6.85
K2 5.7.86

31. Benoit Chamoux France

Gasherbrum II 15.6.85
Hidden Peak 22.6.85
Broad Peak 20.6.86
K2 5.7.86

32. Gerhard Schmatz (b. 1929) W. Germany

Manaslu 22.4.73
Mount Everest 1.10.79
Shisha Pangma 29.4.83
Hidden Peak 18.8.86

33. Turio Vidoni Italy

Broad Peak 27.6.84; 13.7.84
Gasherbrum II 6.6.85
Hidden Peak 19.6.85
K2 5.7.86

34. Ang Rita, Sherpa Nepal

Dhaulagiri 12.5.79; 13.5.80; 19.5.80; 5.5.82
Mount Everest 7.5.83; 15.10.84; 29.4.85
Cho Oyu 13.5.84
Kangchenjunga 24.10.86

Success, Death and the Eight-Thousanders

By John Town, Mountain Data.

First published in *Mountain* magazine, No 110, July 1986.

Table 1: Expeditions to the 8,000m Peaks

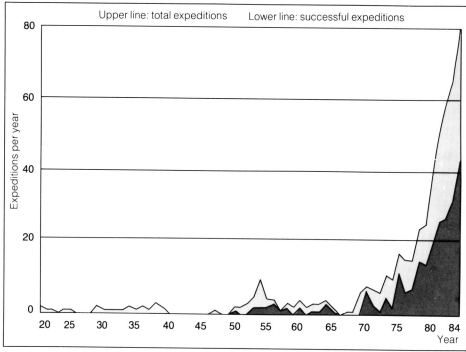

Upper line: total expeditions   Lower line: successful expeditions

Table 2: Expeditions to Individual Eight-Thousand-Metre Peaks

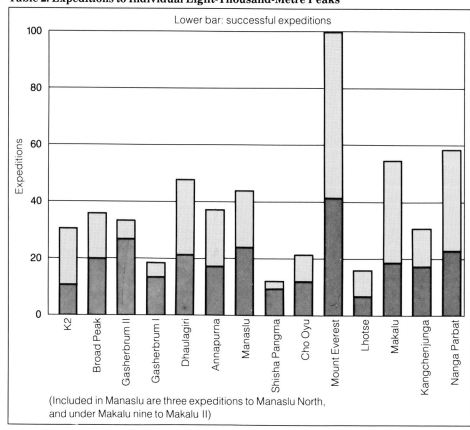

Lower bar: successful expeditions

(Included in Manaslu are three expeditions to Manaslu North, and under Makalu nine to Makalu II)

The Explosion in Himalayan Mountaineering (Tables 1 and 2)

By the end of 1984 Winter season the total number of expeditions to the 8,000m peaks had reached 524. This in itself may not be too surprising, but more worryingly in the four years 1980–84 more expeditions visited these mountains than in the previous sixty years. Table 1 illustrates this recent explosion in graphic terms, and Table 2 how the total numbers are distributed among the various peaks. The effect of this kind of pressure on local culture and environment can only be disastrous.

Success Rates On The 8,000m Peaks
(Tables 3 and 4)

Of the 8,000m peaks, some are more popular than others. Behind Everest lie Nanga Parbat, Makalu, Dhaulagiri and Manaslu. Table 3 shows the percentage success rate by mountain. It is hard to account for the popularity of the above 5 peaks on the likely chance of success. The average success rate for expeditions to all the 8,000m peaks is 47%. To Nanga Parbat (38%) and Makalu (35%) many are called but few are chosen.

It would appear that by picking the right mountain you can have the best of both worlds. On Gasherbrum I and Shisha Pangma you can both escape the crowds and stand a better than 70% chance of success. The dark horse exposed by this analysis is Lhotse. It is not a peak that readily springs to mind, but proportionately more people fail here than anywhere else.

Finally there is K2. Until recently it has attracted only a tiny number of parties, all but the strongest choosing less formidable alternatives. It took 5 attempts to make the second ascent, a situation unparalleled elsewhere. It seems ironic that Messner was criticised in 1979 for choosing the 'ordinary' route and departing from his previous Alpine approach. This 'ordinary' route had received only 2 ascents in the previous 25 years and his team was half the size of any of the 3 previous successful parties.

Crude success rates and expedition numbers do not tell the whole story. The Karakoram was out of bounds for 14 years so the expedition totals do not give a fair comparison of activity levels. This is also the case for Shisha Pangma and Cho Oyu. The overall success rate for a peak is the result of combining data for a number of routes and it is in the comparison of routes that things become more interesting. The overall success rate for Everest is 41%, surprisingly low given the impression that a majority of expeditions succeed on the S Col route. Table 4, a breakdown by route, reveals that despite their early first ascents the N Col route and W Ridge repulse 4 out of every 5 expeditions.

Table 3: Success Rate by Peak

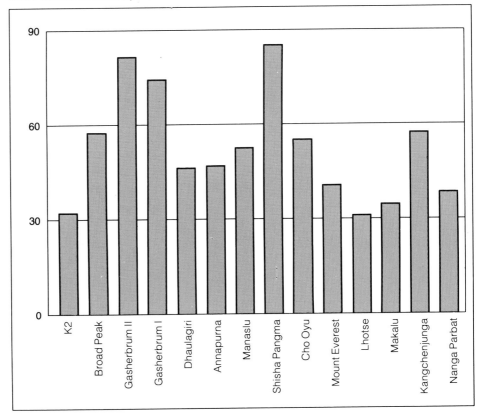

Table 4: Success Rate on Everest by Route

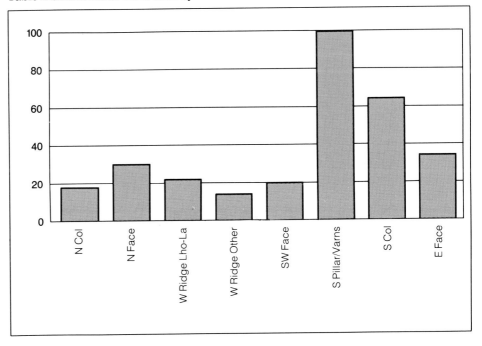

243

Nationality (Table 5)

Table 5 shows the breakdown of expeditions by nationality excluding joint expeditions (51) or international ventures (21). This confirms that the Japanese dominate the scene, followed by the French, German, American, British and Italians. If some effort is made to attribute joint expeditions (not shown) the order of the top 6 remains the same, but the Austrians join the Italians in 6th place. The Germans (12) and Austrians (10) have been involved in the highest number of joint expeditions, though mostly with each other. Categorising expeditions by nationality is bound to be something of an arbitrary process. These days it is the exception rather than the rule to find a team without some multinational aspect. In one sense all expeditions using Sherpas are joint ventures, but to avoid chaos they have only been classed as Nepalese if officially described as such.

Table 5: Expeditions by Nationality

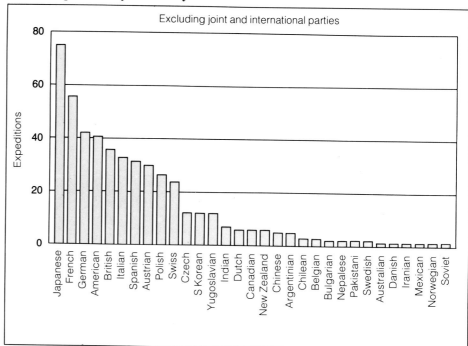

Fatalities by Cause (Table 6)

By February 1986, 280 people had lost their lives on the 8,000m peaks. 60% of the fatalities were due to what are conventionally termed as objective dangers, that is those outside the control of the climber. On the 8,000m peaks, however, you could say that the reduction of objective risk is the most important skill a climber can develop.

There is an inevitable blurring between the categories in this form of analysis. Exposure, exhaustion and illness in varying proportions combine again and again in reports of incidents. Reports of avalanches do not always specify whether the medium was falling snow or serac, the end result being the same in both cases. It came as a sobering thought that Himalayan storms, without other factors, do kill a significant number of climbers, either by pinning them down or literally blowing them off the mountain. Perhaps the saddest aspect of the findings is that over 30 climbers have disappeared or died of unknown causes, with all the additional pain that this must cause.

Table 6: Fatalities by Cause

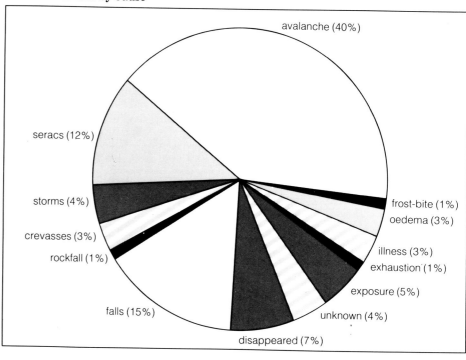

244

Fatality Rates (Tables 7 and 8)

The question that started it all. What proportion of those who go do not come back? Fatalities are invariably reported, but the number departing was available for only 86% of the expeditions reported. These 481 parties had a total of 4,967 members (an average size of 10) and suffered 168 fatalities, excluding Sherpas. The fatality rate is thus 3·4%. This means that one in thirty climbers, rather than one in ten, fail to return from the eight-thousanders – a welcome finding. For those who return again and again the risk is obviously higher.

There is some feeling that differences in national attitudes or experience result in higher fatality levels for expedition teams from certain countries.

The size and frequency of Japanese expeditions inevitably means more accidents than for other nationalities, but man for man they see fewer deaths than British or American ventures.

Table 8 shows the number of deaths on each of the 8,000m peaks.

Table 7: Fatality Rate by Nationality

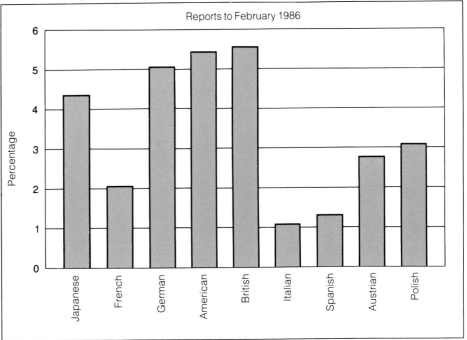

Table 8: Fatalities by Peak

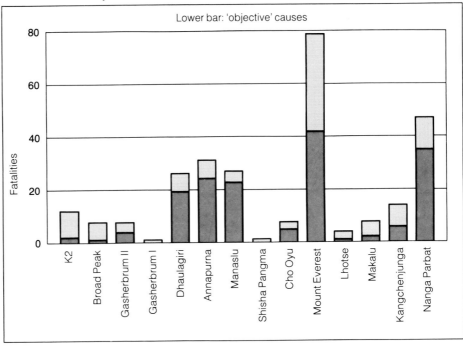

Title of the original German edition:
Überlebt – Alle 14 Achttausander
© 1987 BLV Verlagsgesellschaft mbH, München

First published in Great Britain in 1988 by
The Crowood Press
Ramsbury, Marlborough
Wiltshire, SN8 2HE

Reprinted 1989

English translation © The Crowood Press 1988

British Library Cataloguing in Publication Data.
Messner, Reinhold
   All 14 Eight-Thousanders
   1. Mountaineering. Messner, Reinhold – Biographies
   I. Title II. Uberlebt-alle 14 Achttausander. *English*
   796.5'22'0924

   ISBN 1 85223 106 8

All pictures were supplied by Reinhold Messner and his expedition companions (Michl Dacher, Ang Dorje, Horst Fankhauser, Ursula Grether, Peter Habeler, Nena Holguin, Hans Kammerlander, Friedl Mutschlechner, Oswald Oelz, Reinhard Patscheider, Reinhard Schiestl, Doug Scott) the Deutschen Himalaya-Stiftung and the Vittorio-Sella Archive. Author and publisher thank photographers and people quoted, as well as all those who helped on the expeditions.

The perspectives of the mountains featured in some of the diagrams have been altered in order to show the Messner routes.

Typeset by Chippendale Type, Otley, West Yorkshire.
Printed and bound in Spain by Graficas Estella, S.A. (Navarra)

Snow and Ice Climbing

John Barry

Written by one of Britain's foremost winter
climbers, this up-to-date and highly readable
book instructs the novice and improving
climber in snow and ice skills. With advice on
equipment, techniques including belaying and
protection, selecting a route suitable to your
ability, plus a useful guide to the world's ice
climbing areas, this book will be a welcome
addition to any mountaineer's library.

144 pages
165 photographs and diagrams plus 16 colour
pages

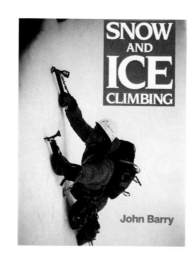

Rock Climbing

Steve Ashton

Through personal anecdote, expert instruction
based on extensive experience, and superb
photography, this book reveals the world of the
rock climber from the first tentative moves
through to the special mental and physical
challenges of Extreme grade climbing.
Chapters cover all aspects, from types of rock,
equipment and techniques, to a survey of
British crags and climbs, making this
comprehensive book essential reading for all
rock climbers.

160 pages
139 photographs and diagrams plus 8 colour
pages

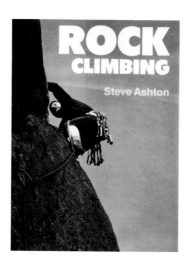

Climbing Fit

Martyn Hurn and Pat Ingle

This book offers a unique opportunity to share
the fitness training techniques of two highly
experienced and respected specialists. With the
help of some of the world's leading climbers,
the authors have devised training programmes
for all climbing disciplines, from Alpinism to
rock climbing. Demonstration photographs
illustrate the exercises, and there is also
invaluable advice on mental training methods.

96 pages
83 photographs and diagrams
paperback

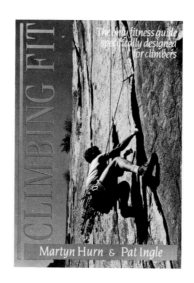